THE NEW SOVIET MAN AND WOMAN

The New Soviet Man and Woman

Sex-Role Socialization in the USSR

Lynne Attwood

INDIANA UNIVERSITY PRESS
Bloomington and Indianapolis

Copyright © 1990 by Lynne Attwood

All rights reserved

No part of this book may be reproduced or utilized in any form or by any means, electronic or mechanical, including photocopying and recording, or by any information storage and retrieval system, without permission in writing from the publisher.
The Association of American University Presses' Resolution on Permission constitutes the only exception to this prohibition.

Manufactured in Great Britain

Library of Congress Cataloging-in-Publication Data
The new Soviet man and woman: sex-role socialization in the USSR / Lynne Attwood.
p. cm.
Includes bibliographical references.
ISBN 0-253-31074-1. — ISBN 0-253-20615-4 (pbk.)
1. Sex role—Soviet Union. 2. Sex differences (psychology)
I. Title.
HQ1075.5.S65A88   1990
305.310947—dc20   90-33693

1 2 3 4 5 94 93 92 91 90

Contents

Preface	ix
Introduction	1
The Concept of 'Sex Upbringing'	2
The 'Demographic Crisis'	4
The Link between 'Sex Upbringing' and the Demographic Crisis	6
The Effects of *Glasnost'* and *Perestroika* on Women	9
The Outline of the Book	13
A Note on Translation and Terminology	14
1 Western Theories of Male and Female Personality Differences	16
Psychoanalytic Theory	16
Social Learning Theory	21
Cognitive Developmental Theory	24
Feminism and Sex Differences in Personality	27
2 Soviet Psychology and Personality Development	32
Historical Outline	33
Ivan Pavlov	40
The Troika: Vygotskii, Luria and Leont'ev	47
The Development of Moral Attitudes and Behaviour	56
Biology and Society in the Development of Personality	60
A Proposed Soviet Theory of Male and Female Personality, According to the Tenets of Soviet Psychology	63

3	**Soviet Psychologists on Sex Differences**	**67**
	B. G. Anan'ev: Sex Differences in Ontogenesis	67
	A. A. Bodalev: Sex Differences in Interpersonal Understanding	69
	V. S. Mukhina: Sex Differences in Choice of Toys	70
	T. G. Khashchenko: Sex Differences in Mental Problem Solving	71
	Sex Differences and Identification with Parents: the Work of A. I. Zakharov	74
	Sex Differences and Identification with Parents: the Work of A. Ya. Varga	77
	V. A. Kuts and V. P. Bagrunov: Sex Differences and Success in Marriage	78
	L. S. Sapozhnikova: Sex Differences in the Development of Moral Behaviour	80
	A. Kelly and T. Snegireva: a Comparison of British and Soviet Approaches to Sex Differences in School Subject Preference	81
	Concluding Remarks	84
4	**The Work of I. S. Kon**	**86**
	Personality, Social Roles, and the Social Construction of Sex Differences	87
	The Role of Biology in the Development of Sex Differences	90
	The Erosion of Traditional Sex Differences in Personality	93
	The Interaction of Social and Biological Influences	96
	More Recent Work	97

5	**Sex-change in the USSR: A. I. Belkin's Theory of Gender Development, and His Treatment of Hermaphrodites**	**100**
	Hermaphroditism and Transsexualism: the Western Approach	100
	Belkin's Approach: Hormones and Sex Differences	101
	The Process of Gender Reassignment	104
	Belkin's Theory of Gender Development	111
	Belkin and Western Writings on Gender	113
	Belkin and the Pro-family Ethos	115
	Belkin and Soviet Psychology	117
6	**Sociological and Demographic Approaches to Sex Differences**	**119**
	Male and Female Personality in Socialist Society	120
	Male and Female Roles in the Family	127
7	**The Pedagogical Approach to Sex Differences**	**133**
	The Early Pedagogical Writings on Sex Differences	133
	Conflicting Opinions within the Early Writings	140
	The Recent Writings	145
	A Summary of the Pedagogical Writings	154
	Pedagogy and Psychology	157
	Pedagogy and the Medical Profession	159
	Warnings Against the Encouragement of Excessive Sex-differentiation in Personality	162
	Summary of the Pedagogical and Medical Approach	163

8	**The Popular Press**	**165**
	The Causes of the Masculinization of Women and the Feminization of Men	166
	The Tensions between Women's Work and Family Roles	170
	Propagandizing the Multi-child Family	172
	Promoting the Full-time Housewife	173
	Writings in the Popular Press which Oppose the Resurrection of Traditional Sex Roles	174
	Concluding Remarks	181
9	**The Practical Application of Soviet Ideas on Sex Roles**	**183**
	The School Course: 'the Ethics and Psychology of Family Life'	184
	The Course Outline	185
	Family Consultation Centres	191
	'Get-acquainted' Services	198
	Discouraging Divorce through the Legal System	200
10	**Sex Role Socialization in the USSR: Summary of the Past, and Prospects for the Future**	**203**
	Zakharova, Posadskaya and Rimachevskaya: Four Approaches to Sex Roles	207
	The Development of Soviet Views on Sex Roles, and Prospects for the Future	209
Notes and References		213
Bibliography		237
Index		255

Preface

According to the Soviet constitution, women and men have equal rights. However, it has proved somewhat harder to establish this in reality than it is to declare it in law. The Western literature on women in the Soviet Union generally concedes that considerable efforts have been made, but that these have been impeded by the survival of certain 'sex-role stereotypes'. Yet little has been said about the ways in which sex-roles are acquired in the Soviet Union. This book aims to fill that gap. It is primarily an analysis of Soviet writings on sex and gender, the climate of thought around them, and their implications for the development of male and female personality differences. It reveals that there has, in fact, been little attempt in recent years to overcome the sex-role stereotypes which stand in the way of equality between the sexes. Concern about the so-called 'demographic crisis' has actually had the opposite effect.

The demographic crisis became a major issue in the Soviet Union from the middle of the 1970s. It found expression in the Soviet press in the form of articles lamenting what were now seen to be negative consequences of women's equality. The strong work orientation which had been encouraged in women, and which was reflected in the virtually universal employment of women in the European republics of the country, was now linked to an increase in the number of divorces and a sharp fall in the birth-rate. This, it was feared, would lead to a severe labour shortage in the near future. At the same time, there was now an alarming variation in the reproductive patterns of the European and Central Asian republics, where comparatively few women work outside the home and the birth-rate remains high.

It is argued here that this led to a reappraisal of male and female roles in the European republics, and a concerted effort to resurrect a more traditional notion of women's role which stressed a more maternal and domestic orientation. The concept of equality between the sexes was redefined, and a new catch-phrase introduced: 'being equal does not mean being the same'. At the same time, Central Asian women were subject to rather different ideological messages – they were put under increasing pressure to reduce their family size, place their children in crèches and go out to work.

Gorbachev's arrival on the scene, and the onset of *perestroika*, have done little to change this revision of women's role in Soviet society, although they have added some new elements to the picture. The envisaged increase in productivity and automation may have reduced anxiety about the future labour shortage, since it is anticipated that fewer workers will be needed; however, that is the only cause for demographic celebration. Concern is still expressed about the increasing proportion of elderly people in the population, and, still more, about the imbalance in the birth-rates in different parts of the country. In addition, a more family-oriented life for women in the European republics will serve a second purpose in the era of *perestroika* – it will help solve the growth in unemployment which will be an inevitable consequence of the rationalization of the Soviet economy. The result is that although *glasnost'* has resulted in more heated debate on the subject, the efforts which began in the 1970s to establish a more domestic mode of life for women have not ceased. Indeed, the literature we look at in the course of this study suggests that they have even intensified.

This book would not have been produced without the help of a number of people. I would like to begin by expressing my gratitude to Dr Nick Lampert. He has been involved in the project from the very beginning, both as supervisor of the doctoral thesis on which the book is based, and as editor of the book itself, and has given me invaluable guidance and support throughout. However, any deficiencies in the end product are due entirely to me and not him.

I would also like to thank Dr John Dunstan and Dr Mary Buckley for offering a wealth of helpful comments on the book, and members of the Women in Eastern Europe Group for their friendly advice on certain sections.

Finally, I would like to acknowledge my enormous debt to friends in Moscow and Leningrad. The long evenings spent in discussion with them over countless bottles of wine (or, as is more often the case in the Gorbachev era, cups of tea) have not only given me invaluable insights into Soviet views on sex roles, but have also helped sustain my interest in both the subject and the country. It is to them that the book is dedicated.

LYNNE ATTWOOD

Introduction

Until recently, the subject of sex differences in personality received scant attention in the Soviet Union. Even in the early years of the revolution, when so much was being questioned, matters pertaining to sex were generally seen as marginal to the needs of the new society. Lenin complained to Clara Zetkin that 'those who are always absorbed in sex problems, the way an Indian saint is absorbed in the contemplation of his navel',[1] were at best diverting energy away from the more pressing needs of the revolution. At worst, they revealed a distinct respect for bourgeois morality.[2]

All the same, Alexandra Kollontai braved public disapprobation and tackled a range of issues concerning the sexes. These included a highly controversial discussion of the future of sexual relations. Yet she too felt that the question of psychological sex differences was irrelevant. In the introduction of her book *The Social Basis of the Woman Question*, she left it 'to the bourgeois scholars to absorb themselves in discussion of the question of the superiority of one sex over the other, or in the weighing of brains and the comparing of the psychological structure of men and women'.[3] Such questions were not the concern of revolutionaries. '(T)he followers of historical materialism fully accept the natural specificities of each sex', she explained. They 'demand only that each person, whether man or woman, has a real opportunity for the fullest and freest self-determination, and the widest scope for the development and application of all natural inclinations'.[4]

This conclusion has lately been challenged. A number of Soviet writers now argue that the psychological structure of men and women is no longer a concern which can be left to the bourgeois scholars. For the Soviet Union as well,

> the study of psychological differences between members of the male and female sex is an important scientific and practical question, no less important than the continuing study of their biological and physical differences.[5]

Past neglect of the subject is blamed on a misguided sensitivity to the issue of women's equality, a false belief 'that the exposition and study of the psychological differences between the male and female sexes is opposed to the principles of women's equality'.[6] This error has led to a range of social, demographic and educational problems. A mountain of books and articles has appeared to redress the balance.

THE CONCEPT OF SEX UPBRINGING

Unlike in the West, where the study of sex differentiation in personality has largely been the province of sociologists and social psychologists, in the Soviet Union it has fallen to educational theorists. Their interest in the subject began in 1964, when the publication of two articles in the pedagogical press by V. N. Kolbanovskii and E. G. Kostyashkin broke a 30-year silence on the subject of sex and gender.[7]

These articles raised the question of whether a form of sex education should be introduced into Soviet schools. They resulted in a heated debate in which sex education – or 'sex upbringing' (*polovoe vospitanie*), as it was more commonly termed – struggled to find a definition. For some writers it meant, or at least included, something approaching sex education as understood in the West. Others defined it as the process by which psychological sex, or gender, is formed in children.

Kolbanovskii felt that both needed attention. On the one hand, he complained about the lack of information given to teenagers about sexual matters, and suggested a possible link between this ignorance and masturbation (which is still heavily frowned upon), sexual perversion and sexual crime. On the other hand, he saw gender as the root of the problem. If boys and girls were to develop appropriate male and female personalities, sex would take care of itself.

> There are certain norms of behaviour that are specific for boys and girls, which should regulate [their] mutual relations . . . in the early age periods of their development. These moral standards and principles, along with hygienic recommendations, should constitute the specific character of sex upbringing.[8]

This has now become the standard definition of sex upbringing. In the words of A. G. Khripkova, one of the most prolific writers on the subject, sex upbringing in the Soviet Union is not synonymous with the 'sex enlightenment' of the West, but is a programme of 'moral upbringing . . . with regard to one's membership of one or the other sex'.[9]

Although a trickle of articles on sex upbringing began to appear from the 1960s onwards, it was not until the late 1970s that pedagogical theorists turned to the subject with a vengeance. Claiming that no real scientific work had been undertaken in the area,[10] they tended to couch their own articles in a more scientific language than was evident in those of the 1960s. However, a dramatic and revealing contrast continues to exist between these writings on male and female personality, and the psychological literature on personality in general. There is, for example, a lack of concord regarding the extent to which personality development is influenced by biological factors on the one hand, and by social factors on the other – the environment, training and so on. There is also a distinct contrast over the personality characteristics which should be considered desirable, and hence should be consciously fostered in people. In comparison with the scientific approach of the psychologists, and despite professing to undertake a scientific analysis of psychological sex differences, the writings of the pedagogical theorists appear to be based on little more than assumptions. They are largely untheoretical. They offer a mere description of psychological sex differences, with the (usually implicit) suggestion that they are biologically determined. But in case social influences begin to interfere, a programme of training is recommended to nurture these differences and produce healthy, dichotomized male and female personalities. The contrast between the two disciplines is particularly interesting since, as we shall see, they have generally enjoyed a close working relationship in the Soviet Union.

This contrast can be explained by reference to the social context in which the pedagogical writings flourished. It is possible to perceive a distinct connection between this approach to sex differences and certain political, social and demographic concerns which also emerged as a major preoccupation of the late 1970s. The stress placed on the 'biological basis' of male and female personality differences and the insistence on their inevitability, while at the same time a programme of training is provided to foster these differences, can be interpreted as a reflection of alarm over the perceived 'feminization' of men and 'masculinization' of women and the adverse social implications of this phenomenon. These are, firstly, that such men and women make poor parents. Secondly, they undergo a high level of divorce. Thirdly, and most important, they produce an alarmingly low birth-rate. These three consequences are to a large extent interlinked. Demographer V. I. Perevedentsev has noted that divorce amounts to a demographic as well as a personal tragedy since 'fewer than 50 per cent of divorced women remarry, and most them have no more children'.[11]

THE 'DEMOGRAPHIC CRISIS'

Perevedentsev has described the demographic crisis as one of the major social problems now confronting the Soviet Union. The demographic situation has undergone a radical change over the past two decades, with the population now failing to reproduce itself. This will ultimately result in an acute labour shortage. Simple population reproduction requires 260 births per 100 couples; this means that a large proportion of families should have a third child.[12] However, in the urban areas of the European republics the one-child family has become the norm. Unless the trend is reversed and the birth-rate considerably increased in the 1990s, a calamity will occur by the second decade of the next century, when the babies of the demographically prolific 1950s reach retirement age.[13] Accordingly, considerable attention is focused on the current teenage population as they head towards their child-bearing years.

A second aspect of the crisis is the disparity in reproductive patterns in different regions of the country. In the south and east of the Soviet Union, particularly the Central Asian republics, the population is still reproducing itself with great vigour. Yet this increases rather than mitigates demographers' concern over the low birth-rate in the European republics. For one thing, a large birth-rate in the Central Asian republics will not help resolve a labour shortage elsewhere unless there is a change in the present unwillingness of Central Asians to migrate. There is a marked lack of geographical mobility even within Central Asian republics, let alone beyond their boundaries. This is no doubt due to fear amongst the rural population that their Moslem traditions and beliefs will be eroded if they move to the cities or to other republics. According to Alec Nove, this has led to the anomaly of an urban labour shortage in the republics which have the highest birth-rate in the country, and the need to import labour from the European republics.[14] On the other hand, the Soviet press has recently drawn attention to growing unemployment in rural Central Asia as a direct consequence of the high birth-rate.[15]

Another reason for the concern over family size in Central Asia is an evident fear that the influence of Islam will grow along with the population. Soviet commentators refer to Moslem traditions and beliefs with evident distaste. M. Vagabor talks of the mass of 'religious superstitions and prejudices' which still hold sway in much of Central Asia,[16] while A. K. Minavarov refers to them as 'vestiges of the past'.[17] The negative attitude to Islam is particularly prominent in the recent glut of articles about the phenomenon of self-immolation amongst young Central Asian women. This has been directly attributed to the perpetuance of outlawed Moslem traditions, such as the selling of daughters for bride price.[18]

At the 26th Party Congress it was decided to aim at establishing as the norm throughout the country the two or, preferably, three-child family.[19] If successful, this would result in a huge decrease in the birth-rate in Central Asia, as well as an increase in the European republics. Family allowances were changed to give women financial inducement to have the optimum number of children. The sum due to a mother on the birth of her second or third child now exceeds that for subsequent children, and one demographer has even suggested that the allowance should be stopped altogether after the third child.[20]

The three-child family is said to be the ideal not only from a demographic point of view, but in terms of the 'qualitative improvement' of the population.[21] Firstly, it will promote the psychological health of the nation. Single children are often spoiled and self-centred, while those in over-large families receive inadequate personal attention from adults.[22] Secondly, it will enhance physical health. A single child tends to be sickly, while the second and third children are not only healthier themselves but also improve the health of the first-born child.[23] More than three children per family, however, is damaging to the health of mothers and children. Repeated pregnancy is said to have resulted in widespread anaemia amongst Central Asian women, which in turn has led to a higher than average infant mortality rate.[24]

The excessive work-load a large family produces also hinders the mother's cultural development and impairs her role as upbringer. This is especially important in Central Asia, since local tradition ensures a strict sexual division of labour which places women firmly in the centre of family life. This gives them a particularly strong influence over their children.[25]

It is also said that a standardized family size across the length and breadth of the Soviet Union will promote greater unity between its peoples.[26] Yet what this seems to mean is that Central Asian cultural traditions will give way to Russian norms.[27] As if in anticipation of this charge, A. G. Volkov argues that large families are not a distinctly Central Asian cultural phenomenon but were once the norm for all peoples of the country.[28] Hence Central Asia is merely entrapped in the past.

The desire to increase family size in the European republics and decrease it in Central Asia has resulted in rather different messages being imparted to the indigenous women of these regions. In the European republics there are moves to encourage more of a maternal and domestic orientation in women, and to persuade them to see work outside the home as of secondary importance. This sex-role socialization in the European republics will provide the focus of this book. At the same time, it is important to note that in the Central Asian republics and in Azerbaijan (the one Moslem republic in the Caucasus), the situation is rather different. There, the emphasis is on drawing women into the economy and into political and cultural life. While the status of the full-time housewife is being raised in the European republics, local activists in Central Asia and Azerbaijan are making efforts to persuade women to leave their children in crèches and kindergartens and to take their place in the work-force.[29]

THE LINK BETWEEN 'SEX UPBRINGING' AND THE DEMOGRAPHIC CRISIS

Of course, it has not escaped the attention of the authorities that certain aspects of Soviet living conditions, and in particular the cramped quarters in which family life takes place, leave much to be desired. It has been acknowledged that to start married life living with one or other set of parents, or in a communal flat, puts a considerable strain on the young couple. This can have an obvious effect on divorce and birth-rates.[30] Accordingly, one of the immediate goals of *perestroika* is to provide every family with its own apartment by the year 2000. There has also been talk of building larger apartments so that families will have enough space for two or three children.[31]

There have been other practical measures as well. In 1981, under Brezhnev, the period of maternity leave was extended. Women who had worked for at least one full year, or were in full-time education, were granted one year's post-natal leave on partial pay (35 roubles per month, or 50 roubles for women in 'inhospitable regions', such as Siberia). They were also given the option of a further 6 months unpaid leave, without losing their jobs or their uninterrupted work record. Child-benefits were increased, especially for second and third children. (The allowances for subsequent children were not altered.) Women with small children were entitled to work from home, or for shorter hours or fewer days per week.[32] These measures were extended at the 27th Party Congress; partially-paid postnatal leave was increased to 18 months,[33] with a strong possibility of this shortly becoming three years,[34] and the pledge was made to increase the number of nursery places until the country's need for them is met.[35]

All the same, Soviet demographers argue that improvements in material conditions do not automatically increase the birth-rate. Indeed, they can have the opposite effect. According to G. Naan, the housing situation has improved considerably since the 1960s, but the divorce rate has virtually trebled.[36] V. Sysenko similarly notes that while incomes have risen 3.8 times since 1940, the birth-rate has almost halved.[37]

This means that the major offensive against the demographic crisis has been fought on the ideological front rather than the practical level. In the words of journalist Ada Baskina: 'The growth of prosperity in itself does not cause an increase in the number of children if we ourselves do not come to the conclusion that the more children there are, the greater happiness in family life'.[38] Likewise, demographer A. Antonov insists that, 'it is essential to form in the country's inhabitants, in effect, a new desire for several children. This is a long and difficult business, but there is no other route to success'.[39]

This has the added advantage of being cheaper than improving material conditions. Gorbachev's promise to satisfy the country's need for nursery places, for example, will not require much expenditure if the 'need' is drastically reduced by women responding to the call to have two or three children and to stay home for three years for each of them. Indeed, when the idea of a three-year maternity leave was first suggested in an article in *Literaturnaya Gazeta* in 1975, it was precisely on the grounds that it would solve the shortage of nursery places.[40] It is not clear whether the three-year leave will be optional or compulsory, but in practice it seems likely to become the latter. The current 18-month leave is supposed to be optional, but there is considerable psychological pressure on women to take it. The complaint has also been made in a letter to *Literaturnaya Gazeta* that it is now virtually impossible to get a child into a crèche until it is 18 months old.[41]

It is argued in this book that the Soviet writings on sex and gender, along with a school course introduced in the 1984–5 academic year on family life, constitute part of this attempt to create 'a new desire for several children' in young women growing up in the European republics. This is not to say that the pedagogical 'theory' about sex differences in personality (which presents them as natural, inevitable, and essential) was conceived solely as a response to the demographic crisis. On the contrary, the earlier writings predate the general alarm over the drop in the birth-rate. Such writings also continue to link the inadequate delineation of male and female personalities with other social concerns besides the purely demographic; for example, male anti-social behaviour is often attributed to the 'feminization' of men. It is more likely that when the drop in the birth-rate was perceived to be a crisis, this provided the pedagogical writers with a concerned and influential audience, which encouraged the proliferation of their views and gave them something of an 'official' status. They had, after all, focused attention on what came to be seen as some of the major antecedents of the demographic crisis – women's increasing independence and economic equality, the emphasis on work as a citizen's primary contribution to society, and the corresponding neglect of women's demographic contribution. They also offered some solutions to the problem. These centred on the rekindling of traditional qualities of masculinity and femininity, and the resurrection of women's flagging domesticity.

The revolutionary ideology on women and sexual equality has accordingly been reworked. The earlier Soviet theorists are charged with having wrongly interpreted equality to mean that women and men should be identical. Obscure writings by Marx, which seem to support the new policy, have been dredged up. The one used most frequently is a questionnaire, 'Confessions', which circulated around school playgrounds in England and Germany in the year 1865, and which Marx was asked to fill in by his daughter. Asked for his favourite male quality, Marx listed 'strength'; his favourite female quality, 'weakness'.[42] A large number of writers – generally, though not exclusively, from within the pedagogical camp – have made a serious attempt to analyse and explain Marx's words, and to justify their own models of masculinity and femininity on their basis.[43] Marxist ideology has thus functioned not as a basis for action, as the Soviets claim is the case, but as a *post-hoc* rationalization of this action.

THE EFFECTS OF *GLASNOST'* AND *PERESTROIKA* ON WOMEN

Pedagogical interest in sex differences in personality, and the subsequent attempt to resocialize women into more domestic roles, began in the relative stability of the Brezhnev period. The death of Brezhnev led to three rapid changes in leadership, and then the onset of *glasnost'* and *perestroika*. The Soviet Union now seems set on the path of transformation in virtually all spheres of life. Yet this has had little impact on the 1970s model of sex role socialization. If anything, it has reinforced it.

As we have seen, the practical measures introduced under Brezhnev, aimed (at least in part) at encouraging women to have more children, were extended by Gorbachev at the next Party congress. The school course on 'the Ethics and Psychology of Family Life' has also been carried over from the Brezhnev era, and, although there have been many complaints about the way it is taught, there is no sign of waning commitment to the idea of such a course. The education journals, in particular *Vospitanie Shkol'nikov*, still offer frequent advice to teachers of the course, and the content of these articles could not be said to have changed in the Gorbachev era.

Demographers claim that the demographic situation in the Soviet Union has been improving. Perevedentsev, for example, points to a modest increase in the overall birth-rate in the early 1980s (from 5 to 6 per cent), which he attributes to the success of the pro-natal campaign in the European republics:

> It was the consequence of the whole range of measures directed at raising the birth-rate and improving the upbringing of the rising generation, outlined by the Party and put into practice in the 11th Five-Year Plan ... The new demographic policy turned out to be effective. Experience has shown that it is possible to control the birth-rate.[44]

A. G. Vishnevskii and colleagues have similarly noted that the number of births in 1986, 20 per 1000 people, was the highest since 1963.[45] Yet anxious articles about the demographic situation continue to appear in the press, despite the fact that one of the fears expressed in the Brezhnev days – that there would be a future labour shortage – must have been offset by the expectation that *perestroika* will bring improvements in worker productivity.

The imbalance in the European and Central Asian birth-rates is still a source of continual worry. Efforts to curb the reproductive output of Central Asian women have actually been intensified since Gorbachev came to power.[46] Concern is also expressed about the decreasing ratio in the European republics of workers to retired people, whose pensions they will have to fund.[47] The call to women in the European republics to increase their family size to an average of three children continues to be loud and clear.

Gorbachev has talked on a number of occasions of a need to get more women involved in politics and the higher echelons of the economy, which could be interpreted as a move away from the resocialization of women into a more domestic mould. However, there have not been any notable practical attempts to achieve this. The pledge made at the 27th Party Congress of February 1986 to increase the provision of pre-school child-care institutions could be seen as a step in that direction, if it were not offset by practical and psychological inducements to persuade women to stay at home for the first two years of a child's life, with the possibility of this being increased shortly to three years. If women were to comply with the request to have three children each, and stayed at home for long periods with each child, the result would be such a protracted leave from work that it is difficult to see how they could also manage to move up the political and professional hierarchies. In fact, some of the economic and social reforms currently taking place in the Soviet Union are working against the professional development of women.

The fact that improved productivity will result in unemployment is discussed with increasing openness. *Rabotnitsa* first raised the matter in its report on the International Women's Congress, which Moscow hosted in June 1987. Western delegates are quoted as saying that mechanization has put many women out of work, and that the increased use of computers has resulted in more of them working from home. This has led to a contraction of child-care facilities, on the grounds that women can look after their children at the same time as working. *Rabotnitsa* confidently claims that this will not happen in the Soviet Union, since unlike in the West, the interests of women rather than employers are put in first place. Part-time work, work from home and flexible hours have been introduced for women, but this has not been done out of economic expedience. It has been done in order to help women combine work and family.[48]

It could be argued, however, that whatever the reasoning, the effect will be the same. Sociologist Igor Bestuzhev-Lada suggests with evident approval that improved productivity in the Soviet Union will release women from their present high participation in the work-force and enable them to concentrate more on child-upbringing.[49] In the West (despite the complaints of the delegates at the International Women's Congress), the female proportion of the work-force has actually increased, since unskilled manual work, which is generally performed by men, has been mechanized faster than the female service occupations; but in the Soviet Union, much manual work is performed by women.[50] In any case, even if it were the case that male workers were more likely to be the first to be made redundant, the tighter state control of the economy in the Soviet Union would make it possible, in the dual interests of boosting the birth-rate and disguising unemployment, to relocate male labour within the work-force and remove women in larger numbers. A recent article in *Izvestiya* claims that around 16 million people are expected to lose their jobs as a result of the rationalization of the economy, the majority of them in manual work – 'and at least 15 million of them will be women'.[51] It seems likely, then, that women will become a secondary labour force in the Soviet Union. However, this will be presented as a positive rather than a negative development for them.

N. Zakharova, A. Posadskaya and N. Rimashevskaya, of the Institute of Socio-economic Problems, fear that this is already happening. In an article in the March 1989 issue of *Kommunist*, they delineate a prominent trend of thought which holds that increased economic effectiveness can only be achieved by shedding the less effective elements of the work-force – 'and that means, in the first place, women'. This lies behind the supposed benefits women have recently been granted in terms of work schedules.

> In order to facilitate this female 'exodus' from social production, it has been suggested that they be granted a series of privileges which will result in the reduction of their work load: the work day will be shortened, the period of paid leave to look after a new-born baby lengthened, and so on.[52]

They present a picture which stands in bleak contrast to *Rabotnitsa*'s insistence that in the Soviet Union women's interests are not subordinate to those of employers. The policy of '*khozraschet*', which has become one of the principles of *perestroika* – i.e., that enterprises are held responsible for their own cost-effectiveness – is making employers reluctant to take on women workers. Women's child-care responsibilities make them less stable members of the work-force, and so employers are worried that they will jeopardize the enterprise's ability to be cost-effective.[53]

Despite Gorbachev's comments on the need for female advancement in the political and economic spheres, the extent of his concern is perhaps indicated by the fact that less than two pages of his weighty book on *perestroika*, published in the West in 1987, are devoted to the effect of the economic and social reforms on women. He begins by recounting the Soviet Union's commitment since the Revolution to the establishment of equality for women, and the achievements which women have made in education, work, and social and political activities. He also reaffirms his desire to have more women promoted to administrative posts, especially in the professions in which they predominate. A network of Women's Councils have been set up to help develop the level of female participation in management and public life. However, reading further, this initial cause for optimism begins to dissipate.

Gorbachev goes on to place housework and child-care firmly on women's shoulders, and makes it clear that their professional work should fit around these 'natural' female roles. While Lenin's intention was that women should be freed from domestic work, Gorbachev's plan is to reduce their professional work-loads so that they have more time for their domestic duties. He writes:

> over the years of our difficult and heroic history, we failed to pay attention to women's specific rights and needs arising from their role as mother and home-maker, and their indispensable educational function as regards children. Engaged in scientific research, working on construction sites, in production and in the services, and involved in creative activities, women no longer have enough time to perform their everyday duties at home – housework, the upbringing of children and the creation of a good family atmosphere. We have discovered that many of our problems – in children's and young people's behaviour, in our morals, culture and in production – are partially caused by the weakening of family ties and slack attitude to family responsibilities. This is a paradoxical result of our sincere and politically justified desire to make women equal with men in everything. Now, in the course of perestroika, we have begun to overcome this shortcoming. That is why we are now holding heated debates in the press, in public organizations, at work and at home, about the question of what we should do to make it possible for women to return to their purely womanly mission.[54]

In fact, the discussions on this subject predate *perestroika* by some two decades. All that is new is that *perestroika* has created a few more social reasons for returning women to 'their purely womanly mission' – i.e., taking them out of the work-force and putting them back in the home.

THE OUTLINE OF THE BOOK

In the first chapter we will briefly outline the Western approaches to male and female personality differences. It is important to do so since many of the Soviet psychologists whose work we look at are influenced by them, and in some cases make frequent reference to them. The Western theories will also provide an intellectual backdrop against which to view the Soviet writings on the development of sex differences. As well as the three main psychological theories, we will also be looking at the contribution which feminism has brought to the discussion.

Chapter 2 turns to Soviet psychology's approach to the subject of personality development in general. It traces the development of Soviet psychology since the Revolution, linking it with the practical problems of constructing a new type of person, and analyses the dialectical-materialist approach to personality development. It discusses the work of the key characters in the pantheon of Soviet psychology – most notably, Pavlov, Vygotskii, Luria and Leont'ev – and at recent developments within the discipline. It then suggests how this dialectical-materialist Soviet psychology would be expected to tackle the subject of sex differences in personality.

Chapters 3 to 8 compare this with the writings which have actually emerged in the Soviet Union on sex differences in personality. They discuss the contributions offered by various disciplines, including psychology, sociology, endocrinology, and pedagogy. As we have noted, the pedagogical theorists have shown the most interest in the subject, and have produced a vast body of material dating from the 1960s. It is suggested that this has formed the basis of a propaganda campaign which began in the middle of the 1970s, aimed at strengthening the family and increasing the birth-rate by attempting to resurrect traditional sex roles.

Chapter 9 then looks at the ways in which the writings on psychological sex differences and the merits of traditional sex roles have entered into practical efforts to boost the birth-rate in the European republics. It looks firstly at the way in which sex-role socialization has entered the school curriculum in the form of a new course on 'the Ethics and Psychology of Family Life'. It then looks at the various organizations which have been introduced to promote a more responsible attitude towards the family amongst the adult population. These include family consultation centres, 'people's universities' and lectures for young people on family life. It also suggests that there is a link between the establishment of 'get-acquainted' services – the Soviet version of lonely-hearts clubs – and the pro-family campaign.

Chapter 10 summarizes the discussions and conclusions of the previous chapters, and attempts some predictions about the future of sex roles and sex role socialization in the Soviet Union.

A NOTE ON TRANSLATION AND TERMINOLOGY

The Russian language is distinctly male-biased. The word 'chelovek' is a generic term which would most accurately be translated as 'person' (though it generally appears in English translations as 'man'); but male pronouns – he, him, his – are used without exception by Soviet writers when referring to the human being in general. It is usually assumed that in Soviet psychology of the personality the use of such terms indicates that gender is considered to play no part in a person's personality development, and that the object of psychological enquiry could be male or female. However, the Soviet texts sometimes give the impression that women do not exist at all, and that the 'chelovek' under scrutiny is exclusively and inevitably male.

Hence while I do not use male nouns and pronouns in my own writing to denote human beings in general, I do so when quoting directly from Russian sources. In other words, I do not attempt to rectify the male bias in the Russian language, which I feel would be totally misleading. To have Soviet psychologists describe the human being as 'he/she' would make it seem that none of them ignore women, that they are all aware of the issue of gender but think it irrelevant to the study of personality.

However, a number of English-language translators of Soviet psychology have translated the pronoun 'ego' as 'his/her', as 'his' or 'her' in alternate paragraphs, or even as 'her' exclusively. This comes as a welcome relief for tired ears on which the words 'he', 'him' and 'man' have grated too often, but I feel that it proves the point – that to change the language of Soviet psychology is to obscure the thought behind it. None the less, in the discussion of Soviet psychology in Chapter 1, much of which is based on psychology texts available in the English language, I have quoted from these translations as they stand.

1 Western Theories of Male and Female Personality Differences

Before we begin to analyse the Soviet writings on sex differences in personality, we should look briefly at the Western theories concerning the development of these differences. This will provide an intellectual context for the Soviet writings. Western psychology and sociology have applied themselves directly to the question of how these differences arise, and hence provide a useful point of comparison with Soviet psychological theory and the pedagogical writings.

PSYCHOANALYTIC THEORY

Sigmund Freud's psychoanalytic approach to the development of sex differences is the inevitable starting point, despite the fact that an interest in the personality of women did not occupy a central position in his work. His study of personality development centred on the male child. The conclusions he drew from this were then applied, with dubious success, to the female situation. All the same, his work in this area had a greater influence than any before it on popular perceptions about the personality of women. His influence has also extended to subsequent psychological research. As American psychologist J. Rohrbaugh notes, 'Much research on sex-roles and sex-differences is based on Freudian assumptions about what is important to study, how to study it, and how to explain what is found.[1]

Fundamental to Freud's theory of the process of personality development is the notion that three different levels of awareness exist in the mind. These are the 'conscious', which contains those thoughts and feelings of which we are readily aware at any given time; the 'preconscious', that which we can become aware of if we apply our minds to it; and the 'unconscious', which contains phenomena of which we are unaware and which manifest themselves only indirectly, in the form of dreams. These three levels of awareness find their parallels in three different mental structures: the Id, the Ego, and the Super-Ego. The Id constitutes the uncoordinated biological drive, largely sexual and aggressive, aimed at the acquisition of pleasure and the avoidance of pain. The Ego constitutes the realistic part of the mind, attempting to organize the demands of the Id and satisfy them as far as possible within the limits imposed by the Super-Ego and external circumstances. The Super-Ego is society's watch-dog, concerned with keeping behaviour within the rules and norms set by society. The Ego and the Super-Ego are not present at birth but must be developed during the early years of childhood.

During these years, the child passes through a series of developmental stages. These are distinguished by the dominance of different erogenous zones, which act as the source of instinctual drives. During the first year of life the child experiences the Oral stage, when the mouth is the main source of pleasure. This gives way to the Anal stage. Then, at the age of three or four, the Phallic stage takes over. Girls as well as boys undergo a Phallic stage, but with some major differences.

For the boy, the Phallic stage begins with awareness of the penis and the pleasurable sensations it can produce. He begins to masturbate. He connects the pleasure with his mother, who has fondled and caressed him since birth. He perceives his father to be a rival for her affections and so comes to resent him, even to the point of wishing him dead. This marks the onset of the Oedipus complex.

The boy initially assumes that everyone has a penis. Then he has his first glimpse of the female anatomy. He decides that the girl must once have had a penis, but lost it as a form of punishment. If her penis could be cut off, so too could his. This line of thought produces Castration Anxiety. Since the boy sees his father as a figure of discipline and power as well as his rival, he focuses this anxiety on him; and, rather than risk losing his penis, he renounces desire for his mother and begins to identify with his father. Hence the Oedipus complex is ultimately resolved by the castration complex. He now strives to develop in himself his father's characteristics and moral attributes. Thus his Super-Ego and sexual identity are formed.

In the girl's Phallic stage the clitoris takes the place of the penis. She masturbates, in Freud's words, 'like a little man'.[2] However, when she notices the male organ she feels humiliated by her own inferior version, and 'from that time forward fall(s) victim to envy for the penis'.[3] While the boy fears castration, the girl believes herself to already be castrated. This constitutes her version of the castration complex. She abandons masturbation, and moves instead towards passivity and femininity. To

Freud, this rejection of the 'masculine' clitoris is essential for the woman's progression to genuine womanhood.[4]

Since the boy is already in the Oedipal stage when he experiences castration anxiety, it serves to resolve his Oedipus complex. Fear of castration forces him to renounce desire for his mother and transfer identification to his father. The girl, however, is still in the Phallic stage when she experiences her castration complex, and it has the opposite effect of propelling her into a kind of Oedipal stage. The shame and humiliation she derives from her lack of penis is directed against her mother, whom she holds responsible for bringing her into the world so inadequately equipped. Her desire for a penis is sublimated into the desire for a child; she thus turns to her father in the hope that he will satisfy this yearning. Accordingly, 'Her mother becomes the object of her jealousy'.[5]

The girl, therefore, must undergo a much more complex process of mental development than the boy. Although he also has to renounce his mother as the object of sexual attachment, he retains his attachment to women in general; his initial erotogenic zone, the penis, is also retained throughout life. The girl, however, renounces not only her mother but all women as love-object. In addition, her erotogenic zone must change from the clitoris to the vagina. While the castration complex is a traumatic experience for both sexes, then, the outcome for the girl is potentially more hazardous. Three possible paths to adulthood stand before her. The rejection of her clitoris as an inferior organ might also lead to a rejection of 'her sexuality in general as well as a good part of her masculinity in other fields'[6] – i.e. she becomes sexually frigid and abnormally passive in other areas. She could, alternatively, cling defiantly to the hope of some day growing a penis and thus develop a 'masculinity complex' which, in severe cases, results in lesbianism. (As Rohrbaugh suggests, were Freud around today he would probably see the insistence of some women on entering 'masculine' careers as an indication of the 'masculinity complex'.)[7] Only the third, 'very circuitous path' leads to 'the normal female attitude, in which she takes her father as her object and so finds her way to the feminine form of the Oedipus complex'.[8]

Yet even the 'normal female attitude' is beset with problems. While castration anxiety for the boy serves to destroy, suddenly and completely, the Oedipus complex and 'leads to the creation of his Super-Ego and thus initiates all the processes that are designed to make the individual find a place in the cultural community',[9] the girl's Oedipus complex undergoes no such abrupt destruction but is gradually abandoned through a process of repression, or else its effects linger into adult mental life. Hence

> for women the level of what is ethically normal is different from what it is in men. Their Super-Ego is never so inexorable, so impersonal, so independent of its emotional origins as we require it to be in men. Character traits which critics of every epoch have brought up against women – that they show less justice than men, that they are less ready to submit to the great exigencies of life, that they are more often influenced in their judgements by feelings of affection or hostility – all these would be amply accounted for by the modification in the formation of their Super-Ego which we have inferred above.[10]

In addition, the woman bears through adult life a sense of inferiority, which she applies to women in general and so 'begins to share the contempt felt by men for a sex which is the lesser in so important a respect . . .'[11] Penis envy develops into jealousy, which is a much stronger element in the mental make-up of women than of men.[12] It also results in such supposedly 'feminine' characteristics as shame (an attempt to hide their physical inferiority), physical vanity (since they attempt to value the charms they do have more highly to compensate for their early sense of inferiority) and lack of creativity. Penis envy also combines with the inadequate development of the woman's Super-Ego to hinder the formation of a sense of justice:

> The fact that women must be regarded as having little sense of justice is in no doubt related to the predominance of envy in their mental life; for the demand for justice is a modification of envy and lays down the condition subject to which one can put envy aside.[13]

Last but not least, the aggressive, masculine activity which is repressed with the rejection of clitoral masturbation turns inwards and is directed against the self. 'Thus masochism, as people say, is truly feminine.'[14]

Even in Freud's day, some women were loathe to accept this description of 'normal femininity'. Freud had to warn his readers against 'the denials of the feminists, who are anxious to force us to regard the two sexes as completely equal in position and worth'.[15] All the same, there have been attempts by feminist psychologists, such as Juliet Mitchell, to rehabilitate Freud's theory on the grounds that it has been misread and misunderstood.[16] Unfortunately an appraisal of Mitchell's argument lies beyond the scope of this book.

The Soviet response to psychoanalysis has been largely negative. The principal objection has been that psychoanalysis fails to account for social factors in the development of personality. B. L. Vul'fson, for example, writes that:

> In speaking about the formation of the personality, Freud completely ignored the role of the environment and social conditions in the child's life. He reduced everything to the action of biological instincts and unconscious impulses and, at best, acknowledged a certain influence from the inter-relations within the family.[17]

Social influences are, in fact, accorded a negative role, in that they supposedly suppress the child's basic biological urges.[18] Freud's emphasis on the unconscious, and in particular on the existence of a primordial region of the mind which exists in virtual isolation from the external world, is also shunned as an example of blatant idealism.[19] Furthermore, Freud is accused, along with other 'bourgeois ideologists', of attempting to construct a theory of 'generalized human nature' independent of class, culture or tradition. Only physiology and biology are granted the prerogative to do this in the Soviet Union.[20]

The pedagogical theorist Kolbanovskii, whose work on sex upbringing we mentioned in the introduction, suggests another reason for the Soviet antipathy towards Freud. Soviet scholars could not accept this 'hypertrophy of the sex-life of man', and in particular his claims about childhood sexuality. These, it was felt, amounted to a 'slander of the innocent infant'.[21] Yet in Kolbanovskii's view, this principled rejection of Freud's ideas had an unintended negative consequence. It meant that for many years his colleagues refused to acknowledge that children were sexual beings in any way. The object of their study became a sexless child, 'neither a boy nor a girl, but a creature of neuter gender'.[22] This situation, as we shall see, has now changed. Yet in overcoming their abhorrence of sex, the pedagogical writers seem to have forgotten many of the other Soviet objections to Freud. It might be expected from the critique of writers like Vul'fson that a Soviet analysis of the development of male and female personality would avoid the pitfalls of biologism and idealism and look primarily to the influence of social and environmental forces. This expectation is shattered by the pedagogical writings. In fact, Vul'fson's criticism of psychoanalysis could be levelled almost equally at them.

It should be noted that although Freud remained a *persona non grata* in mainstream Soviet psychology, members of the Uznadze psychology institute in Tbilisi, who have a reputation for unorthodoxy, were showing renewed interest in psychoanalysis throughout the 1970s. As well as republishing Freud's works, they brought out a four-volume study of their own on the unconscious, and hosted an international symposium on the same subject in 1979.[23]

Now, in the climate of *glasnost'* and *perestroika*, this interest is spreading. The psychologist L. A. Radzikhovskii insists that Soviet psychology has to take stock of Freud's enormous contribution, not only to psychological research but to all aspects of life and culture. Failure to do so will ensure its isolation from the rest of the world, and the Iron Curtain will stay firmly in place around people's minds. Stalin's personal opinions were largely responsible for Freud's status as Soviet psychology's 'public enemy no. 1'; and by the time Stalin was dead it was too late, since 'we had already constructed our science as if psychoanalysis did not exist'.[24] Yet psychology has to take a stern look at its past if it is to finally enter adulthood.

> The 'early childhood' of Soviet psychology, as with the other human sciences, was a difficult time. Standing by its cradle, to put things delicately, was a very 'cruel' father – the Father of the People. The fear which began then, and the authoritarian lines which were established, have remained till now in our consciousness, and have produced in it a deep neurosis. Only the full truth, only a process of reflection which covers everything, can cure the 'Oedipus complex' in Soviet psychology.[25]

SOCIAL LEARNING THEORY

In contrast to psychoanalysis, social-learning theory stresses the cultural and environmental influences in the development of sex-roles. It is opposed to the notion that biology underlies sex roles and sex differences in personality. To quote A. Bandura, one of the principal exponents of the theory:

> From a social learning perspective, human nature is characterized as a vast potentiality that can be fashioned by direct and vicarious experience into a variety of forms within biological limits.[26]

A child learns about behaviour through observation of other people. However, performance of such behaviour is dependent on reinforcement. This distinction between learning and performance is the basic explanation for sex differences in behaviour. Boys and girls learn many identical behaviour patterns; they have ample opportunity to observe both male and female models. Their performance of sex-appropriate behaviour, however, relies on the different 'response consequences' or reinforcement contingencies in operation.

A study by Bandura illustrates the point. A group of children were shown a film in which an adult exhibited extremely aggressive behaviour. Some children then saw the model being severely punished for this, others saw the model being rewarded, and the third group were shown no response at all to the behaviour. Afterwards, the children in the second and third groups were found to imitate the model's behaviour to a significantly greater extent than the children in the first group. Boys, especially those in the first group, were more inclined to imitate this behaviour than girls. The children who had reproduced the model's behaviour were then rewarded for doing so. Now, without being further exposed to this behaviour, all three groups began to perform similar levels of imitative response, and the difference between boys and girls was substantially reduced.[27] As Rohrbaugh comments, 'Clearly all the children learned the aggressive actions; but girls were reluctant to perform any of those actions until it was clear to them that in this unusual situation they would be rewarded rather than punished'.[28]

Another reinforcement is the level of adult attention, either positive or negative, which a certain type of behaviour produces. Serbin and O'Leary monitored teacher–pupil interaction in nursery schools, and found that aggressive or disruptive behaviour by boys got more attention than that by girls. Although the attention was negative, it seemed to encourage the boys. When teachers were instructed to ignore the aggressors and concentrate on the victims, such behaviour decreased. Girls, on the other hand, used dependent behaviour to get attention: 'teachers were more likely to react to girls when they were within arm's reach, either literally or figuratively clinging to the teachers' skirts'. When this attention was withdrawn, the dependent behaviour also ceased.[29] Differential reactions to aggression and passivity in boys and girls seem, then, to reinforce sex-typed behaviour.

Reinforcement by powerful models is another factor. Television is particularly important in moulding sex-typed behaviour. Not only does it greatly increase the range of models available to children, but it also provides models who 'are so effective in capturing attention that viewers learn much of what they see without requiring any special incentives to do so'.[30]

A variety of studies have indicated that models who are considered powerful, or who seem to have great prestige, command more attention and thus make better models. (As Rohrbaugh notes, this is the principle behind advertising campaigns in which a celebrity claims to use a particular product: 'Noticing (and coveting) the success of a particular model, the consumer will imitate his or her behaviour by buying the advertised product'.)[31] For girls, power can be a more important factor than sex in the selection of models. Bandura suggests that this reflects the greater tolerance in our society towards cross-sex behaviour on the part of females, and a greater positive reinforcement of masculine role behaviour.[32] A number of studies support this suggestion. It has been found that parents are more disturbed by boys engaging in 'girlish' activities than vice versa, and that boys are monitored more closely than girls for the development of appropriate personality traits.[33] This probably reflects the lower value accorded feminine activities in general.

Behaviour which is rewarded in one situation or by one person will not be rewarded in all situations or by all other people. Children thus build up 'habit hierarchies'.[34] Behaviour which has been rewarded most in the past stands at the apex of the hierarchy and will be the first to be tested in a new situation. If the expected rewards fail to materialize, the behaviour pattern which lies next in the hierarchy will be produced. As a child grows older, different patterns of behaviour are expected and thus rewarded, and the child's habit hierarchy adjusts accordingly. Behaviour patterns also alter on account of increased contact with peer group models or adults beyond the family sphere. A child is exposed to a variety of models, and while one or more may constitute the primary influence, behaviour will rarely stem from one source. This accounts for the fact that even same-sex siblings can exhibit very different patterns of behaviour.[35]

Self-regulation also plays a role. This is facilitated by the adoption of labels for certain types of behaviour. These can have very different meanings for males and females. As Mischel notes:

> It is apparent that numerous activities, goals, interests, and the like acquire differential value for the sexes by being differentially associated with positive and negative outcomes and labels. Labels like 'sissy', 'pansy', 'tough', or 'sweet' acquire differential value for

the sexes, and their application can easily affect the value of other previously neutral labels.[36]

Knowing the connotations of these labels determines whether people allow themselves to perform the types of behaviour subsumed by them. Hence while these self-controls are initially created by external influences, they become internalized and serve as a mediating link 'between the cause (previous response consequence for that behaviour) and the effect (future performance or non-performance of that behaviour)'.[37]

Some critics have charged social learning theory with being over-mechanistic and turning the individual into a robot, a passive recipient of society's norms and values. However, although it does portray the social environment as the ultimate cause of human behaviour, it does not see the individual as a passive receptacle into which society pours a set of values, norms and patterns of behaviour. Bandura describes the process of personality development as one of 'reciprocal determinism', whereby 'behaviour, other personal factors, and environmental factors all operate as inter-locking determinants of each other'.[38]

COGNITIVE DEVELOPMENTAL THEORY

Cognitive developmental theory was originally formulated by the Swiss psychologist Jean Piaget to account for personality development in general. It was subsequently applied by the American psychologist Lawrence Kohlberg to the study of sex differences. It focuses on the way in which a child learns to interact with and utilize surrounding objects and people and thus build up an orderly pattern of networks and relationships out of the chaos of sights and sounds he or she is born into. The ability to organize surrounding phenomena comes gradually through a process of biological maturation and a series of cognitive stages.

In common with social learning theory, the cognitive developmental approach sees sex differences in personality as culturally rather than biologically determined. It does not see them as the result of socialization, however, but as a spontaneous development which results from the child's attempts to sort out and understand his or her own experiences. 'The child's sex-role concepts are the result of the child's active structuring of his own experience; they are not passive products of social training.'[39]

Children establish their gender identity through the same process of intellectual development by which they learn about other conceptual categories. This is linked to their level of cognitive maturation as well as to cultural factors. Rohrbaugh offers a clear description of this process:

> Just as a child must learn about the inanimate objects in the world, so must a child also learn about human bodies. At the same age (two to seven years) when a child learns that physical objects always exist independently of their physical presence, he or she is also learning about the unchangeable characteristics of human bodies.... Once the physical constances of human bodies are understood, a child can begin to connect behaviour and emotions with those physical characteristics. Thus by age four a child learns that the world is made up of people who are physically male or physically female. Applying this category to him or herself, a child develops 'gender identity', or a stable self-categorisation as male or female. A child, once having understood that he or she will always be of one gender, begins to value objects and characteristics that go with that gender.[40]

According to social learning theory, children produce sex-appropriate behaviour largely because of the rewards which accrue from doing so. The cognitive developmental approach sees the rewards as merely a secondary reinforcement. The fact that children perceive certain types of behaviour to be linked to their own sex is sufficient reason for them to want to perform them. Once they have reached the cognitive level necessary to perceive male and female sexes as separate, stable categories, with different sets of characteristics, they are anxious to acquire these characteristics themselves.

> [They] begin to show clear preference for same-sexed playmates and toys, games, clothes, occupations, and other things characteristic of their own sex. They also begin to show an aversion for things associated with the opposite sex, including many activities that they happily participated in previously, rejecting them now on the grounds that 'they're for boys' or 'they're for girls'. All of this usually goes on with little or no deliberate instruction or reinforcement from adults and sometimes in spite of it.[41]

Hence according to cognitive developmental theory, cognitive factors themselves have a causal role in the process of sex-role development.

A number of objections can be levelled at this theory. Firstly, it takes no account of studies which indicate that much reinforcement is performed by adults without their own knowledge, and sometimes contrary to their intentions.[42] It could also be argued that it frequently ignores the cultural factors which contribute to children's ideas of the world around them. Kohlberg suggests that children develop an image of men being more dominant and powerful than women because at the age of four to five they define social attributes in terms of concrete body images. Social power is thought to result from physical power, which in turn results from physical size. They also equate size with age; so since men are generally larger than women, they perceive them as older. Kohlberg concludes that 'children's stereotypes of masculine dominance or social power develop largely out of this sterotyping of size-age and competence'.[43] It has nothing to do, it seems, with the male dominance and social power they can readily observe in the society around them.

It turns out that children do not necessarily imitate behaviour which they associate with their own sex. According to Kohlberg, they tend 'to imitate or model persons who are valued because of prestige and competence, and who are perceived as like the self'.[44] For the boy this presents no problem, since persons who are considered to have prestige and competence are generally male. However, the girl must find herself in something of a dilemma, since her father has the prestige and competence, but her mother is like herself. Which of the two is she to model herself on? Kohlberg's answer is that the girl initially imitates her mother, but at around the age of five to eight she begins to transfer her attention to her father as primary model. This explains the fact that girls are generally less sex-typed in their activities than boys. Kohlberg adds that this does not interfere with her feminine values and self-concept because 'while the boy defines his masculinity in terms of competitive achievement and acceptance in male groups (i.e. being 'one of the boys'), the girl defines hers in terms of male acceptance and approval'.[45] Yet as Rohrbaugh notes, this means that Kohlberg 'reverses the basic principle that he uses to explain male development. The boy values and imitates people who are *similar* to himself, while the girl values and accommodates herself to people who are *opposite* to herself'.[46]

FEMINISM AND SEX DIFFERENCES IN PERSONALITY

The brief outline we have provided in this chapter of the Western writings on male and female personality differences show that there have been significant variations in ideas about how these develop. However, while there is considerable speculation and assumption about the role of biology in determining the differences in male and female personality, there is little that constitutes conclusive evidence. On the other hand, it is evident that social and cultural influences do play a vital role in the development of sex differences in personality.

This provided the cornerstone of the feminist approaches to the development of sex differences which developed in the 1970s. These held that girls and boys are conditioned into certain personality traits and patterns of behaviour which dictate their different adult social roles. Girls learn, for example, to be passive, servile, emotional, and to fear competition. Boys, on the other hand, are brought up to be active, competitive, and to crave leadership. The roles which reflect these qualities differ enormously in scope and status. In Kate Millett's words, the woman has traditionally been confined to 'domestic service and attendance upon infants', which 'tends to arrest her at the level of biological experience'. In contrast, the man has a limitless range of possibilities; 'the rest of human achievement, interest and ambition' is his.[47]

Feminist writers have differed over whether the roles allotted to women have inherently less value than those of men, or only appear to have because of men's power to bestow status on the roles they perform themselves. They also disagree as to the extent to which men could be said to suffer, like women, as a result of the restrictions of role segregation. Some suggest that they pay for their greater share of power and status with the stunted development of their emotions, while others have argued that the male monopoly of power and status renders sympathy for the male plight rather inappropriate.[48] There is a consensus, however, that sex-role differentiation has perpetuated patriarchal social relations. This has led most feminists to argue that the establishment of genuine equality between the sexes requires the abolition of culturally determined differences, and that only then will people develop their full potential as individuals:

> All the true diversity that people are capable of experiencing and expressing ... is repressed by gender.... The good qualities deemed masculine – courage, strength and skill, for instance – and the good

qualities seen as feminine – tenderness, the ability to feel and express feelings – should be the qualities available to all and recognised and acclaimed wherever they occur, regardless of the sex of the person.[49]

They have found their theoretical support in social learning theory. Its stress on the flexibility of human personality, and of the paramount role of social forces in its development, offers the most optimistic route to change and the achievement of equality between men and women. Yet feminism has also made a significant contribution of its own to an understanding of the development of sex differences. The 'consciousness raising' groups, which were a prominent feature of the early years of the movement, helped women to develop an understanding of the ways in which they had been conditioned into the performance and acceptance of subordinate roles. Armed with this knowledge, they could attempt to reject these roles and consciously learn the personality traits which had hitherto been colonized by men and which are essential for achievement in the world beyond the family, such as assertiveness and self-confidence. In a recent review of the early years of the movement, Dale Spender attributes to 'consciousness raising' a significance which extends beyond the realm of the women's movement. Feminists actively challenged the notion that human nature is immutable by attempting to 'reprogramme' themselves. In this way they have contributed to society's understanding of the nature of consciousness and knowledge.[50]

Concern has been expressed that social learning theory tends to have an over-mechanistic approach to the development of sex differences. As Michele Barrett and Mary McIntosh explain, 'it tends to assume a pre-given content that is mechanically transmitted from one generation to the next: "roles" already exist in society, and the task of "socialization" is to funnel people into them as actors in a play whose script is already written'.[51] As we have seen, adherents of the theory reject this criticism and argue that it acknowledges a 'reciprocal determinism' between the environment and the individual's personal features.[52] It is still more useful to see the biological and social input into personality not as empirically distinct phenomena, but as an on-going, dialectical process. If there is a biological imprint on the personality it clearly does not operate in isolation from a particular social context. This means that the 'nature versus nurture' debate is virtually irrelevant, since the two are so interconnected – in the words of the feminist sociologist Ann Oakley, 'nature affects nurture'.[53] Lynne Segal describes the process thus:

> the biological basis of human behaviour is not only experienced and understood through social meanings but is itself determined and transformed by human society and human action. The growth and decay of human capacities are moulded within the possibilities and constraints of particular societies. They are not two separate or separable entities.[54]

A strong element in the work of the controversial radical-feminist theorist Shulamith Firestone is that what is natural is not inevitable. She claims that natural sex differences are indeed behind sex role differentiation. The difference in male and female reproductive functions produced the first division of labour, and women were dependent on men for their physical survival before the invention of reliable contraception released them from constant child-bearing and its attendant 'female ills'. This resulted in the power imbalance which persists today.

> But to grant that the sexual imbalance of power is biologically based is not to lose our case . . . . Humanity has begun to transcend Nature: we can no longer justify the maintenance of a discriminatory sex class system on grounds of its origins in nature.[55]

As we shall see in the next chapter, Soviet psychologists – faced with the challenge of producing a theoretical basis for the creation of the New Soviet Person – have reached similar conclusions to social learning theorists and the early feminist writers about the flexibility of the personality and the mutability of biological input. They are also committed to the all-round development of personality. However, this has not prevented the arrival of a sharply contrasting biologistic theory of sex differences in personality. Ann Oakley's study of Western feminism draws attention to the fact that throughout history, biological accounts of male and female personality differences have proliferated at times when women have been seen as particularly demanding and assertive, and have thus represented a challenge to the status quo:

> in situations of social change, biological explanations may assume the role of an ethical code akin in their moral persuasiveness to religion. They provide powerful, easily understood arguments about

the undesirability of change by fuelling a retreatist emphasis on the immutability of the natural world.[56]

This could also apply to the Soviet Union, since the insistence on natural and immutable sex differences in personality has emerged within a social context in which traditional masculinity and femininity have quite obviously undergone enormous changes.

It should be noted here that the Western feminist movement has also undergone some considerable changes in recent times. It has become increasingly fragmented in the 1980s, and new strands have emerged which contradict many of the ideas we have discussed above. Instead of seeing personality differences between men and women as cultural constructs, which need to be eradicated in the interests of achieving equality, it is argued by certain groups of feminists that there are, indeed, fundamental differences in the psychological make-up of the sexes, which are rooted in nature. Female personality is portrayed as innately more nurturant, cooperative, peaceful, attuned to nature, and – in short – morally superior to that of men. Lynne Segal describes the situation as 'a Manichean struggle between female virtue and male vice, with ensuing catastrophe and doom unless 'female' morality and value prevail'.[57]

It is not difficult to understand how such a view could have emerged. However convincingly social learning theorists and feminists have demonstrated the social influences which shape male and female personality differences, this has not dislodged men from their positions of power and dominance. Nor has it made them any less prone to violence, or dulled what seems to be a passion for war. Celebrating the superiority of female nature must be rather more rewarding than insisting on men's capacity to change. However, it not only ignores evidence about the social input into personality, but also fails to take account of the different ways in which masculinity and femininity are expressed in different classes, races and ethnic groupings. It also does nothing to challenge women's position as the subordinate sex. Segal continues:

> This is all the more troubling because a parallel cycle seems to have occurred in the first organised feminist movement at the turn of the century, when struggles for women's equality with men were gradually superseded by campaigns to revalue and improve women's position in the home.[58]

This sounds not dissimilar to the current situation in the Soviet Union. Indeed, the support which can be derived from the new feminist tracts has not gone unnoticed. In a recent article in *Voprosy Filosofii*, N. S. Yulina explains with evident approval that Western feminism has passed into a second phase, and that the original slogan, 'equality of the sexes', has been supplanted by a new one, 'equality in difference'. The article goes on to promote a pro-family, pro-natal orientation for women, and argues that 'tearing the woman away from the hearth, and getting her accustomed to performing social roles which are new for her', can do irreparable damage to the human race, since it suppresses the woman's vital biological functions connected with the family. The adoption of new social roles 'can lead to dangerous syndromes, if it does not take into consideration the laws of nature'.[59]

2 Soviet Psychology and Personality Development

As we saw in the last chapter, psychology in the West has played a prominent role in the study of the development of sex differences in personality. However, in the Soviet Union it has been notably silent on the subject. It has fallen to pedagogical theorists in recent years to draw attention to the importance of sex differences as a factor in personality development. In order to understand the significance of their ideas, however, it is necessary first to have an understanding of how Soviet psychology has dealt with the problem of personality in general.

Psychology and pedagogy have enjoyed a good working relationship in the Soviet Union since the Revolution, the former providing theoretical justification for the practical proposals of the latter. Since the genesis of their own interest in sex differences, pedagogical theorists have criticized the sexless approach of psychology. They explain it as an off-shoot of psychology's rejection of Freudianism, in particular its 'inherent hypertrophy of the sex life of man';[1] or as a misguided over-sensitivity to the issue of women's equality.[2] Whatever the reason, the absence of a sex dimension in Soviet psychology of the personality has, in the view of the pedagogical writers, done severe damage to the healthy development of the personalities of men and women. They predict that psychology will soon come to realize its error and adapt to accommodate what they see as vital psychological differences between boys and girls.

It is difficult to see how this could be done without changing the tenets of Soviet psychology. As we shall see, its approach to the development of personality is completely incompatible with the pedagogical writings on the development of male and female differences in personality. Given the close and complementary relationship which psychology and pedagogy have traditionally enjoyed, one might expect that psychological theories would have exerted at least some influence over pedagogical writings on sex differences in personality. This, however, does not seem to be the case.

In this chapter we will explore the Soviet psychological approach to personality development, indicate the major milestones in its history and the most important figures in its pantheon, and illustrate the strong working relationship which developed between psychology and pedagogy in the years following the Revolution. An attempt will then be made to apply this theoretical framework to a study of male and female differences (much as, in the West, Kohlberg has applied Piaget's cognitive-developmental theory to the subject of sex differences). This will serve to highlight the inconsistencies between the Soviet psychological approach to personality and the pedagogical approach to sex differences.

HISTORICAL OUTLINE

Psychology existed as a discipline in the Soviet Union before the Revolution, but this event marked a total upheaval in its function and approach. Latter-day Soviet psychologists describe their subject in the pre-revolutionary era as 'steeped in idealistic philosophy'; it 'was used along with religion to shape the consciousness of people in the interests of the ruling classes as a means of reinforcing the class stratification of society, the privileges of the intellectual elite, and of combating the revolutionary movement'.[3] After the Revolution its brief was, instead, to reshape the consciousness of people in the interests of socialism – to create a 'New Soviet Person'. Such a person would have 'a high-principled personality, placing the social, the public interest first, and sharing the aims and principles of the communist ideology.[4] The New Soviet Person would also have an all-round personality in which all qualities and potentialities had been fully developed.[5]

The problem of personality development thus became a major issue within psychology. Its specific role was to provide a theory for this process, which would be put into practice by educational workers in schools and through work with families. Hence the practical significance of psychology was stressed, and the need for a unity between the two disciplines of psychology and pedagogy.

By 1923 psychology was set firmly on a Marxist foundation. The psychologist P. P. Blonskii was converted to Marxism in the early years of the Revolution by N. K. Krupskaya (a prominent pedagogical theorist, and the wife of Lenin), and argued that psychology must involve a class analysis: 'in a class society, "man in general" is an empty abstraction, for man's social behaviour is determined by the behaviour of his class'.[6] In a lecture delivered by K. N. Kornilov to the First All-Russian Congress on Psychoneurology in 1923 on 'Psychology and

Marxism', it was argued that psychology could only become a real science if it were organized on materialist, determinist and dialectical lines.[7]

At the same time, great attention was paid to the work of the physiologist Pavlov, whose laboratory of Higher Nervous Activity was established in 1921 and who continued to receive large government grants until his death in 1936. Although himself not a professed Marxist, Pavlov's work on higher nervous activity was considered to play an important role in the creation of a Marxist psychology since it rejected idealist notions of personality and showed that human mental processes rest entirely on a materialist base. Both before and after his death, Pavlov's name has erroneously been used in support of various strands of extreme behaviourism, particularly in connection with his work on conditioned reflexes. However, his influence has remained strong in the Soviet Union, and his theory still forms the basis of much contemporary Soviet psychology.

Despite the broad adherence of psychology to Marxist principles which Blonskii and Kornilov initiated, there was not an absolute coherence of views. The dominant idea of human nature was of something very plastic and malleable. This accorded with the Marxist principles of historical materialism and dialectics, which stressed the social nature of human beings and that everything in existence is in a continual process of change. It also provided an optimistic stance towards the creation of a New Soviet Person. However, biology had a traditional influence over the discipline which some psychologists were reluctant to relinquish, and which stood in contradiction to the new emphasis on social factors in personality development. The conflict between the two camps was couched in Marxist terms, as a disagreement over the correct interpretation of materialism. One side, that which was favoured by the Party, took it to mean that the person was largely a product of the material conditions of life. The other understood it as an indication that personality rested on a more biological basis. By the late 1920s the former interpretation had gained fairly general acceptance.

There was also considerable controversy over new developments in psychology in other countries. Reflected in Soviet psychology, as in other spheres of science and in the arts, was the general atmosphere of excitement and experimentation which prevailed in the Soviet Union in the 1920s. Within this context, any new and seemingly progressive developments in Western psychology were analysed and discussed with great interest in the hope that they might offer some enlightenment on the subject of the remodelling of personality. Psychoanalysis, for example, was greeted with initial enthusiasm by a number of eminent psychologists, including A. R. Luria and A. B. Zalkind. The appeal of Freud's theory lay largely in its negation of free will, of self-directed activity; the concept of the unconscious stood in opposition to the notion that people can consciously determine their own behaviour. As Zalkind wrote, 'Freud's psychic pan-determinism is the best antidote to the entire doctrine of free will'.[8] However, psychoanalysis was finally rejected as inherently idealistic and individualistic, and thus incompatible with Marxism. It was considered to ignore the role of the environment and social conditions on human development, reducing thought and activity to the product of biological instincts and unconscious impulses. Its stress on the unconscious, in particular on the existence of a primordial region of the mind which exists in virtual isolation from the external world, was denounced as blatant idealism. Freud was also accused, along with other 'bourgeois' ideologists, of attempting to construct a theory of generalized human nature independent of class, culture, tradition, etc., while in the Soviet Union only physiology and biology were permitted to do this.[9] As Zalkind's musings show, Freudianism also quite simply offered too pessimistic a view of the mutability of human nature to be a useful theoretical tool in the creation of the New Soviet Person: 'The Freudian can tell you why a person is the way he is, but can give you little help in making him what he should be.'[10] The unconscious was now dropped and the conscious resurrected to play a supporting role in human behaviour, as a mediator between external stimuli and behaviour. To quote Zalkind once more:

> For Freud, the conscious is subordinate to the unconscious. For Freud, man is preserved from the demands of society in a private little world in which he constructs a special strategy of behaviour. For Freud, man is a pawn of internal, elemental forces.... How can we use this Freudian concept of man for socialist construction? We need a socially 'open' man who is easily collectivised, and quickly and profoundly transformed in his behaviour – a man capable of being a steady, conscious and politically independent person, politically and ideologically well trained. Does the Freudian man meet the demands of the task of socialist construction?[11]

The adherents of an extreme environmentalist view of personality development in the 1920s sought support in the work of Pavlov, whose theory of conditioned reflexes was taken as evidence that human behaviour was conditioned by external stimuli and not by conscious mental processes. By extension, personality was seen as almost exclusively the product of the environment. They did not completely reject biological factors, generally adhering to a 'two factor theory' – that personality was the product of both environment and inheritance. To many, however, inheritance was granted a nominal role, and people were seen as largely passive agents under the control of environmental forces.

The debates within psychology were reflected in educational practice. In line with the new psychological stress on environmental factors in shaping human personality, schools underwent a transformation. While they were characterized in Tsarist times by strict discipline and training, they were now seen as microcosms of the new socialist society, and the emphasis was on creating an environment in which socialist qualities would thrive. As with psychology, there was much attention paid to Western trends which seemed progressive. John Dewey's 'Project Method', for example, was tried out in Soviet schools: children would work on projects rather than undergo formal tuition.[12]

A new discipline called pedology emerged to complement pedagogy and construct a Marxist theory of childhood which could be translated into educational practice. Pedologists worked alongside teachers, and performed intelligence tests on children, again based on Western methods. They explained children's failings not in terms of the children's own efforts or in the teaching methods employed, but almost exclusively in terms of the environment. Children's performance could thus be improved only by exerting influence on the environment. An extreme version of this held that children could not actually be taught anything, but only learnt through 'the fact of [their] existence'.[13] Their own efforts were as futile as those of their teachers. Artemov warned that:

> it is erroneous to assume that the child's attempt to increase his powers by exertion will yield positive results. In actuality this effort will disrupt the relationship of the child to his environment, and the results of his labour will be decreased.[14]

Some even argued that the school was an obsolete institution and would ultimately, like the state, 'wither away'. V. N. Shul'gin, for example, thought the school would be replaced by children's participation in productive work in the community, and that education should not be seen as a special process but was inseparable from life itself. Society itself was an educational institution and all its citizens were students.[15]

Other pedagogical theorists argued against such a strict environmentalist position, however. Krupskaya, for example, while granting the social environment the major influence over personality development, urged that the role of biological inheritance also be acknowledged. The child's personality (which she defined as a totality of internal qualities through which external influences manifest themselves) also becomes a factor in its own further development, in that it interacts with both the social environment and its own natural foundations and in doing so transforms them both, thereby promoting its own process of change. The socializing function of the environment operates only through the child's active participation in it. She advocated an educational process which relied not only on the effect of the environment but combined this with conscious, organized upbringing.[16]

Krupskaya did not, however, seek a return to the strict discipline and authoritarian structure which had characterized the pre-revolutionary Russian school. As well as promoting organized upbringing, she also argued that children should be encouraged to organize themselves, and gain pleasure from this. She counterposed a development of inner discipline in socialist schools against the external discipline of the Tsarist schools. This inner discipline could be developed, she suggested, through collective work.[17]

Another pedagogical theorist who went against the tide of Soviet pedagogy in the 1920s, but whose name is now revered, is A. Makarenko. His pedagogical outlook developed from his actual experience of running the Gorky colony for homeless delinquent children in the 1920s. Having failed to mould his horde of desperadoes into a shining socialist brigade by means of the libertarian, progressive educational ideas which abounded at the time, Makarenko reverted to an authoritarian – in fact, quasi military – regime. Lessons and work sessions were compulsory, and a spirit of collectivism sought through a combination of direct education and collective labour organized on paramilitary lines. The collective spirit of Makarenko's camp, and the combination of education and work which he established there, were not in conflict with the progressive mood of the 1920s, but his methods of achieving them certainly were.[18]

By the 1930s, however, the contours of Soviet psychology and pedagogy were shifting. The experimentation of the 1920s found itself increasingly out of step with the growing centralization and authoritarianism of Stalin's regime. The *laissez-faire* approach to education was no longer appropriate in a society which felt an increasing need for training, stability and control. Schools returned to a formal curriculum and examination system, and the roles of teaching and conscious learning were reasserted. In 1936 the 'Decree against Pedological Perversions' destroyed the power of pedologists and re-established the leading role of teachers in the educational process. While the environment had been blamed in the 1920s for children's failings, now teachers themselves were held responsible.

Viewing the environment as virtually the sole agent in personality and intellectual development had, in fact, become something of an embarrassment by the 1930s. The Bolsheviks were now largely responsible for the environment; and yet undesirable personality traits still existed, as well as differences in achievement between different ethnic groups. M. Efimov's critique of F.P. Petrov's explanation for the underachievement of Chuvash children contains the following tirade:

> Petrov explains the underachievement of a great number of Chuvash children as the result of current socio-economic conditions, i.e., of those conditions which were created under Soviet rule, by workers under the leadership of the Communist Party. It is precisely these conditions, according to F.P. Petrov, which account for the low average performance of the children who were studied. F.P. Petrov, not understanding and not wishing to understand the real conditions for the development of workers' children in the Soviet Union, speaks from the point of view of counter-revolution.[19]

Particularly after 1936, when Stalin declared the achievement of socialism, the environment could no longer be held to account for any perceived failures in the attempt to improve human nature. The passive conception of the child, 'deprived of any life and activity of its own',[20] gave way to a more dynamic approach which permitted children more active roles in relation to the environment and hence some control over their own behaviour and destiny. The previous position was now deemed appropriate only to a capitalist analysis of human nature:

> The entire reactionary nature of this approach to man is clear. Man is an automaton who can be caused to act as one wills! This is the ideal of capitalism! Behold the dream of capitalism the world over – a working class without consciousness, which cannot think for itself, whose actions can be trained, according to the whims of the

exploiter! this is the reason why it is in America, the bulwark of present-day capitalism, that this theory of man as a robot has been so vigorously developed and so stubbornly held to.[21]

Consciousness was now embraced as the essence of human personality. The two-factor theory of personality which prevailed in the 1920s, i.e. that personality is the product of environment and inheritance, evolved into a four-factor theory incorporating the notions of training and self-training. The role of inheritance in this process took the form of potentialities; only through training could they be realized in the form of abilities. As we shall see, this view has held to the present day amongst Soviet psychologists.

By the 1940s, Lysenkoism had found full official support in the Soviet Union, and left its imprint on psychology along with all other disciplines. Lysenko was himself a biologist; his theory, which has passed into the annals of eccentricity, was that genetic changes could be wrought in plants through changes in the environment, and that chromosomes were hence not of ultimate importance. His experiments involved subjecting wheat to low temperatures in order to produce seeds which could then be planted and grown in the colder regions of the Soviet Union. Hailed by Stalin as a Marxist approach to heredity, this theory began to emerge in all fields of scientific endeavour. Its significance for psychology lay in the notion that human biology could also be transformed through environmental changes and was therefore open to scientific control. Hence a psycho-physiological approach was instituted, in which a person's individual biology was seen as raw material in the process of development, which was entirely susceptible to environmental influence through the medium of training. The 1920s notion of the environment was now extended to incorporate parents and teachers, whose influence in the form of training constituted environmental pressure. As Bauer notes, the prevailing approach in this period was 'to concentrate attention on the mutability of innate characteristics and to direct efforts toward what can be done by training, with the notion that there are no limits to what can be done'.[22]

After Stalin's death, and his denouncement by Khruschchev, psychology was able to emerge again as a discipline separate from both physiology and pedagogy. It turned its attention once more to the theories and methodologies of Western psychology; the work of Piaget in particular was received with great interest (and almost equal criticism). Intelligence testing, which had been outlawed by the 1936

'Decree against pedological perversions', was also revived. Again, the methods used are generally imported from the West (but evidently not in sufficient quantity to satisfy those now working in the field of child psychology. The most consistent request I have received from Soviet psychologists has been for material on methods of intelligence testing in the West).

Soviet psychology retains many legacies from its past. There is still a strong physiological influence, for example, though this has diminished in the years since Stalin's death. The work of Pavlov still exerts considerable influence over Soviet psychology, and remains among the most quoted of early theories. A more recent psycho-physiologist, B. G. Anan'ev, the most prominent member of the psychology faculty at Leningrad University from 1944 until his death in 1972, has also made considerable impact. His main interest lay in the influence of age and, to a lesser extent, sex on the development of the individual organism. We will be looking at his writings on sex differences in the next chapter, though they are very much in line with his general physiological approach to mental development.

A sexually undifferentiated approach to the subject personality remains a prominent feature of Soviet psychology, though there are a few exceptions. I. S. Kon, for example, who is variously described in Soviet texts as a sociologist, social-psychologist, ethnographer and sexologist, has produced a considerable body of work on the development of sex differences in personality, though much of his writing consists of a review of the Western material rather than an attempt at a Soviet theory. We will also discuss the work of Kon in a later chapter.

Before we look at some of the more recent work within Soviet psychology, we should examine in greater detail the major figures in the discipline's past, those who were instrumental in establishing psychology as a discipline and whose influence is still strongly felt.

IVAN PAVLOV

Pavlov's teacher, I. M. Sechenov, is often referred to by Soviet psychologists as the founder of scientific psychology because of his work on higher nervous activity in the middle of the nineteenth century. It was Pavlov, however, who developed Sechenov's ideas and whose name is now most associated with the theory.

As Soviet psychologists have pointed out, in pre-revolutionary Russia psychology was suffused with idealism. The mind and body were seen as separate entities, constituting the spiritual and physical spheres of human existence. The spiritual, with its anthropomorphic overtones, was virtually inaccessible to scientific analysis. Pavlov's approach to the study of the mind was a complete break with this tradition. He insisted that the mind consists merely of higher nervous activity; therefore it can, and must, be studied by the same objective methods as the material processes of the body, and in relation to them.

Pavlov was a determinist as well as a materialist. He insisted that there is 'a cause for every given action or effect'.[23] Behaviour is the response to external stimuli. In higher animals this response can take two forms; it can be either a conditioned or an unconditioned reflex. An unconditioned reflex is an inborn physiological reflex, a 'function of the lower parts of the nervous system' which requires no mental (or higher nervous) activity. It is permanent and unchanging, formed during the course of phylogenesis (i.e. the development of the species). A conditioned reflex is a more or less temporary and highly changeable connection between the organism and the environment, which originates in the brain. It is formed during the course of ontogenesis (i.e. the development of the individual organism). In physiological terms it amounts to a coupling of two points of excitation which occur simultaneously at different sites in the central nervous system. This probably takes place in the synapses of neurones in the cerebral cortex (the outer layer of the brain). These conditioned reflexes enable the animal to form myriad connections with its environment during the course of its life, in order to maintain an equilibrium between itself and the environment and hence promote its chances of survival. Once a connection is no longer required it ceases; its perpetuance depends on constant reinforcement. Hence the brain can be seen as a highly plastic organ, responding and adapting to any changes in the environment. To quote Pavlov himself:

> This temporary relation and its law (reinforcement by repetition and weakening if not repeated) plays an important role in the welfare and integrity of the organism; by means of it the fineness of the adaptation between the organism and its environment becomes more perfect. If the temporary relations of some object are of great significance for the organism, it is also of the highest importance that these relations should be abandoned as soon as they cease to

correspond to reality. Otherwise the relations of the animal, instead of being delicately adapted, would be chaotic.[24]

This theory developed largely out of a series of experiments conducted by Pavlov on dogs, which focused attention on the adaptability of the salivary gland. The functions of saliva are to lubricate food and to neutralise any irritating substances it may contain, in order to ease its passage to the stomach and facilitate its digestion. Some foods produce more saliva than others, depending on how dry they are, how acidic, and so on. The production of saliva, and the variation in the amount produced, constitute an unconditioned reflex on the part of the saliva glands which is triggered off by the food itself. The variation in the amount of saliva according to need involves no reasoning on the part of the animal, no higher nervous activity; it is an entirely physical function.

A conditioned reflex occurs when the dog salivates at the mere sight or smell of food. The salivary gland functions because the dog has established a connection between the food and its secondary properties, which act as a signal for the food itself. One of Pavlov's experiments involved a puppy which had never eaten meat and failed to salivate at the sight and smell of it. Only after it had been fed meat could it establish a connection between the meat and its secondary properties, and could begin to salivate when it encountered these.

Pavlov went on to create connections between completely different stimuli. He succeeded in getting dogs to associate certain sounds with food, and to salivate on hearing them; he even managed to establish a connection between pain and food, so that the dogs salivated at the feel of a pinprick or even an electric shock. (Such discoveries have obvious implications for the understanding of fetishism and masochism in humans.)[25]

Pavlov's experiments demonstrated an amazing degree of sensitivity in the brain's ability to couple two different stimuli. Two completely disparate points of excitation could be linked to such a degree of accuracy that a dog conditioned to salivate on hearing a metronome set at a 100 beats per minute would be unaffected by a tempo of 96. Similarly, a dog which had come to associate food with a pinprick could be conditioned to salivate only when pricked on one particular point of its body and no other, however close to the signal area.[26]

The temporary nature of conditioned reflexes was also established through experiments with dogs. If a conditioned stimulus (i.e. the bell, the pinprick) was used too often without being reinforced from time to time with the absolute stimulus (the food), the conditioned reflex would fade out. It is this temporary nature which grants conditioned reflexes such an important role in ensuring an animal's safety, since it allows the animal maximum adaptability to the extremely complex conditions of its external world.[27]

The complexity of the animal's relations with its environment results in continual competition between different stimuli. This results in a constant necessity to choose, or to inhibit, certain reflexes in favour of others. This accounts for variations in response, both on the part of different animals in the same situation and of the same animal in a number of similar situations.[28]

Although much of both animal and human behaviour functions through conditioned reflexes, these play a larger role in human life than in animal life. Animals rely more on instincts, i.e. behaviour operating through inborn reflexes, which are better developed in them than in humans. Humans also possess at least two inborn reflexes which are identical to those in animals. These are the 'goal-seeking reflex' and the 'reflex of liberty'. The former can take the form of an urge to grasp and appropriate, and can lead to hoarding and stealing. This means we are all natural thieves; all that stops us from stealing is upbringing, i.e. conditioning which inhibits the urge to appropriate. The 'reflex of liberty' is a particularly important innate reflex; 'without it, the smallest obstacle encountered by the animal would suffice to modify the course of its life completely'.[29] However, Pavlov also claims to have evidence of a 'reflex of servility'. This protects the weaker from a stronger being; a small dog, for example, will sometimes lie on its back on the approach of a larger dog to signify submission, so that the other dog will have no reason to attack. Pavlov saw serfdom in pre-Revolutionary Russia as a manifestation of this reflex in humans.[30] Pavlov's insistence on an innate basis for social problems such as stealing, and for a tendency towards passivity in the face of potential aggression, does not receive much coverage in the Soviet literature on his work. It is probably something of an embarrassment, or is at least seen as overly pessimistic, in a society which has had a vested interest in seeing human personality as largely moulded by the environment and as infinitely malleable.

Pavlov did, in any case, stress that conditioned reflexes play a more prominent role in human life than inborn reflexes. The mechanism through which conditioned reflexes take place is identical for humans and animals. However, there is one major difference, in that humans have a signalling system which animals lack in the form of speech. A word, by representing an object, will act as a signal for it – or, more precisely, will act as a signal for its secondary properties – and hence activate a conditioned reflex. A hungry person, for example, will salivate at the mere mention of food. In Pavlov's words:

> In the animal, reality is signalized almost exclusively by stimulations and the traces they make in the cerebral hemispheres, which directly lead to the special cells of the visual, auditory or other receptors of the organism. This is what we too possess in the shape of impressions, sensations and ideas of the world around us, both in the natural and the social – with the exception of oral and written speech. This is the first system of signals of reality, common to man and animals. But speech constitutes a second system of signals of reality which is peculiarly ours, and is a signal of the first signals.[31]

This second system of signals offers a much greater potential than the system which humans share with animals. As a result of the adult human's life history, 'any verbal formula is bound up with every external and internal stimulus reaching the cerebral spheres, and may take the place of any of these, so that it may call forth the activities, the reactions of the organism, that are conditioned to those stimuli'.[32]

Speech is thus the predominant signal system in the formation of conditioned reflexes in humans. According to Wells, this sets Pavlov and Freud firmly in opposition, since Pavlov 'maintains that the determining element of mental activity is not the lowest level, human "instincts", but rather the highest system, the speech system. Consciousness, not the "unconscious", plays the leading and dominant role in man's psychic life'.[33]

Pavlov did not deny the existence of the unconscious, however. On the contrary, he saw it as a vital component of psychic activity, a knowledge of which was essential for a full understanding of human psychology. Without it the psychologist would be limited to exploring the vast caverns of the brain with a torch which illuminated only a small area. 'With such a torch', he wrote, 'it is hard to study an entire locality.'[34]

A major implication of Pavlov's work is that people (except in cases of physical or mental disability) are born equal. To quote Wells again, 'according to this scientific philosophy, there are no innate differences in the higher nervous mechanisms of classes, races, nations or the sexes'.[35] A. N. Leont'ev referred to the work of Pavlov when he argued that ability is essentially a matter of education. Wells summarizes his argument thus: 'Psychic qualities, abilities to locate sounds accurately in space, to reproduce vocally sounds of a given pitch, ability in arithmetic and other intellectual capacities, are not inborn, but are acquired in the course of one's life through conditioned reflexes.'[36] Hence similar conditions will produce in different people a similar range of abilities, while variations in ability are the result of exposure to different conditions.

Leont'ev developed Pavlov's theory and introduced the notion of stages and links in mental development. If early links in the development of an ability in children are absent or badly formed, the ability will never emerge. This can be rectified by taking the child back to the stage at which the link should have been formed, and trying again. Leont'ev cites experiments which in this way cured children of problems such as backwardness in arithmetic, and even an inability to sing. The children's former 'tone-deafness' resulted from insufficient exposure to musical sounds in their pre-school years; hence the external conditions necessary for the development of an ability to sing were absent.[37] We will discuss the theory of stages in greater depth in the next chapter. We should note in passing, however, the challenge that such experiments pose to the notion of inborn abilities, and the implications of this for a theory of the development of psychological sex differences.

Although Pavlov stressed that all people (other than those with congenital abnormalities or deficiencies, are born with the same mechanisms for higher nervous activity and hence have the same physical potentiality for intellectual development, he did take note of certain inborn differences in temperament in both animals and humans. He delineated four different temperament types, borrowing their names and essential properties from the ancient Greek physician, Hippocrates. These types are: choleric, phlegmatic, sanguine, and melancholic. They are produced by the actions and combinations of the three basic properties of the nervous system – the strength, equilibrium and mobility of the processes of excitation and inhibition. They are characterized thus:

1. *Choleric*: Such an individual has a strong but unequilibrated nervous system. Both processes of excitation and inhibition are powerful, but the former predominates. Hence a choleric type is excitable and impulsive.
2. *Phlegmatic*: This type is strong and well-equilibrated, but somewhat inert. A phlegmatic individual is thus calm, with a tendency to react slowly to stimuli.

3. *Sanguine*: Strong, equilibrated and mobile. A sanguine person appears lively and active.
4. *Melancholic*: This person has a weak nervous system, in which inhibition predominates.[38]

Pavlov stressed that these temperament types accounted only for differences between individuals; they could not be used to explain variations in the intellectual development of different races, and hence to support notions of racial superiority or inferiority. Such variations were entirely the product of different social environments. The same would presumably be true for personality differences between men and women.

These temperament types also do not actually determine a person's personality. Although it might be fairly easy to ascertain an animal's temperament type, human personality is a much more complicated phenomenon, which is influenced to a much greater extent by the social environment. As Wells explains, people can develop certain character traits through conditioning – for example, strength of will, perseverance, and endurance – which can compensate for weaknesses in their nervous processes. 'Strength of the nervous system is an asset in a human being, but the social values, character and personality traits and consciousness of what is expected of one, play the decisive role.'[39] A recent Soviet account of Pavlov's work includes the assurance that:

> Character is the most complex system in the human psyche; and the leading role in its formation is played by the influence of the life-conditions and the activities of the person. The properties of temperament are essentially transformed by their inclusion in a person's character. As a result, no kind of temperament serves as an obstacle to the development of socially valuable qualities of personality, nor equally of its negative properties. The genetically-determined properties of temperament are only preconditions of upbringing, teaching, the formation of character, and the development of intellectual and physical abilities.[40]

Before leaving Pavlov, we should briefly summarize his work and its implications for a Marxist psychology. It is materialist; it rejects the notion of a dualism of mind and body. It argues that the mind constitutes higher nervous activity and must be studied by the same methods as, and in relation to, other physical nervous processes. It is determinist; it argues that every effect has a cause, and that human behaviour is a complex of reflex reactions to external stimuli. It therefore sees human consciousness as a reflection of external reality, a product of the complex interactions between the individual and external stimuli, which cannot be studied in isolation from the environment. It argues that mental processes adapt to any changes in the external environment by creating ever new conditioned responses to it. Hence human consciousness must be seen as culturally and historically specific, and must be studied within its social and historical setting. Finally, if human consciousness adapts to changes in the environment, it follows that the social transformation wrought by socialism will necessarily result in a change in human consciousness – i.e., it provides an optimistic theory for the development of a new socialist person.

> The chief, strongest, and most lasting impression we get from the study of higher nervous activity is the extraordinary plasticity of this activity, its immense potentialities; nothing is immobile, intractable, everything may always be achieved, changed for the better, provided only that the proper conditions are created.[41]

THE TROIKA: VYGOTSKII, LURIA AND LEONT'EV

L. S. Vygotskii, A. R. Luria and A. N. Leont'ev – collectively known as the 'troika' – have exerted an influence over Soviet psychology almost, if not as great as that of Pavlov. Of the three, Vygotskii's name is the best known beyond the Soviet Union, although he entered psychology late in life and enjoyed a short, if prolific, ten years of work before he died of tuberculosis in 1934. He had a varied background, having been a philologist, teacher and lawyer before turning to psychology. This might account for his success in the field; Radzikhovskii and Khomskaya suggest that the post-revolutionary psychologists who had the least ties with traditional pre-revolutionary psychology produced the most notable achievements.[42] His main contribution is his work on child development. This constitutes, in the words of Sutton, 'a formulation of the origins of the human mind which has, with only minor alterations, continued to serve as the basis for the dialectical materialist psychology of the Soviet education system'.[43] Hence it will also provide the foundation of the attempt we will make shortly to apply Soviet psychological theory to an understanding of psychological sex differences.

Vygotskii's theory holds that a child's mental development is a process of adaptation to, and interaction with, the mass of contradictory elements which comprise its social environment. The child's previous experience constantly interweaves with the new input from the environment; hence the new mental structures which emerge from this relationship are totally dependent on the child's own history. The environment therefore has only an indirect determining effect on psychological development. In the words of Bozhovich and Slavina, 'experience is a sort of "prism" which breaks up the action of the environment and itself directly determines the psychological development of the child'.[44]

This development takes place not as a continuous, uninterrupted process, but in a series of stages. This gives Vygotskii's work a superficial resemblance to that of the Swiss psychologist Piaget. However, unlike Piaget (of whom he was strongly critical), Vygotskii rooted his stages in dialectical materialism, and saw them as analogous to the economic stages through which, in Marxist analysis, society passes en route to communism. Marx argued that in any given society one economic stage is transformed into another when the material forces of production come into conflict with the existing relations of production, or property relations. These act as fetters which stunt the development of the forces of production, until the impasse is broken by a period of social revolution. This causes a complete transformation in society, not only in the economic foundation, but also in the corresponding superstructure. Vygotskii proposed that similar contradictions emerge in the interaction between individual children and society, leading to similar 'revolutions' and transformations in structure, in this case in the children's minds. These transformations constitute different stages in development. Vygotskii, then, set out to extend Marxism, to take it into the arena of individual mental development. As Sutton says, 'Vygotskii made it quite explicit that he wanted to create his own *Capital*'.[45]

There are four major stages. The first is from birth to the age of one; the second, from one to approximately three; the third, from three to seven; and the fourth from seven to adolescence. Within each stage the mental capacity of children grows very slowly. Their skills and knowledge increase, but this constitutes quantitative change (growth) rather than qualitative change (development). Their relationship to the external world remains much the same. These stages are broken by periods of much sharper, more violent change. A fusion of elemental mental structures leads to the emergence of new mental characteristics, of 'higher mental functions', which are qualitatively different. This process is irreversible, as is clear from Vygotskii's description: 'The initial stage is followed by that first structure's destruction, reconstruction, and transition to structures of the higher type.'[46] The children's relations with the external world are transformed.

The new mental characteristics of children necessitate new activities and ways of interacting with the people and objects around them. As Bozhovich explains,

> each developmental stage is distinguished by a unique and particular orientation of the child within the system of relationships assumed for a given society. Accordingly, each period of a child's life has its own specific content: specific relationships between the child and the people around him, a dominant kind of activity for each stage of development (play, study, work, etc.) Each stage has its particular system of rights the child exercises and duties he or she must perform.[47]

The 'dominant activity' is that which will maximize the child's development within a particular stage, and should be encouraged by the adults connected with the child.

The transition periods between stages are marked by certain common features. Children become rebellious, irritable and capricious. These negative features are the symptoms of frustration, which occur because the new needs emerging in the children cannot be met within their present stage of development.

In the first stage a child's 'dominant activity' is emotional association with adults. They attempt to guide the infant through the mass of stimuli in the surrounding environment.

> In the buzzing confusion that surrounds the infant during the first few months of her life, parents assist her by pointing and carrying the child close to objects and places of adaptive significance (toys, refrigerator, cupboard, playpen), thus helping the child to ignore other irrelevant features of the environment (such adult objects as books, tools and so on). This socially mediated attention develops into the child's more independent and voluntary attention, which she will come to use to classify her surroundings.[48]

The infant takes the first step along the path of communication with others by learning indicatory gestures. This might begin when an unsuccessful attempt to grasp something is observed by an adult who comes to the child's aid and passes the object. In Vygotskii's words, 'pointing becomes a gesture for others'.[49] Its function thus changes; 'from an object-oriented movement it becomes a movement aimed at another person, a means of establishing relations'.[50]

In the second stage the child's dominant activity is handling objects. In this way he or she learns the socially-evolved uses of simple objects, and how to control hand movements and manipulate objects with them. The first step is thus taken towards the development of an ability to think.[51] Memory also emerges in a rudimentary form. Mukhina, a follower of Vygotskii, kept a diary of her children's development and noted that before they reached the age of one year and four months she could remove familiar objects from their immediate environment without them noticing, but after one year six months this was no longer the case.[52]

Between the ages of two and three the emergence of an 'ego system' is observed. The child becomes aware of him or herself as an independent entity, a subject. The word 'I' begins appearing in the child's speech. This ego system is a central new structure, effecting a major change in the relationship with the external world. The child now has a conscious awareness of his or her own desires, and wants to act on them. However, another new structure emerges soon after – 'self-esteem' – which, being strongly bound up with adult evaluation, clashes with the ego system. This conflict in the child results in an ambivalent attitude towards adults and contradictory behaviour.

In the third stage, play supplants activity with objects as the leading activity. Although children's desire to do things for themselves makes them more independent of adults, the emotional relationship remains very strong; 'adults continue to be a constant centre of gravity around which the child's life is built'.[53] Hence to Vygotskii, play does not constitute a special children's world removed from reality, as Piaget holds. On the contrary, it is a means of learning the rules and goals of the adult world and involves laws at least as strict. Leont'ev described play as 'a school in which [children] practically acquire the norms of socialist behaviour'.[54] It evidently also gives them considerable tuition in sex roles. He continues: 'What matters to the child in this new kind of play is to act as exactly as possible the way his father or his brother, a chauffeur or an officer, acts . . .'[55] Bozhovich similarly notes that:

> In playing out a role, the child distinguishes the rules and norms that are accepted in his/her social environment and makes them the rules of his/her own play behaviour. For example, in assuming the role of a mother, a little girl will show concern, kindness, and attention for

her 'child', take care of it, prepare its food, scold it, punish it for bad conduct, and try to be just. In other words, in play she tries to embody the behaviour she has adopted as an example.[56]

Play is not the only means through which children assimilate these social norms of behaviour. Vygotskii also places considerable emphasis on adult reinforcement.

In the course of daily life, adults place many demands on children . . . . The child is encouraged to meet these norms, and for their refraction is rebuked or even punished. During this period, encouragement by adults, especially parents, means so much to the child that he/she tries very hard to earn it with his/her behaviour.[57]

Role models also occupy a prominent place in Vygotskii's theory. They become 'ideal forms' of behaviour: 'a constantly acting motive which stimulates [the child's] behaviour and activity, determines his values, the schema of his relation to reality. It is thereby the most important factor of the child's personality'.[58]

As children assimilate norms of behaviour, these become internalized. They appear to the children to be their own, rather than rules of conduct which are externally imposed. The children begin to act in a socially accepted way not only to receive adult approval but because they derive a sense of self-satisfaction from doing so. This is the genesis of moral conviction.

This internalization of social norms is particularly important in Vygotskii's theory. He held that all higher mental functions begin as activities between children and other people, which children gradually internalize.

Every function in the child's cultural development appears twice: first, on the social level, and later, on the individual level: first, between people (interpsychical), and then inside the child (intrapsychical). This applies equally to voluntary attention, to logical memory, and to the formation of concepts. All the higher functions originate as actual relations between people.'[59]

The development of speech is one example. Vygotskii observed that children's early use of speech is entirely social, i.e. directed towards others; but as they develop, this social speech becomes increasingly internalized so that 'instead of appealing to the adult, children appeal to themselves; language thus takes on an intrapersonal function in addition to its interpersonal use'.[60] This represents the major disagreement between Vygotskii and Piaget. To Vygotskii, children are social beings from the moment of birth; their development as human beings depends entirely on their contact with others. Piaget, on the other hand, sees infants as autistic, living in a world of their own made up of subjective experiences and desires. Only gradually, and autonomously, do they become aware of objective reality and develop social thought. 'In Piaget's view . . . events taking place before a child's eyes are unable to teach him, are unable to break down the ego-centric character of thought – in a word, a child is 'impervious to experience'.[61]

As the pre-school stage develops, children begin to feel the need for a more adult, socially oriented way of life. Play ceases to provide them with satisfaction; it was only an imaginary participation in adult life, and now they want the real thing. The impossibility of having it produces the crisis which propels them into the next stage, that of the pre-school child. This is characterized by the leading activity of systematic instruction. The direct role of the adult in the child's development is reasserted, but 'at a much higher level of organisation, with particular emphasis on the child's potential to learn rules and the principles that he can now potentially utilise to direct his own behaviour'.[62]

School, and the relations children experience there, both with peers and teachers, are their greatest influence at this stage. For this reason it is important for them to achieve status at school. If they cannot be good students – they have problems with the work, for example, or they are disturbed by a negative relationship with someone in the school environment – they are likely to seek status in alternative, negative ways. Some children reject school completely and seek an alternative social environment outside the school with other misfits.[63]

In the early years of school the teacher's influence on a child is primary, and exceeds even that of the parents. By the fourth year, however, approval on the part of peers is more important: '. . . collective relations are formed, and the emotional well-being of the school child begins to be determined by the position he occupies in the class collective. The social attitude of the class becomes the regulator and organizer of his behaviour'.[64] Hence it is the task of educationalists to ensure that the attitude of the collective is correct, and conducive to the reinforcement of positive behaviour patterns.

Bozhovich holds that the importance of status as a factor in child development occupies a prominent position in Vygotskii's work, though he does not always refer to it explicitly. She cites his study of three fatherless children whose mother suffered periodic bouts of psychic disturbance. The oldest boy took over as 'head of the family' having complete responsibility when his mother was ill. While the other children were timid and shy, his elevated status resulted in his becoming mature, confident and reliable.

Thus, although Vygotskii did consider the child's understanding and experience of this situation the main factors in his development, he nevertheless analysed the child's *status*, which conditioned his experiences, and his attitudes towards reality, in order to understand the causes of the child's behaviour and development.[65]

A later study by Kovalev and Myasishchev looked at twin sisters who exhibited very different personality traits. One had been put in the position of the elder sister and was expected to supervise her 'younger' twin. The difference in status and demands placed on the two sisters produced radical differences in their personalities.[66]

The contribution of the other members of the Troika to Soviet psychology is not as great as that of Vygotskii, nor is their work so relevant to this thesis. None the less, it is worth a brief exposition. Luria is best known for his work on the development of speech. He was particularly interested in the changing role of speech in controlling the behaviour of the developing child, and in the formation of new mental processes. He was also considerably influenced by psychoanalysis. For a time he corresponded with Freud himself, and in 1925 produced an article which attempted to combine psychoanalysis with Marxism. What has been described as his 'first discovery', the combined motor method, drew strongly on Jung's association experiments. It consisted of asking subjects to respond to a word stimulus by squeezing a pneumatic bulb as well as saying the first word which occurred to them. The theory was that if the motor reaction of squeezing the bulb was conditionally connected with the word response, studying the variations in latency periods between stimulus and motor response would reveal hidden emotional experiences. Together with Leont'ev and other colleagues, Luria conducted a series of such experiments with students undergoing examinations, criminals, neurotics, and children.[67] He also conducted a free-association experiment (using only verbal responses) on rural, urban and homeless children to analyse variations in their speech and intellect. If the experimental method was taken from psychoanalysis, the conclusion was rooted in Marxism: 'Only by tackling the problem of the role played by concrete socio-historical conditions in transforming behaviour can we hope to arrive at an adequate appreciation of how behaviour patterns are shaped.'[68]

This is emphasized still more by his study in the early 1930s of how collectivization and the cultural revolution were reflected in the mental development of members of a rural community in Uzbekistan. In accordance with the Marxist view that human consciousness is a reflection of reality, he aimed to show how it adapted to the transformation in social conditions. He found that changes in basic forms of activity, literacy, etc. produced a shift from a purely concrete, object-orientated experience to more abstract and general forms of thought. New mental abilities appeared – reasoned thinking, and the ability to analyse objectively one's own motives and actions. Luria took this as evidence that

> the basic categories of human mental life can be understood as products of social history – they are subject to change when the basic forms of social practice are altered and thus are social in nature .... Psychology comes primarily to mean the science of the socio-historical shaping of mental activity and of the structures of mental processes which depend utterly on the basic forms of social practice and the major stages in the historical development of society.[69]

Leont'ev's contribution to psychology rests chiefly on his theory of activity. It owes much to Vygotskii and is to some extent an extension of Vygotskii's work, but it is also accorded considerable status in its own right. In listing the fundamental principles of Soviet psychological theory in 1982, Davydov placed Leont'ev's contribution in a position of prime importance:

1. The mental processes of a person (consciousness) are formed and develop in the process of carrying out practical, transforming *activity* with objects, which is social by nature;
2. The mental processes are a *reflection* of objective objects and phenomena which exist in the practical activity of the person;
3. The material substratum of consciousness is the nerve processes of the human *brain*;
4. The mental development of a person has a *concrete-historical* nature;
5. The scientific study of the activity, consciousness and personality of the person must be carried out by *objective methods*.[70]

Leont'ev saw activity, consciousness and personality (*deyatel'nost'*, *soznanie* and *lichnost'*) as the major concerns for psychology, with activity in first place. Failure to accord it this status would lead to reductionism – reducing human behaviour to stimulus and response – or to idealism, the depiction of certain human mental functions as abstract phenomena. The first type of activity is external, practical activity with objects. This activity becomes internalized; an object is transformed into a subjective image. From this process all internal forms of mental activity derive. Internal activity is then externalized; a person's image of the object, through activity, becomes reified. Leont'ev describes the process thus:

> In activity an object is transformed into its subjective form or image, while at the same time activity passes into its objective results and products. In this regard activity emerges as a process that effects a reciprocal transformation between the subject-object poles. In production, the personality is objectified; in the personality, the thing is subjectified, as Marx expressed it.[71]

Activity thus functions to orient the subject, the individual, to the world of objects. Leont'ev sees human behaviour as a three-component process, with activity providing a link between stimulus and response. He stresses that this is a two-way link; society should not be seen as an external world to which the individual must adapt in order to survive, in the same way that animals adapt to the world of nature. If this were so, human activity would merely be the result of reinforcement or non-reinforcement, however indirect. The vital point is that there is a process of interaction between the individual and society through activity.

> In a society a person does not simply find external conditions to which he must adapt his activity, but rather, these very social conditions bear within themselves the motives and goals of this activity, its means and modes. In a word, society produces the activity that shapes its individuals.[72]

This brief exposition of Leont'ev's theory of activity is sufficient to complete a rough outline of the development of Soviet psychology in its early years. We will now move to more recent developments in the discipline. We will concentrate on two areas which seem particularly relevant to the subject of this book. One is the work on the development of moral attitudes and behaviour in children. The other is the perennial problem of the relative influence of biological and social factors in personality.

THE DEVELOPMENT OF MORAL ATTITUDES AND BEHAVIOUR

The study of the development of moral attitudes and behaviour in children has always been a focus of attention within Soviet psychology, given the commitment to create a new socialist type of person. Since it involves an understanding of how children learn to exhibit socially accepted norms of behaviour, it will be of particular use when we come to apply the tenets of Soviet psychology to an understanding of how sex roles are developed, i.e. how boys and girls come to produce behaviour which is considered appropriate for their sex.

The creation of this new Soviet person – that high-principled being who places the public interest first and shares the aims and principles of communist ideology – has not proved an easy task. Even before the advent of *glasnost'*, Soviet writers were willing to admit that success still lay in the future. Newspapers and magazines have long carried stories about individuals and social groups who fail to conform to the ideals of socialist morality. This is still more the case within the current climate of self-appraisal, where the cancerous growths of drug-addiction, prostitution, etc. are laid before the public eye. Accordingly, how to form appropriate moral attitudes and behaviour in people is a major concern for psychologists. The link between psychology and pedagogy has remained strong in this area, and has led to much use of the 'psycho-pedagogical experiment', i.e. one which is conducted by psychologists on children in their own school environment.[73]

The early psychological and pedagogical writers of the Soviet Union still provide the theoretical foundation for work in this area. The names of Vygotskii and Makarenko, in particular, are found in most accounts of recent experimental work. They are most frequently evoked to endorse the views that genuine moral behaviour occurs only when children internalize the demands of adults and act under their own guidance rather than through external compulsion, and that the collective and play hold positions of paramount importance in the formation of moral values in children.

Bozhovich has offered a detailed exposition of Makarenko's observations on the role of the collective as a medium between adult demands and individual internalization of these demands. He delineated four stages. In the first stage, adult demands are seen as external to the collective. In the second, the leading individuals or group within the collective adopt the demands and impose them on the other members. By the third stage, the collective as a whole has accepted the demands and imposes them on any remaining miscreants. In the final stage, the individual members have all internalized the demands. They perceive them as their own individual moral judgements, and hence impose them on themselves.[74] Bozhovich accepts this description, but suggests that it does not go far enough. It does not actually describe the process by which the motives are created in children to accept and internalize the moral demands of adults.[75] Much recent work in the area constitutes an attempt to do this.

Use of play and the collective remain at the centre of many such attempts. Makarenko argued that play 'must . . . be organized in such a way that, while remaining play, it nevertheless develops the qualities of the future worker and citizen'.[76] El'konin and others have performed experiments which suggest that play develops moral qualities in children because they are so anxious to submit to the rules of a game that they will subordinate their own desires to it. This is particularly so if the game involves a group of children rather than just one or two.[77]

E. V. Subbotskii is one of the more prominent young psychologists to emerge in this field. He argues that play in itself does not create moral qualities in children. Studies by both Western and Soviet psychologists demonstrate that children who adhere to moral norms of behaviour in their play do not necessarily continue to do so in real life. This is not because they do not understand the norms, or are inherently immoral; it is because they have not sufficiently internalized the rules. Play in itself seems unable to effect this process of internalization.[78]

On the basis of his own experiments, Subbotskii concludes (again reminiscent of Vygotskii) that the status accorded to children – their position in the network of social relations with peers and adults – is of prime importance. If children are seen by society, as personified by the adults around them, to be models and defenders of moral attitudes, this affects their self-evaluation. They come to see themselves as mature and responsible, and begin to act accordingly. If a child then breaks the norms of behaviour, 'he destroys also [his own] attitude to himself "as a bigger person"'.[79] Hence children's evaluation of themselves as responsible people who uphold the rules provides an inner sanction against their breaking them. This, suggest Subbotskii, is 'the basis of moral motives of behaviour. It is precisely this which constitutes those 'internal instances' which ensure the fulfilment by the child of moral norms in the complete absence of external control.[80]

Subbotskii tested this hypothesis by putting children who had been known to transgress norms when they thought they could not be seen into the role of models and defenders of these norms in relation to other children. the experiments were only partially successful; they effected a change only in children who had not been severe transgressors and were 'already on the verge of crossing over into a moral attitude'.[81] However, Subbotskii notes that they took place in laboratory conditions and over a short space of time, and so could not be expected to form moral behaviour in all the children who took part. 'After all, the formation of a moral attitude, as with any change in the personality of a child, is a prolonged process, presupposing a deep transformation in the life and activity of the child . . .'[82] On the whole, he was satisfied with the experiments. 'The results support our proposition, according to which a change in the position of the child, "awarding" them the function and defender of rules, leads to the formation of moral motives.'[83]

Following the example of Leont'ev, other psychologists have attempted to achieve the internalization of adult demands in children through incorporating them into goals to which the children already aspire. Leont'ev himself found that some children resisted the study of physics, despite the demands of their teachers, until they found that it was necessary for the construction of model aircraft which could actually fly. This led them to study physics under no external compulsion.[84]

It has also been suggested that competition can develop motives for internalizing moral demands, though it can also produce a number of adverse effects. Mukhina notes that in Western countries competition and individualism are seen as an ethos in themselves and are inculcated in children; this, however, causes them to exhibit aggressive and immoral behaviour.[85] Makhlakh and Prokina argue that such negative behaviour can be avoided in Soviet children if the following measures are taken. A goal should be selected which has social significance and which the entire collective agrees upon. Competition should take place between groups rather than individual children. Finally, the progress of these groups should be evaluated individually, without comparing them to each other.[86] (If the last measure is implemented, however, it is difficult to see where the concept of competition fits in.)

Mukhina, on the other hand, holds that competition on an individual level is necessary for children and, despite the possible dangers, should be encouraged. She reached this conclusion though experiments with groups of children. Each child in the group was given a number of dolls equivalent to the number of children in the group, each doll representing a member of the group. The children were asked to position the dolls in such a way as to symbolize their roles in a certain game. They were able to do this individually, alone, and seemingly unobserved. Almost without exception they gave the doll which represented themselves the most important role in the game, regardless of their actual status in the group and the possibility of their assuming a role of such significance in real life. In Mukhina's view, this refutes the commonly-held psychological view that certain children always take the lead in games either because they have a natural inclination towards leadership, or because they seek to counteract a sense of inferiority.[87] In fact, the majority of children aspire towards leadership. This is because at the pre-school stage of development the need for recognition of status is transferred from relations with adults to relations with peers. Adults are more unequivocally supportive of the child, while peers vacillate between mutual support and competition since the already established 'need to be like everyone else' has been joined by a 'need to be better'. Hence

> as a child interacts with his peers, his developing need for recognition finds expression in an aspiration toward some position in the group of peers that is important for all the children. However, the phenomenon is not obvious, since, for the most part, the child conceals his aspirations toward this important place from others.[88]

Mukhina concludes that competition and ambition are important for children and should be encouraged; psychologists will just have to find ways of overcoming the negative personality traits which can result from them. '[A]mbitions are necessary; the need for recognition is an important human need, which determines the success of the development of a full all-round personality.'[89] If psychologists have really had the success they claim through the psycho-pedagogical experiment (Kovalev, for example, was apparently able to ascertain what produced such negative traits as shyness, impulsiveness and rudeness, and to eliminate these through retraining),[90] this should not be too difficult.

BIOLOGY AND SOCIETY IN THE DEVELOPMENT OF PERSONALITY

This brings us to the question of biological and social influences in the formation of personality, which has particularly important implications for understanding the development of sex differences in personality. The conviction that training and retraining can inculcate positive character traits and eliminate negative ones necessitates a continued notion that human personality is very plastic and malleable, conditioned primarily by the social environment rather than internal factors. However, this view has always been somewhat controversial. The debates of the 1920s revolved largely around this issue; when they died down (or, more accurately, were strangled by Stalinism), the subject did not disappear forever but merely lurked in the background, a skeleton in the cupboard of psychology and its related disciplines. In recent years the cupboard door has creaked open again.

The psychologists who have taken part in the debate are in fairly broad agreement with each other. Their views generally fit within the pattern of psychological thought which we have already traced from the works of Pavlov and Vygotskii. A person's biological make-up is granted a role in the development of personality, but it is generally seen as subordinate to that of the social environment. From the moment of birth people are social beings, taking their position in a human world. The biological in them is not destroyed, but is included in a social system of relations and connections.[91] Hence a dialectical interdependence exists between the social and the biological, but an unequal one in which the influence of the social envirnonment is able to suppress the biological input in personality when this proves a hindrance to social progress. In Fedoseev's words,

> In the course of social activity, the person actually *transforms*, but does not abolish, the natural or biological within him or herself. Hence the interdependence, the continuity, between the biological and the social does not disappear but historically develops.[92]

Biological factors are not strong enough to resist this transformation. Fedoseev states firmly that: 'There is no evidence whatsoever that the biological traits of a person can act as irresistible barriers to social progress.'[93]

This unity of the biological and the social is evident in the development of abilities. People do not possess innate abilities, though they may have certain potentialities which will assist in the development of abilities. The abilities themselves can only be formed through interaction with the social environment, i.e. during the course of activity. Their formation represents a qualitative change in the person's psychological development.[94] Posnanski asserts that, 'The theory of dialectical materialism . . . excludes the existence of abilities before the appearance of the activity which first makes the ability effective. Abilities are formed and develop only in the process of the activity which requires them.[95]

A strongly opposing view can be found within the biological sciences. This was brought to public attention in 1980, by a controversy provoked by the publication of an article by N.P. Dubinin in the journal *Kommunist*. A geneticist himself, Dubinin expressed alarm at a recent trend amongst his colleagues to account for human personality in largely genetic terms. He argued that this contradicted the basic tenets of dialectical materialism and Marxism-Leninism, which see human potential as limitless, by promoting the notion of innately superior and inferior people. He suggested that they had been influenced – indeed, duped – by 'bourgeois ideologues' in the West, who promote a neo-eugenicist approach to the study of human personality for racist and elitist ends.[96]

Dubinin's article refers by name to a number of scientists. Among these are Yu. Kerkis, who tries to explain criminal tendencies in terms of genes, and B.V. Efroison, who does the same with morality. His attack is primarily directed, however, against V.M. Polynin, one of the editors of a popular science journal *Priroda* and author of a work of the same ilk called *Mama, Papa i Ya*. Polynin approaches the development of human beings, in the words of Dubinin, like a cattle breeder. In openly eugenicist terms, he calls for the sterilization of all people who are 'unsuitable, those of little value',[97] arguing that in this way genetics can 'improve' the human being and contribute towards the development of an ideal person. Anticipating the objection that a popular work of this sort should not be taken too seriously, Dubinin points out that the foreword of the book is written by a well-known and respected academic, B.L. Astaurov, who asserts that 'the content of the book is in reality very serious' and argues that, 'heredity is a special sphere with its own unalterable laws . . . . Nothing can be achieved through upbringing, or exercising the body'.[98]

Dubinin does not confine his attack to the strict geneticists. He is also critical of the 'two-factor' theorists, who promote a sociobiological view of personality development. In the 1920s, adherents of the two-factor theory generally granted a far larger role to social rather than biological influences on personality; however, Dubinin argues that the two-factor theorists of the present day have an excessively biological approach. Like the geneticists, they hold that people's genetic programme governs their social behaviour, and that

> consciousness is merely the result of the 'unwinding' of the genetically conditioned 'endowments' (zadatkov) of the higher nervous functions, in dependence on environmental factors. Social conditions appear in this scheme to be external in relation to the ready-prepared, genetically conditioned human qualities.[99]

He quotes two such writers, E. T. Lil'in and P. B. Gofman-Kadoshnikov, who insist that, 'No environmental conditions whatsoever . . . can produce a prominent artist, singer, mathematician or sportsman from a child who does not have the corresponding inherited instincts . . .'[100] Evidently the work by Leont'ev on children's singing abilities, and the corresponding theory of learning through stages, have had little impact on the thinking of such writers.

When Dubinin's article first appeared, it generated considerable controversy. The President of the Academy of Sciences accused Dubinin rather than his colleagues of being non-Marxist, and an application by the editor of *Kommunist* to join the Academy of Sciences as a corresponding member was rejected, apparently because of his role in the publication of Dubinin's article. On the other hand, the French Marxist philosopher Lucien Sève gave Dubinin his full support, and a rather more cautious endorsement of his position appeared in a report of the June 1983 Plenum of the Central Committee from K. U. Chernenko[101] (who was soon after to enjoy brief fame as General Secretary). This initial level of interest was not sustained, but contributions on the subject have continued to appear in the Soviet press from time to time. Dubinin's concern about the 'two factor' theorists is echoed in an article by D. I. Fel'dshtein, which appeared in *Sovetskaya Pedagogika* in 1984:

> Asserting that the genetic programme directs the social behaviour of the person, the authors of such a dualistic approach to the problem of the combination of the biological and the social in the person try to revive eugenics . . . [they] seek the improvement of human nature through selection and have created a base for social-Darwinism, racist theories and the practice of genocide.[102]

Talent is interpreted as 'a happy combination of genes', with abilities 'encoded' or programmed in the biological make-up. '[T]he formation and development of abilities is a process of the maturation of qualities which are defined by the level of "the genetic equipment". This "equipment" defines the spiritual qualities of a person, whether he is gifted or not.'[103]

Fel'dshtein claims that the spread of this insidious bourgeois theory to the Soviet Union has not been confined to biologists but includes some psychologists and pedagogical theorists, and, still more alarming, has begun to orientate activities in schools. He suggests that some teachers adhere to the theory as a way of letting themselves off the hook, freeing themselves 'from responsibility for the low level of their own upbringing work'.[104]

The obvious conclusion which can be drawn from this discussion is that there is no single Soviet approach to an understanding of the biological and social influences on the development of personality. However, the conflict we have outlined above could be described as an interdisciplinary phenomenon, rather than a disagreement within psychology. Despite Fel'dshtein's fears, psychologists – at least, those who appear in print – still adhere to the dialectical materialist approach to personality development. This sees the social environment as the primary determinant of personality and finds its roots in the work of Pavlov and Vygotskii. We will how attempt to apply this to an understanding of the development of sex differences in personality.

A PROPOSED SOVIET THEORY OF MALE AND FEMALE PERSONALITY, ACCORDING TO THE TENETS OF SOVIET PSYCHOLOGY

In the previous pages we have explored the development of Soviet psychology in the years since the Revolution, and seen how the need to tackle the problem of creating a 'New Soviet Person' led to considerable interest in personality development. However, although Western psychologists of the same period began to turn their attention to male and female differences in personality, Soviet psychologists remained indifferent to this aspect of their subject. Their concern was supposedly a sexually undifferentiated child, although one who, in accordance with the male bias inherent in the Russian language, was described in distinctly male terms.

If Soviet psychologists intended their theories to be applicable to both men and women (and did not just forget about the existence of women), we can deduce from their work a Soviet understanding of psychological sex differences. This would centre on two premises: that

Soviet psychologists deny both the desirability, and the inevitability, of these differences.

The first premise is an obvious conclusion of the conviction that the new Soviet person will have an all-round personality, in which his or her qualities and potentialities are fully developed. This would hardly be possible within the confines of the cultural definitions of masculinity and femininity which we explored in the Western material. Soviet psychologists would surely reject the attempts by certain of their Western colleagues to reduce female psychology to a range of traits and characteristics associated with their reproductive organs and functions.[105] This pledge to the full development of the Soviet citizen's personality has not foundered in more recent years; we have seen it repeated, for example, in Mukhina's discussion of the social development of the child. It is also significant that several of the personality traits which are commonly linked with women in the West have been described as negative characteristics by Soviet psychologists, who are intent on eradicating them. Kovalev, for example, considered shyness and impulsiveness to be negative traits leading to undesirable behaviour in children, which should be eliminated through a process of re-education. Vygotskii saw over-emotionality as similarly negative, and attached great importance to teaching children how to control their emotions through the use of play. Mukhina, on the other hand, perceives a number of supposedly 'masculine' traits to be positive and even essential for the healthy development of all children; these include competition, ambition, and the desire for status.

Of course, these examples might also point to a tendency (not unfamiliar to Western readers) to value that which is generally associated with the male, and devalue that which is associated with the female. Soviet psychologists would evidently not see such sex-typing as inevitable, however, since they argue that the characteristics can be suppressed or developed through a process of socialization and training.

A glance through the previous chapter reveals much support for the contention that Soviet psychologists cannot, according to the tenets of their own theories, see sharply differentiated male and female personalities as inevitable. As we saw, while the relative weight of the two factors has altered to some extent during the development of Soviet psychology, what has emerged is the notion that personality is formed by a dialectical interaction of social and biological influences. (The former may be taken to include the effect of the environment, training, and self-training.) Although certain voices of protest can be heard from within the natural sciences, psychologists continue to credit social influences with the more important role. This position has been largely consistent since the theories of Pavlov and Vygotskii were first expounded.

Pavlov, we will recall, considered that people are born equal (apart from those with physical or mental disabilities). The development of differences occurs during the course of their life-time, through their interaction with the environment and the formation of conditioned reflexes which enable them to survive within that environment. Male and female children would thus be born equal; their psychological differences would constitute conditioned responses to the demands of the environment, including those dictated by its social norms and institutions. Since conditioned reflexes are temporary and dependent on continued reinforcement, alterations in the social demands made on men and women will inevitably lead to changes in their behaviour and abilities. Leont'ev's introduction of the idea of links and stages in mental development is also relevant; the fact that men exhibit less nurturant behaviour, to give one example, could be explained by their having missed a vital stage in the development of this characteristic, in the form of childhood role-play with dolls. Pavlov does delineate different temperament types, but emphasizes that these only account for differences between individuals. In any case, they do not determine personality, which is a far more complex phenomenon and is largely dependent on social conditioning. A recent Soviet exposition of Pavlov's work talks of the social transformation of the properties of temperament by upbringing and teaching etc. This is echoed in Fedoseev's description of the person transforming the natural or biological within him or herself in the course of social activity. Activity is stressed again and again by Soviet psychologists; only through activity can innate potentialities be developed into abilities.

Hence even if there were innate male and female psychological differences and tendencies towards certain patterns of behaviour, they would be unable to withstand the influence of the environment if it was organized in such a way as to encourage the break-down of sex-role stereotypes – which it would have to be if the all-round development of personality was to be achieved. Given the emphasis on the development of abilities through activity, and the importance accorded to play in the preparation of children for adult roles, we would imagine that schools and kindergartens would use play activity to develop a vast range of abilities in children of both sexes to equip them with the full gamut of future roles and functions. The importance of the social environment in developing certain modes of thought, as well as abilities and patterns of behaviour, is evident from Vygotskii's assertion that mental activity is always social.

Finally, the Soviet rejection of Freudianism is also worth a mention. It was seen as incompatible with Marxism for its failure to acknowledge the role of the environment in the development of personality; for its reduction of human thought and behaviour to the level of biological instincts and unconscious impulses; and for its lack of optimism regarding the human potential for change. Evidently, then, a Marxist approach to psychological sex differences would have to acknowledge their amenability to environmental influence, would not reduce them to biological instincts connected with reproductive functions, and would see them an fundamentally mutable. As Posnanski has asserted, 'even naturally caused differences of birth, e.g. racial, can and must be abolished by a new historical development'.[106] The same must surely be true of psychological sex differences.

These are the logical conclusions of an application of Soviet Marxist psychology to an understanding of psychological sex differences. How does it correspond to the actual writings which have appeared on the subject? We will turn to these in the next chapter.

3 Soviet Psychologists on Sex Differences

As we have already mentioned, Soviet psychologists have shown little interest in producing a comprehensive study of the origins of sex differences in personality, and the process by which these develop. However, a number of them have looked at sex as a possible factor in other areas of psychological concern; for example, the development of skills in childhood, the tackling of mental problems, and the strength of children's identification with their parents. Such studies appear to be on the increase in accordance with the government interest in the family and with the introduction of the school course on family life. Several of the psychologists whose work we look at point to the current topicality of their subject. Many of them adopt one or more of the Western theories we looked at earlier as their theoretical framework. Kohlberg's cognitive-development theory appears with particular frequency. One psychologist, however, sees the Soviet position as fundamentally opposed to that of the West, which is epitomized as a feminist desire to promote psychological sex neutrality. In contrast to the expectations we expressed earlier – that Soviet psychology should, according to its own tenets, see psychological sex differences as neither desirable nor inevitable – we will find from these studies that it considers them to be both inevitable and vital. Often the professed purpose of these psychological studies is to indicate conditions and methods more conducive to the successful accomplishment of sex-role socialization.

These studies do not combine to form a body of knowledge on any aspect of sex differences. They constitute single, rather isolated ventures into the arena of sex differences. Hence it seems appropriate to divide the chapter according to author rather than theme. In the conclusion we will try to draw some general threads from the material.

B. G. ANAN'EV: SEX DIFFERENCES IN ONTOGENESIS

The late psychologist B. G. Anan'ev has shown considerable interest in sex differences, though his approach to the subject has a more physiological perspective than is generally found in the West. He is particularly concerned about the role of sex differences in ontogenesis, i.e. the development of the individual organism. He sees them as a constant factor in the regulation of all internal processes of the human organism, as well as some aspects of the interaction of that organism with the outer world. He talks, for example, of sex differences in sensory-motor functions in children, such as visual perception. He argues a biological sex difference in certain abilities such as sewing or threading a needle, in which he claims girls have a natural superiority. Boys, on the other hand, react more precisely to moving objects, and walk faster than girls. Girls have a greater ability to withstand pain and suffering, and to fulfil boring, monotonous tasks. This is linked to their greater ability to control muscular or motor reactions. Many sex differences are related to different rates of maturation of the organism. For example, boys have a more advanced field of vision up to the age of six or seven, when girls suddenly begin to show an advantage. Girls are initially better at catching objects, but boys overtake them at around the age of 15.[1]

Anan'ev does not ignore the influence of the environment, however. He concludes that the greater propensity for motor-control amongst girls may be partly due to the effects of upbringing and training; the behaviour of girls is under tighter adult regulation and takes place within a greater number of adult interdictions, which helps to develop this 'braking process' (*tormoznoi protsess*). Similarly, after citing Jung's finding that male responses are faster than female in word-association experiments, he adds that the sex factor is almost entirely superseded by that of education. Both sexes respond faster with increasing age and intellectual development.[2]

Anan'ev fails to provide any convincing evidence for the biological nature of such differences. While his major work, *Chelovek kak predmet sosnaniya*, refers to the results of many Soviet and Western studies (the latter generally very dated – one, on greater female longevity, was published in 1898!), he rarely describes the experiments from which these results derive. When he does, the conclusions he draws are questionable. For example, he refers to a study by former colleagues at Leningrad University, Bodalev and Kurbanov, which compares the drawings of 600 boys and girls of pre-school age divided into three different age groups.[3] The children's drawings were found to be considerably influenced by the sex of the child. On the whole they drew people of their own sex; boys in particular very rarely drew girls.

The subject matter was also highly sex-differentiated, with boys favouring industrial and war scenes and girls choosing pastoral and domestic subjects. Seventy per cent of boys in the six-to-seven age group drew industrial landscapes, compared with only 6 per cent of the girls. Instead girls drew houses, trees, flowers and natural landscapes. They also lavished greater care on the clothes and hair-styles of the people in their drawings, which Anan'ev takes as an indication that visual perception and the ability to perform delicate hand movements are better developed in girls. However, even a casual observer in the Soviet Union cannot fail to notice the abundance of feminine frills and bows which adorn girls of the youngest age. Surely this would suggest to children of both sexes that such attention to appearance is an exclusively female concern, which could be reflected in their drawings? Anan'ev only mentions the difference in choice of subject matter in relation to the oldest group of children, the six- to seven-year-olds. By this age they will already have had ample exposure to the influence of sex stereotypes to form ideas about sex-appropriate attitudes and behaviour – especially according to the tenets of Soviet psychology, which sees children as active agents in their own learning process who seek to acquire what they see as appropriate attitudes and behaviour. If the difference in choice of subject matter rested on natural male and female differences, would it not be evident in children of all ages?

A. A. BODALEV: SEX DIFFERENCES IN INTERPERSONAL UNDERSTANDING

It is interesting to note that A. A. Bodalev, one of the two names connected with the study referred to by Anan'ev, is himself a social-psychologist, most noted for his work on interpersonal understanding (i.e. on how people perceive one another). A glance at his work suggests that his explanation of sex differences in children's drawings would be rather different. He argues that interpersonal understanding, like all else in the external world, is mediated by people's own personalities. The same individual will be perceived differently by different people in accordance with the personality traits, expectations, and level of knowledge of the people who are perceiving them. They will notice certain traits and not others because of their 'preferences for certain psychological qualities', which stem from 'the particular conditions under which the individual's own personality has been formed'.[4] Bodalev refers to a study of school children's perceptions of other people, which revealed many discrepancies in the qualities and behavioural traits they attributed to them. He suggests that these differences result from the history of their own development, which taught them to be more alert to certain types of quality and behaviour than to others. This in turn stems from the 'assimilated moral values and norms present in the society of which the pupils themselves are a part'.[5] One would expect, then, that Bodalev's explanation of the sex differences in children's drawings would refer to variations in the values and norms promoted by society in the two sexes, which would encourage differential observations of other people and of the external environment in general.

In a later study, Bodalev does directly address the subject of sex differences in interpersonal relations.[6] For men, he claims, the level of closeness which is desirable or acceptable is lower than it is for women. It also declines with the passing years. For women, in contrast, there is a tendency to need greater closeness over the years. In a long-term relationship there are periods of withdrawal for both men and women. For husbands, the first of these tends to come in the sixth or seventh year of marriage. For women it comes later, not until the tenth or eleventh year. In both cases closeness is generally restored, though there are further periods when it slackens. Bodalev does not say how he reaches these conclusions, but it is obvious to what use they could be put by family councillors. Bodalev makes no bones about the practical purpose of his studies. Having reached the conclusion that identification is stronger with people who are perceived as subjectively important, he suggests that attention should be paid to why certain people are considered more important, and what influences this enables them to exert. This 'would enable us to purposefully organize influences, with a presumably high educational effect, on an individual through the circle of persons who are significant for him'.[7]

V. S. MUKHINA: SEX DIFFERENCES IN CHOICE OF TOYS

Passing comment should be given to an article by V. S. Mukhina in *Voprosy Psikhologii* on the use of toys in child development. In the last chapter we discussed a study by the same psychologist about the importance of competition and ambition in child development. In that work Mukhina made no comment on the sex of the children in her experiment, and it can only be assumed that her conclusions were meant to be valid for both boys and girls. However, in this more recent article she draws a clear sex distinction. She claims that when a child is playing alone, sex is the most important determinant in the choice of toys and games. The boy likes to play with guns, knives and toy cars; he enjoys banging a hammer, building a toy house or garage, and pretending to drive a car. The girl prefers to play with dolls and toy furniture, and her games include tidying up the doll corner, looking after a sick teddy bear, and encouraging her dolls to be good. Parents are urged to be on their guard if their children fail to correspond to these norms of behaviour. 'If the boy plays with dolls or furniture, it is necessary to keep an eye on him. If he starts to imitate his elder sister at play, you should try to interest him instead in games for boys. The same is true for the girl, who, doting on her elder brother, plays with a bow and arrow and starts to throw stones . . .'[8] Unfortunately Mukhina gives no indication of the consequences if parents are not sufficiently vigilant.

T.G. KHASHCHENKO: SEX DIFFERENCES IN MENTAL PROBLEM SOLVING

Another psychologist who has directly addressed the issue of sex is T.G. Khashchenko. He looks at the influence of sex on mental problem solving. His experiments involved 45 adults divided into 15 groups of three; five groups were exclusively male, five exclusively female, and five were mixed. The groups were asked to provide explanations for problems such as the following: 'A cardboard sugar-cube carton is standing on the edge of a table, with part of the body hanging over the edge. It stays like that for some time, then falls. You open the lid, and find nothing inside. What made it fall?'[9]

According to Khashchenko, the male groups were generally more active than the female, and their members interacted with each other in an attempt to find a viable solution to the problem. The all-female groups used a 'brain-storming' approach, posing individual, uncoordinated responses. In some cases a women would arrive at the right answer, but because this was not taken up by the rest of the group the problem remained unsolved. Khashchenko gives an example of a female group approach:

A. It was the air.
B. Something had held it back at first?
A. A tortoise, but then it ran off.
C. A cockroach! The box lost its balance!
A. It was glued, but it came unstuck . . .
C. Someone went near it and brushed against it.
B. Something was inside it.
A. The air blew it.
C. Or there was a bit of sugar which spilled out.
B. Perhaps it was a ghost?
C. The box probably fell because its balance was disturbed.
B. There was a butterfly which flew past. Or a mouse chewed at it and then ran off.

The all-male groups, in contrast, were said to develop a distinct division of functions, with one man adopting the role of 'generator of ideas' and the others evaluating and criticizing these ideas. The role of 'generator' sometimes moved between the members of the group, but it usually settled on one person, the 'leader', who dictated the method of solving the problem. for example:

A. There was nothing in the box.
B. At least, not at the end.
C. But why should there have been something?
B. It hasn't been spelt out that there was no sugar.
. . .
A. Perhaps there was a draught? . . . There was no outside influence. It fell by itself.
C. It could not fall by itself.
B. Perhaps there was something in it?
A. Something that could disappear.
B. A bug.
A. But where did it get to?
B. The box might have been open.
C. According to the rules of physics it could not have fallen by itself.
A. Could it have been something that could evaporate?
C. Maybe acid?
B. It might simply have dried up, and the heavy end became lighter. No! The influence is external. What was it and where did it get to?
C. What is this ! There is nothing outside; there was something inside!

A. There was, otherwise it could not have fallen.
C. What?
A. Something mobile.
B. A worm?
A. No. Where could it have got to?

The approach of the mixed groups differed, Khashchenko tells us, according to the ratio of male to female. If the group consisted of two women and one man, it tackled the problem in the same way as an all-female group. If there were two men and one woman, the group functioned in the same way as an all-male group. In this case the woman would show much interest in the variants suggested by her partners and a high level of interaction, proposing ideas of her own in response to the remarks of her partners.

Khashchenko concludes from his experiment that sex is one of the factors in joint creative thought. He evidently has little faith in the problem-solving abilities of women. Devoid of male influence, they are incapable of working together in a logical and cooperative way. They function best, it seems, as supports to male decision makers; in male-dominated, hierarchical structures they are able to achieve a higher level of involvement, ingenuity and interaction. Khashchenko's conclusions have rather disturbing political implications; they are not exactly supportive of women occupying positions of power and responsibility in the economic and political spheres.

However, Khashchenko's methodology is open to some criticism. His sample is not large; there are evidently only two examples of either the male-predominant or female-predominant mixed groups. This is surely not a sufficient basis for the firm conclusions he draws from his study. The differences he perceives in the male and female approaches could be purely coincidental. His frequent use of the terms 'generally' and 'typically' also suggest that the patterns he describes were not universal. His conclusions also seem decidedly subjective. It should be noted that despite the superiority Khashchenko implicitly assigns to the male problem-solvers, in the example he gives they succeed no better than the women in reaching a unanimous solution. A growing irritation can also be detected between the members of the group; could this not prompt the conclusion that male joint activity, instead of being more successful than that of women, is actually hampered by an excess of aggression?

We have seen from Bodalev's work the powerful influence which a person's expectations have on his or her observations and perceptions of the behaviour of other people. The differences Khashchenko perceives could be the figment of his sex-typed expectations, derived from cultural stereotypes of the level of activity, logicality, and inclination towards leadership to be found in men and women. If they really do exist, they are, in any case, likely to have a social origin – i.e. to be linked to society's expectations about appropriate male and female behaviour and the training and socialization enacted in accordance with these. If so, they would – according to Soviet psychology – be amenable to resocialization. Women's activity in the decision-making process would also release hitherto undeveloped potentialities and transform them into abilities.

SEX DIFFERENCES AND IDENTIFICATION WITH PARENTS: THE WORK OF A. I. ZAKHAROV

A study by A. I. Zakharov is also worth looking at. This explores the effect of age and sex on a child's identification with the same-sex parent.[10] The study has a practical propose; Zakharov points out that knowledge about the age and conditions in which children are particularly sensitive to the influence of the same-sex parent will be useful to psychologists and pedagogues counselling families on upbringing matters.

Zakharov is evidently influenced by the work of certain Western psychologists, in particular that of Kohlberg. He agrees with Kohlberg that children establish their own ideas about sex roles at around the age of five or six, and that these ideas then condition their behaviour; and that the development of these ideas is dependent on the process of cognitive maturation. However, he also supports Bandura's view, rooted in social learning theory, that types of behaviour – including those linked with a person's sex – are primarily acquired through imitation of a model or models. To Zakharov, cognitive development theory and social learning theory are complementary rather than incompatible.

Zakharov's study rests on a structured interview with 961 children between the ages of three and sixteen years, from two-parent families, attending eight kindergartens and two schools in Leningrad. 462 of the children are male and 499 female. On average there are 36 boys and 38 girls from each year. The following questions were asked.

Soviet Psychologists on Sex Differences   75

1. If you were to play the game 'family', who would you be – mother, father, or yourself? (The order in which these options were presented to the children was varied.)
2. Who do you live with at home?
3. Who, in your opinion, is the head of the family, or is there no head?
4. When you grow up, do you want to do the same as your father/mother (the same-sex parent) or something different?
5. When you are grown-up and have a boy/girl (corresponding to the child's own sex) of your own, will you bring him/her up the same as your father/mother brought you up, or differently? (For pre-school children, this was worded 'play with, do activities with'.)
6. If you were by yourself at home for a long time, which of your parents would you be anxious to see first? (For pre-schoolers, 'who would you wish to come into the room first?')
7. If you were to suffer a great sorrow, misfortune or unhappiness (for pre-schoolers, 'if someone was nasty to you'), would you tell your father/mother (same-sex parent) about it, or say nothing?
8. The same question, but with the opposite-sex parent.
9. Are you afraid that your father/mother will punish you, or are you not afraid of this?
10. The same question, but with the opposite-sex parent.

The first five questions were designed to judge the children's perceptions of the competence and prestige of their parents; the last five, to judge their emotional relationship with their parents. The questions were not posed in the order given above.

Zakharov concludes that the level of identification with the same-sex parent alters according to the age and hence cognitive and emotional development of the child. The ability to perceive oneself in another's place, and to take on this person's role, is formed at approximately five years. This is, accordingly, the age when children begin to show the most intense role indentification with the same-sex parent, picturing themselves in that parent's place, imitating that parent's action, etc. This is manifested particularly in sex-typed play with peers. The same-sex parent is, according to Zakharov, the essential and most accessible model for learning sex-typed activities. The need to imitate the parent reduces as children develop their own habits and structure of behaviour (though within the limits of what is considered appropriate for their sex), and identification with the parent decreases. The time-span of this process differs somewhat for girls and boys. For boys the period of greatest identification is five to seven, while for girls it takes place over a longer period, from three to eight. Identification winds down for girls at the age of nine, and for boys at the age of ten. It does not cease completely, though, since children need more time to form a model of behaviour and a stereotype of ideas about their sex role. Evidently girls achieve this faster than boys; by the age of 13 to 15 girls are relatively independent of identification with their mothers, whereas for boys identification is still significant.

Identification operates partly on a conscious level, as children attempt to cultivate their models' qualities in themselves, and partly on an unconscious level, in the form of an involuntary imitation of those qualities through a desire to orient their own personalities. Identification with the same-sex parent is easier if children perceive this parent to be the head of the family, to be competent and prestigious.

Zakharov holds that identification is impaired in children of both sexes if one parent becomes more emotionally attached than the other to the child. However, in societies which view mothers as the primary nurturers and providers of emotional sustenance, is this not the norm? Zakharov gives only one example, that of an anxious mother who binds her son to herself to such an extent that he is denied relationships with his father and peers. The child is therefore unable to work out the habits of behaviour appropriate for his own sex, especially if the mother dominates in the family and is jealous of any signs of paternal influence. This can produce in the boy 'a feminine disposition' and 'infantilism'. On the other hand, it could lead to a pronounced level of self-assertion amongst peers as a form of compensation. The same can occur as the result of excessive strictness and authoritarianism on the part of either parent.

That identification is particularly strong at the age of five is taken by Zakharov as proof of the falsehood of Freud's 'Oedipus complex'. Far from being the object of envy and hostility, the same-sex parent is the object of preference. Boys might say they wish to 'marry' their mothers, but this is in order to imitate the behaviour of their fathers. It is a socio-psychological rather than a sexual impulse.

Like Kohlberg, Zakharov is evidently more concerned with the psychological processes involved in the development of identification and the acquisition of sex roles than with any attendant social factors.

None the less, his failure to acknowledge such obvious social conditions as the different roles men and women play within the Soviet family, and the discrepancy in the amount of time mothers and fathers are available to their children (subjects discussed at length by sociologists), is still surprising, especially given the importance which Soviet psychology has historically placed on the social environment. Zakharov seems to assume that both parents are equally available to their children as models, and that difference in male and female patterns of identification are due to innate sex differences in the children rather than to variations in the social and familial roles of men and women. It evidently does not occur to him that the more protracted period of identification of girls with their mothers could be linked to the more ready availability of the mother as a model.

SEX DIFFERENCES AND IDENTIFICATION WITH PARENTS: THE WORK OF A. YA. VARGA

Zakharov, as we have noted, supports certain of the Western theories about the development of psychological sex differences. So too does A. Ya. Varga. In a short paper as a postgraduate student she outlines the subject of psychological sex differences as a preliminary step towards a study (which was not completed)[11] of identification with parents as a factor in the formation of psychological sex.[12] Varga holds that male and female personalities are culturally produced, and vary according to different cultural settings. She is familiar with the work of a number of Western theorists, though often this is quite dated.

Freud's approach to sex differences is discussed but rejected, mainly on account of his emphasis on the Oedipus complex in the process of identification. Varga acknowledges the cognitive developmental approach, which sees the child as an active agent in its own socialization process. However, she does not hold this as the crucial factor in the development of sex typed behaviour. Instead she veers towards a social learning position. She sees imitations of the same-sex parent, and parents' differential behaviour to male and female children, as the crucial factors in the development of sex-role identification.

Varga finds support for her views in the work of the anthropologist Margaret Mead, whose 1935 study of variations in male and female behaviour amongst different New Guinea tribes convinced her that sex differences in personality are 'cultural creations to which each generation, male and female, is trained'.[13]

She also refers frequently to work done in the West with hermaphrodites, which has shown that a distinct male or female gender identity can develop in contradiction of the actual biological sex of the person.[14] She also accepts the claim of Western doctors working in this area, that gender is irreversibly fixed in early childhood (she gives the deadline as three years). Curiously, although she is aware of the work of A. I. Belkin (which we look at shortly), she makes no reference to the fact that he claims to have accomplished successful gender reassignments on teenagers and young adults – something which, in Varga's view, should be impossible.

Varga is also aware of the work of American psychologists Elinor Maccoby and Carol Jacklin, to whom many Western feminist writers acknowledge a great debt. After comparing the results of more than two thousand studies on supposed sex differences, they concluded that many such differences are myths which have no basis in the reality of male and female behaviour, and that those which do rarely have any biological foundation.[15]

Given the Western works which have influenced Varga, her comments concerning the usefulness of her own research are particularly interesting. It is particularly relevant at the present time in the Soviet Union, she suggests, given the problems surrounding the successful sex upbringing of children and the organization of psychological consultations with parents. Although some of the ideas she refers to have been put forward in the West as a challenge to the existing sex-role stereotypes (for example, the psychological sexual neutrality of a new-born baby, the development of gender identity through imitation of parents, the differential parental reinforcement of male and female behaviour), Varga seems to suggest that they could also inform a more successful cultivation of these stereotypes.

V. A. KUTS AND V. P. BAGRUNOV: SEX DIFFERENCES AND SUCCESS IN MARRIAGE

V. A. Kuts wrote his Candidate's dissertation on the relationship between male and female personality differences and the achievement of successful marriage. He looks at the way in which these differences influence professional orientation and attitude to family life, and argues that a better understanding of them will contribute significantly to the improvement of marriage relations.[16] In an article co-authored by V. P. Bagrunov, he calls for conscious and determined sex-role socialization.[17] Like the other Soviet psychologists, they cite a number of Western texts; but all of these are obscure and ancient (dating from 1892 to 1950), and promote a staunch biologist view of sex differences in personality. Curiously, they also refer to the work of Soviet writers such as Zakharov and Belkin, who are very much aware of the more recent developments in Western psychology on sex differences. They tell us that Zakharov has demonstrated that parents do not behave differentially towards their male and female offspring, and that this encourages feminization in boys and masculinization in girls, which, according to Belkin, leads to a loss of sex identity and a range of other associated problems. Parents must therefore be taught about the psychological peculiarities of boys and girls, and how to respond to these appropriately. In particular they should be made aware that the male psyche is more dependent on genetics, and the female psyche on the influence of the environment. This means that they should be alert to their sons' natural inclinations and potentialities, and endeavour to encourage their self-development. On the other hand, armed with an awareness of girls' susceptibility to training, parents should set about constructing and forming their 'essential habits' through continual control and various methods of encouragement. In other words, boys should be allowed to establish their own direction in life and to develop any skills and abilities in which they express an interest, while girls should be pushed along a culturally-prescribed path of stereotypical habits. Bagrunov and Kuts do not see such exhortations as incompatible with the principles of women's emancipation, however; only with a false understanding of emancipation, which confuses social equality with an identity of behaviour in men and women.

Incidentally, Maccoby and Jacklin (whose work we just referred to in connection with Varga's research) also found some evidence to suggest that boys have a natural superiority over girls in visual-spatial ability, and girls over boys in verbal ability. However, in their view, popular psychological belief holds that girls are more influenced by their biology, and boys by their external environment (a claim for which they were unable to find any evidence). This stands in complete contrast to Bagrunov and Kuts's contention.

L. S. SAPOZHNIKOVA: SEX DIFFERENCES IN THE DEVELOPMENT OF MORAL BEHAVIOUR

L. S. Sapozhnikova did not set out to study sex differences in the development of moral behaviour, but seems to have stumbled across them by chance. The aim of her study was to ascertain the extent to which adolescent school-children understand the norms of moral behaviour, and are willing and able to act on them. Her sample consisted of 120 pupils from the sixth to eighth grades (i.e. from ages 12 to 15).[18] After observing the behaviour of these pupils, she found that they fit into four distinct categories. The first group, almost a quarter of the pupils (24.5 per cent), consciously regulated their behaviour according to moral convictions. Moral rules of behaviour had been internalized, and had become personally important. These pupils generally displayed positive, desirable behaviour. The second group is the largest, with 31.8 per cent of the total. These pupils had a sporadic commitment to moral norms. Active moral engagement, i.e. the control of their own behaviour according to their understanding of moral rules, appeared in certain situations, but there were also displays of negative behaviour. The students in the third group – 24.2 per cent – were not guided by moral convictions. Their behaviour was generally impulsive, with frequent negative displays. They were aware of the moral rules, but these did not yet function as incentives for behaviour. 'Changes had not yet taken place in the moral development of these pupils, and the need to act under the influence of their own convictions had not yet appeared.'[19] The fourth group, or 19.8 per cent of the students, were still insufficiently aware of the moral norms of behaviour to be able to apply them to their own lives. They were not even conscious of a discrepancy between morally desirable behaviour and their own actions.

Despite 'the generally accepted view' that girls are more self-disciplined and diligent than boys, Sapozhnikova found that the pupils in the first group – those who acted in accordance with internalized moral norms, i.e. with demands they made on themselves – were almost all boys. This, she concludes, is because girls have a greater tendency to accept discipline from other people, and so making demands on themselves has less importance. It might also be harder for them to regulate their own behaviour because they are more emotional than boys, which impedes the process of self-regulation.

Sapozhnikova makes no attempt to define 'moral norms' and 'morally positive behaviour'. Nor does she give details about the actual behaviour of the pupils, or explain how she could tell from this behaviour whether the pupils had internalized the moral norms or perceived them as external compulsions which they acted on to gain rewards or avoid punishments. She also gives no break-down according to sex of any group except the first. In the absence of such detail, the article raises more questions than it offers answers. However, it is interesting to note that the supposed greater emotionality of girls is seen here to have a negative aspect; i.e., it impedes the internalization of moral norms. Sapozhnikova also concludes from her study that one way of stimulating children's ability to internalize and follow moral rules is to encourage their independence. Without this, rules will always be external to them and so less effective. 'The development of independence is . . . an important precondition for developing stable moral behaviour.'[20] It will be interesting to compare this with the pronouncements of pedagogical theorists on what personality traits are appropriate, and should be developed, in girls and boys.

A. KELLY AND T. SNEGIREVA: A COMPARISON OF BRITISH AND SOVIET APPROACHES TO SEX DIFFERENCES IN SCHOOL SUBJECT PREFERENCES

Despite the adherence of several of the Soviet psychologists we have looked at to certain Western theories about the development of psychological sex differences, an article in *Literaturnaya Gazeta* claims that there is a fundamental conflict in Western and Soviet approaches. It demonstrates this by juxtaposing articles by British and Soviet psychologists on the subject of sex differences in school subject preference.[21]

Alison Kelly, representing the British view, explains the unequal achievement of girls and boys in science subjects in terms of social influences. Girls are socialized into having little confidence in themselves; believing the sciences to be more demanding, they are scared to compete. Unlike boys, they are not encouraged in early childhood to play with toys which necessitate and hence develop the spatial ability associated with sciences. Children are also socialized into developing stereotyped ideas about what is appropriate for boys and girls, and their desire to conform to the norms established for their sex prevents them from challenging such ideas. Finally, science teachers, in accordance with their own stereotypes, give greater encouragement to male pupils than female.

Tat'yana Snegireva argues an opposite view; that the different levels of achievement of boys and girls in science reflect natural differences in the interest and inclinations of the sexes. Boys have a naturally greater visual-spatial ability than girls, which becomes evident at the age of 12 or 13; girls, on the other hand, have more verbal ability. Snegireva also suggests (like Bagrunov and Kuts) that girls are more amenable to training and education than boys, while the psychological development of boys is more dependent on their biological endowments. This means that the disadvantages girls have in science subjects can be partly offset through the educational process. This explains why girls generally do better than boys at school, despite the fact that boys are able to 'grasp things better' than girls.

Snegireva does not grant these natural sex differences absolute power. Individual differences between people can to some extent override those linked to sex. The type of activity a person is involved in also plays a role. Hence certain teaching methods can reduce the sex component in subject choice and achievement. None the less, she is convinced that boys will continue to excel in science subjects, and that this is how things should be. Women's achievements are quite sufficient as they stand. Their equality has already been established – providing a certain 'adjustment' is made for sex. To prove this, she cites a series of sociological studies undertaken by the Academy of Pedagogical Sciences which found that while an interest in physics and maths was more evident in boys, girls do not 'lag far behind'. Of the 10,000 or so school children in the study, half of the boys and one third of the girls showed a preference for science and maths. Girls constitute the minority in schools that specialize in science subjects, but make up for this by forming the majority in these departments in pedagogical institutes. (Given that the overwhelming majority of teachers are female, this is hardly surprising.) Snegireva also notes that female scientists beyond the teaching profession are located in the applied sphere rather than in theory, which remains a male preserve; and that although there are now many female doctors, there are few female surgeons. There are female engineers, instrument makers, electro-technicians, statisticians and economists, she tells us, but in light rather than heavy industry. Such facts are a reflection of women's natural inclinations. Snegireva explains that young women follow in the footsteps of their mothers and grandmothers, choosing careers which do not oppose their family functions, their psychological properties and their feminine interests. She does not comment on the fact that these female professions and areas of employment are lower-paid and less prestigious than those of men. Curiously, when she turns her attention to agriculture we learn that women receive considerable government assistance in the blossoming of their natural inclinations; it is Soviet policy, 'while giving women every possibility for professional development', to encourage their participation 'only in those areas of agriculture where reasonable conditions for women's work exist', and in types of activity where they will not have to compete with men.[22]

Snegireva also talks of the school course on the Ethics and Psychology of Family Life, which at the time of her article was shortly to be introduced. This, she says, will help children to understand their special male and female roles. She assures her readers that this is not an attempt to resurrect old, moribund ideals of masculinity and femininity, but to preserve everlasting values in a changing world.

Summing up the differences between the English and Soviet approaches, she argues that 'our clocks . . . show different historical times' with respect to the changes which have taken place in the position of women, and the lessons which have been learned from those changes. For the Soviet Union the main lesson 'is that equality does not mean identity, and everything that is traditional is not obsolete only because it is traditional'.[23] The 'progressive women's movement' in Britain, not understanding this, places unreasonable demands on school-girls which only a few, at best, will be able to fulfil. Hence while Kelly's article draws attention to the limitations placed on the achievements of British girls in traditional 'male' school subjects by social expectations of male and female interests and abilities, Snegireva argues that the limitations have a biological basis which (despite the powerful influences of education and training) cannot and should not be eradicated. This is the complete antithesis of our hypothesis that if Soviet psychology were applied to the area of sex differences it would, on the basis of its established tenets, deny both the desirability and inevitability of psychological sex differences.

According to Snegireva's article, the very definition of women's equality in the Soviet Union involves the recognition of natural female limitations, and an 'adjustment' of the terms of equality in accordance with them. If this is so, it amounts to government endorsement of horizontal and vertical segregation in employment, with female labour concentrated in certain, relatively low paid sectors of the economy, and in the lower echelons of occupational hierarchies, on the grounds that such segregation is a reflection of natural male and female differences.

Encouraging girls to challenge the social definitions of their role is useless, and serves to render girls failures by setting them goals they cannot hope to achieve. Instead, the Soviet Union is intent on emphasizing traditional female roles through the 'family life' course. So much for the development of all-round personality, and the mutability of natural differences.

CONCLUDING REMARKS

Despite the differences in subject matter of the above studies, it is possible to draw some conclusions about Soviet psychology and the study of sex differences in personality.

Psychologists in general have shown little interest in developing an understanding of the extent to which these sex differences are biologically or culturally constructed, and the process by which their development takes place. The existence of sex differences is generally taken as given; the main concern has been to determine what influence these have on other psychological problems.

This is not surprising. Academic research is inevitably influenced by the social context in which it takes place. In the West, recent interest in the development of sex differences has largely been due to the Women's Movement.[24] Feminists have had a vested interest in discovering how psychological sex differences and roles have come about, along with the status and power imbalance between the sexes which accompanies them, since this is an essential prerequisite to transforming them. Opposing theories have also appeared as a backlash against feminism. Ann Oakley argues that biological theories of male and female personality differences have flourished throughout history at times of 'nascent feminist uneasiness', or when women have begun to make political demands. For example, an academic concern with the relative intelligences of men and women coincided with the Suffragette movement.[25]

Psychology has not become the primary discipline in the Soviet Union to take on the study of sex differences; none the less, it has shown more interest in the subject since the official concern about family matters began. A British psychologist has noted that although science in the Soviet Union is not 'a monolithic part of the state apparatus pursuing one "official line"', political considerations do have some influence over research interests. '[T]he decisions of the plenum of the CPSU are discussed in the pages of the academic psychology journals, as they do affect psychology – particularly in applied areas such as educational or occupational psychology.'[26] Many Soviet psychologists who have ventured into the field of sex differences point to the particular relevance of their studies in the current social context, when the family and demography are giving cause for concern. Unlike Western feminists, who have tried to reach an understanding of the development of sex differences in order the better to change them, Soviet psychologists suggest that such an understanding can be used to inculcate these differences more successfully, and to strengthen the institutions of marriage and the family.

4 The Work of I. S. Kon

The work of I. S. Kon merits a separate chapter for two main reasons. Firstly, he is one of the few Soviet scholars to have devoted much time to an analysis of sex differences in personality. Secondly, he spans a number of disciplines, and so fits awkwardly into any single category. He has been described as a social-psychologist, sociologist, ethnographer, and (increasingly) sexologist. This profusion of titles is not inappropriate, since Kon strives to maintain an interdisciplinary approach. He is aware of, and frequently cites, research undertaken in a variety of disciplines, both in the USSR and in the West, and laments the failure of other social scientists to learn from the work of their colleagues in related fields. For example, in one hard-hitting article in *Pravda* Kon anticipates the failure of the school reform proposals, introduced in 1984, unless pedagogical theorists and teachers join forces with psychologists and sociologists to produce an integrated study of children and the various agents of socialization. He goes on to attack the Academy of Pedagogical Sciences for virtually sabotaging the development of such a co-ordinated project by ignoring the work of neighbouring disciplines – notably sociology and social-pedagogy – rather than serving as a centre for the assimilation and assessment of all work in this area.[1]

In view of Kon's interest in the interdisciplinary approach, it is intriguing that he displays no apparent interest in the large body of writings on psychological sex differences which pedagogical theorists have produced. Indeed, he denies or belittles its existence when he asserts, in the introduction of a number of his articles, that no scientific work has appeared on the subject.[2]

On the other hand, he is well-acquainted with the Western theories on male and female personality which we looked at in Chapter 1. To some extent his writings represent a translation and presentation of these theories to a Soviet audience. He also has an evident awareness of the Marxist view of personality which informs mainstream Soviet psychology. However, as we will see, he displays a number of contradictions and inconsistencies in his own approach to the subject of sex differences in personality. It may be that he has been hampered by a conflict of interests. On the one hand, he adheres to the main tenets of Soviet psychology's approach to personality development, which leads him to assert that sex roles, like other social roles, are socially constructed. This inevitably makes him critical of biological explanations of the genesis of sex roles and gender differences, amongst which he includes the functionalist approach which was prevalent in sociological role theory in the United States in the 1950s. On the other hand, Kon's writings also reflect the social context in which they first appeared. Within the climate of concern over the 'demographic crisis', differentiation in male and female personalities has generally been seen as highly functional, representing an important factor in the maintenance of strong and stable family structures. As we shall see in due course, his later work might be said to bear the imprint of a more open atmosphere.

PERSONALITY, SOCIAL ROLES, AND THE SOCIAL CONSTRUCTION OF SEX DIFFERENCES

Kon's interest in sex differences developed from his work on personality and social roles in general. Like Soviet psychologists, he sees personality as a predominantly social phenomenon. He describes it as a combination of socially significant traits in the individual, formed during the course of interaction with other people. This individual personality is engaged in a continual process of interaction with the wider environment by means of the social roles the person performs. These act as a two-way passage, leading 'from the objective social structure which does not depend of the individual characteristics of people, to the structure of the psychological motives of the individual, and back again'.[3] The development of the individual's complex of social roles is dependent on four main factors. These are, firstly, the role expectations which society (as a whole, or in the form of smaller social groupings) has of a person who occupies a certain social position. These expectations are external to the individual. The second factor is the way the individual perceives a role, how he or she defines it and the rights and obligations which ensue from it. The third is the individual's attitude towards a particular role; whether it is accepted or rejected, is considered important or otherwise, and whether it harmonizes with or opposes the person's other roles. Finally, fulfilment of a role, i.e. role behaviour, depends both on the social definition of the role, and on the individual's perception and experience of it in a concrete situation. Society is seen as a complex set of interdependent and interrelated sub-systems. One and the same person simultaneously participates in many systems and has many different roles. This means that each role remains somewhat external to the person, it does not determine the personality. Hence if a person leaves his or her family or discards a hobby, this does not result in that person becoming somebody else.[4]

This stress on the social nature of personality and of the roles an individual adopts in society is reflected in Kon's writings on sex differences. He draws a distinction between biological sex and psychological sex, and rejects the 'vulgar biological approach' which reduces psychological sex to an inevitable consequence of biological sex.[5] Children are not automatically male or female, in the psychological sense; they *become* male or female. This takes place through a process of upbringing, or 'sex socialization', interpreted by the children through a prism which consists of a combination of their own previous experiences, the environment, and their individual features.[6] The corresponding sex roles are adopted in the same way as other social roles – through a combination of social expectations and individual assessments of these roles. Not even sexual orientation, i.e. an interest in the same or the opposite sex, is innate. It is something children learn, along with sexual morality, sex rituals, and sex techniques.[7] The development of psychological sex involves:

> a certain sex identification, i.e. a feeling and consciousness of one's membership of one or the other sex; the psycho-sexual orientations connected with this (e.g. an interest in the opposite sex); and socio-sexual orientations, i.e. the internalization of a system of sex roles, in the light of which the individual differentiates the criteria of 'masculinity' and 'femininity', evaluates him or herself according to these categories, and adopts the corresponding activities and social status etc. These qualities are not innate; they are formed only through interaction with other people, under the influence of upbringing and of a wide range of social conditions.[8]

Accordingly the study of sex roles should take place on three levels. These are the 'macrosocial level' – the way a society allocates its social functions along sex lines; the 'inter-personal level' – the way a person's sex roles interact with those of other people in a concrete situation (the way a woman performs her roles as wife and mother, for example, will depend on how the duties of her family are divided and on the roles of father, husband and child which are performed around her); and the 'intra-personal level' – the way a sex role is internalized by the individual in accordance with his or her life experiences and the influence these have had on his or her perception of that role.[9]

Kon delineates three alternative theoretical approaches to the study of psychological sex differences. Although the names he chooses for them are not the same, the theories match those we discussed in Chapter 1. The first he terms identification theory, but adds that it has its roots in psychoanalysis. It stresses the roles of the child's emotional attachment to his or her parents and to imitation as a way of mastering modes of behaviour. The second is the theory of sex-typing according to social training, i.e. social learning theory. The third is self-categorization, alias Kohlberg's cognitive developmental theory.[10]

Each of these theories is accorded some merit, but none is seen as a sufficient explanation of the development of sex differences in itself. The first is accused of a lack of clarity, of confusing the concepts of assimilation, imitation and identification. Kon lists a number of points which the theory fails to acknowledge. Firstly, the defensive identification of a boy with his father because he is afraid of him (i.e. the Oedipus complex) has little in common with imitation based on love. Secondly, the imitation of the qualities of a particular person usually combines with the learning of that person's social role (for example, of the father's role as figure of power). Thirdly, the primary role model for the boy is not always the father, but could be another man. Finally, children's behaviour is far from always a mirror of what they observe in their adult models. For example, single-sex groups of boys clearly do not come into being as an imitation of a tendency amongst adult men to avoid female company.

The 'theory of sex-typing' is criticized for having an over-mechanistic approach, for seeing the child as an object rather than a subject of the socialization process. It fails to account for individual differences and deviations from sex-role stereotypes which cannot be linked to the type of upbringing the child received. It also ignores the fact that many stereotyped features form accidentally, independent of training and encouragement.

The 'theory of self-categorization' is seen largely as a synthesis of the other two. According to this theory, a child's ideas about sex appropriate behaviour depend both on his or her own observations of the behaviour of the men and women who have been chosen as models, and on the approval or disapproval which the child's own actions produce in other people. Yet its amalgamation of the best of two theories does not spare it from a weakness of its own; it fails to account for the sex-differentiated behaviour which can be observed long before children have formed a firm sex-identification.[11] Kon is not explicit about when this firm sex-identification is formed, but if it is linked to an understanding of the irreversibility of sex, this would make it around the age of six to seven. By one and a half years children are apparently aware of their own sex, although they cannot fully explain what it means. By three or four they are able to recognize the sex identity of other people, but associate it with external symbols such as hair and clothes and are not aware that it is irreversible. Only by the age of six to seven are they sure of this.[12]

In line with Kon's general interdisciplinary approach, he suggests that these theories are seen not as alternatives but as mutually complementary approaches, describing the process of sex-role socialization from different perspectives – the theory of sex-typing from the upbringer's point of view, for example, and the theory of self-categorization from the child's.[13]

The work of the American functionalist sociologist Talcott Parsons, which was very popular in the 1950s, is discussed and rejected as an example of latter-day biologism. Although Parsons does not explicitly argue a biological foundation for sex differences, his functionalist view of sex differentiation, with its female-expressive and male-instrumental polarization, suggests that such differentiation is normal and universal, and 'This inevitably leads to the thought that some kind of biological laws rest on its foundation'.[14] The functionalist approach is seen as conservative, ahistorical and culture-bound. It implies the universality of a sex role differentiation peculiar to the United States (and, one might add, to a particular class), and it provides an ideological justification for the continued social dependence of women. It takes no account of the changes which have been occurring in the professional and social roles of North American women in recent years. It is, furthermore, unsupported by the evidence even of some American studies.[15]

THE ROLE OF BIOLOGY IN THE DEVELOPMENT OF SEX DIFFERENCES

It is clear, then, that Kon adheres to the idea that sex differences in personality are largely the result of social influences, and that he repudiates biologistic approaches to the subject. However, he then goes on to make a distinct volte-face, and puts forward a viewpoint which bears strong similarities to the functionalist sociology he has just rejected.

It is a mistake, he argues, to see sex-role differentiation as an exclusively social phenomenon, which would disappear if the conditions which originally produced it were transformed.[16] While some aspects of sex-role differentiation are just 'survivals from the past', others are 'the essence of an expression of deep differences which, in a situation of social equality, not only do not disappear but probably appear yet more clearly'.[17] He admits that the extent to which sex differentiation is biologically determined is unknown, and refers to the study by Maccoby and Jacklin which found no evidence for many popular assumptions about sex differences. However, the fact that psychology does not prove something does not render it false. In some cases the influence of biology is irrefutable. For example, 'The dependence of the social on the biological is particularly clear regarding the reproduction of the race and the upbringing of children'.[18]

Kon's conviction that women have a natural propensity for domestic work lies behind his rejection of the 'platitudinous moralization about the "irresponsibility" of men' to which sociologists are prone in their writings on male and female roles in the family. They do not take enough account of 'the social specifics of the paternal role' in its historical setting, nor of the 'psychological data about the greater emotional expressiveness of women'. Animal studies testify to the existence of natural differences in behaviour between the sexes, since nurturant behaviour is generally more evident in the female of the species.[19]

Biological input into male and female differences is not limited to reproduction and its related functions. Nature has given men and women a range of different personality traits and abilities. Men have a naturally greater aptitude for mechanical habits and knowledge, while women are better at precise and delicate hand movements, at perception, and at fluency of speech. Natural psychological differences render boys more keen on active, tough games connected with competition and risk, while girls prefer quiet activities and submit more readily to the influence of people around them. Men of all ages are more assertive and persistent than women, and more emotionally stable.[20] Comparisons of boys and girls' diaries show that girls are more introspective, more concerned about other people's opinions of them, experience more difficulty in their relationships with other people, are more prone to depression, and worry more about their appearance.[21] Women's greater emotional fragility makes them more prone to neurosis, and results in a greater need for a stable social environment and human contact.[22]

Boys have a great need for competition and a feeling of superiority. Kon chastizes teachers and Komsomol leaders for their failure to realize this, which leads them to place girls – who on the surface seem more suitable, since they are more conscientious and ready to follow instructions – in the important power positions in school and youth organizations. Boys, as a result, either become passive, or revolt against female dominance (not only of their mothers and teachers but also of 'preaching girls in the Komsomol!'). Unable to express their masculinity through legitimate channels, they turn to illegitimate, delinquent channels.[23]

Most of Kon's assertions about natural male and female differences are challenged by the Soviet psychological writings we looked at in Chapter 2. He talks about certain male and female abilities which are supposedly rooted in biology. Yet according to mainstream Soviet psychology, abilities are only formed during the activities which require them. The mechanical abilities in boys and dexterity in girls which he observes could be the result of differences in their upbringing. Kon himself notes that toys are strongly sex-differentiated (as other Soviet writers have pointed out, those intended for boys include machines and technical designs, while those aimed at girls generally consist of dolls, miniature animals, and furniture).[24] Such differentiation is reinforced by the 'Trud' class at school. Boys and girls are taught separately, and while boys learn metalwork and how to operate machines, girls learn how to type and sew. Although in theory children are free to choose which class they attend, there is considerable psychological pressure to choose that which is considered appropriate for their sex.[25]

As we saw earlier, Soviet psychology has applied itself to the problem of helping school children control their emotions. Kon does not suggest that it could, and should, tackle the problem of women's over-emotionality. Yet neurosis would hardly seem an appropriate characteristic in those responsible for rearing the next generation.

Kon's assertion that boys have a powerful need to compete and to feel superior, and that teachers should accommodate this by giving them the key positions in the school and Komsomol, also contradicts the study by psychologist V. S. Mukhina, who found that all children, male and female, have a need to feel they are doing better than others, and to gain status and recognition amongst their peers.

Kon makes little attempt to provide evidence for his assertions. He does (like Anan'ev) briefly describe the study by Bodalev and Kurbanov, which compared the drawings of male and female children; he interprets the difference in subject matter as a reflection of a natural sex difference in interests.[26] However, as we have already noted, the children were old enough to have imbibed social stereotypes of male and female interests, and so the drawings could be a reflection of the successful assimilation of social norms rather than of biological differences. Kon himself has noted that a child's norms and orientations are learned in very early childhood, 'literally with the mother's milk'.[27]

At times, Kon takes the fact that sex differences still exist in the Soviet Union, despite the country's commitment to women's equality, as sufficient evidence in itself that they are natural.

> An unprecedented widening of the sphere of social activity of women entailed a profound breaking-up of traditional stereotypes and a drawing together of 'male' and 'female' social roles in society and the family. However, the sociological studies which document this process . . . at the same time show that a definite role difference is maintained. Alongside the widening of the sphere of common areas, in which men and women are represented more or less identically and perform equally, there are also predominantly male and predominantly female professions; the family roles of men and women are noticeably different; and the subjective importance of familial and work roles are not absolutely identical for them. For example, men more often talk with their friends and acquaintances about work, and women – who are also workers – about family matters.[28]

The implication is that conditions of upbringing and employment etc. are now identical for men and women, so that any discrepancies in their behaviour must be due to natural differences.

THE EROSION OF TRADITIONAL SEX DIFFERENCES IN PERSONALITY

Kon notes that there has been a considerable erosion of traditional masculine and feminine personality types, even if they do rest on biological foundations. While traditional female traits are still highly valued (such as beauty, softness, tenderness, and the showing of affection), and constitute the nucleus of a male understanding of femininity, women are also taking on some of the stereotypes of masculine behaviour, especially those needed in their professional lives – intelligence, a high level of energy, and an enterprising outlook. Some changes have also taken place in the male psyche, though this is a slower process. Strength, bravery, aggression, fortitude and energy are still important, especially for teenage boys who are intent on differentiating themselves from all things female, but in adulthood the self-evaluation of the male alters. 'The man begins to value in himself other, softer qualities, like tolerance, the ability to understand another person, and emotional responsiveness, which previously seemed to him to be signs of weakness.'[29] This break-down of the strict polarization of male and female traits opens up the possibility of a more diverse combination of traditionally male and female traits within an individual.[30]

Again, Kon is prone to inconsistency about whether such changes are positive. On the one hand, he argues that sex differentiation is unhealthy, since it creates psychological barriers between the sexes. Sociological studies show that families which do not adhere to rigid sex-role differentiation have a healthier psychological climate.[31] Confusion about the new roles can cause some worry, but once couples stop trying to match their relationship to a traditional ideal, and to organize their family life in accordance with what suits them personally, things will improve.[32]

On the other hand, Kon claims that the erosion of sex differentiation can create a number of serious problems. It can lead to uncertainty in role expectations, producing in some people a feeling of physical discomfort and uneasiness. If family concerns remain a predominantly female issue, 'despite all our efforts' (though which efforts he is referring to is far from clear), then 'women who are not prepared for this in childhood are doomed to frustration and confusion'.[33] The increasing independence of women also 'undermines the traditional division of paternal and maternal roles',[34] which represents a direct threat to the family. At times he suggests that rather than welcome an erosion of traditional masculinity and femininity, we should treat them with increased respect:

> Many family dramas ... are connected with the fact that men do not know the most elementary things about the physiology and psychology of women. Women, for their part, are not always

taught about the great sensitivity of men towards everything which is connected with their ideas about masculinity: a too energetic and assertive woman (especially in love) is involuntarily perceived as a transgressor of male 'sovereignty'.[35]

This does not offer much hope to the cause of women's equality.

Another inconsistency appears in discussions on the extent to which traditional roles can be eroded. At times Kon is certain that some differences will always exist; for example, women will always be more practical and competent than men in domestic matters.[36] At others, he makes it clear that nature is not strong enough to resist social pressures, and that it must be assisted by 'corresponding variations in the upbringing of boys and girls within the boundaries of their mutual instruction.'[37] One of the tasks of educationalists must therefore be 'to train (*vospityvat'*), and train again, girls to be girls and boys to be boys, so that we will then see in them the women and men we want to see'.[38] This is hardly consistent with Soviet psychology's commitment to the all-round development of personality.

The authority of Marx is invoked to support the notion that sex differentiation is a good thing. The questionnaire we mentioned in the introduction, which plays such a prominent role in the justification of sex differences in the writings of pedagogical theorists, also makes an appearance in Kon's work. 'Nobody', insists Kon, 'has supported the emancipation of women and the widening of the spheres of their social activity more consistently than Marx. But Marx himself, naming the most valuable qualities of man and woman, gave in the first place "strength", and in the second, "weakness"'.[39] Unlike the pedagogical theorists whose work we will look at shortly, Kon makes no attempt to explain these statements.

The women's liberation movement in the USA comes under attack for its mistaken promotion of a transcendence of psychological differences between men and women. It sees sex-role differentiation as a hierarchy which places women in the subordinate positions, and holds that women's inequality is determined largely by upbringing. Its aim is to draw together the different activities of men and women, both in and outside the family, and to achieve an ultimate 'androgeny', whereby no stereotyped behaviour differences based on sex would exist.[40] Kon approves of some aspects of feminism, such as the 'Marxist categories' which are often used; he also accepts some of its arguments, such as the hierarchical aspect of traditional sex roles. However, he rejects the idea that sex-role differentiation can and should disappear.

A division of labour between the sexes pre-dates the oppression of women, he argues, and hence the eradication of this oppression need not entail the disappearance of all sex-roles. In words reminiscent of Snegireva, whose view on sex differences we looked at in Chapter 3, he explains that 'equality does not mean identity', and 'not everything which is traditional is wrong'.[41] His ultimate concern seems to be the threat to the family which feminism poses. 'It is not coincidental', he suggests, 'that the ideas about the complete disappearance of the differentiation of sex roles is often concluded with a thesis about the disappearance of the monogamous family . . .'[42]

THE INTERACTION OF SOCIAL AND BIOLOGICAL INFLUENCES

One of Kon's clearer statements about the relative influences of biology and culture in the development of male and female personality differences is that nature provides the foundation of male and female personality, but that 'the house erected on this foundation is a storehouse of human life, culture and upbringing. And the "architect" depends entirely on cultural norms and conditions taken from society, and even on fashion trends'.[43] At the time of these writings, the 'architectural' trend in the Soviet Union stresses women's domestic and nurturant qualities, in the interests of family stability and an improved birth-rate. Kon's writings make repeated reference to the family when discussing the consequences of changes in male and female personality, expresses concern that these may go too far, and insists that teachers 'train, and train again', girls and boys to grow into the adult men and women 'we want to see'.

However, he is also concerned that a person's individuality should not be stifled by an over-zealous inculcation of masculine and feminine personality traits. Educationalists are exhorted to work on developing the personality on two fronts: 'the front of general development (including also the professional aspect) of the personality, and the front of the particularly "female". And the same applies with boys'.[44] Kon's ideal would appear to be a retention of traditional forms of masculinity and femininity, but in a muted version which permits a degree of flexibility and a limited cross-over of supposedly male and female characteristics.

However, it is likely that some of his professed views are a reflection of the ideological climate within which they have appeared, and that he has been forced to walk a narrow tightrope between what he has wished to say and what he had to say so as not to contradict the Soviet line on sex differences in personality. He himself notes that the main concerns of the West in the area of sex differences are different from those in the Soviet Union; while 'in the West one hears complaints about the continuing oppression of women', in the Soviet Union there is more anxiety about the '"feminization" of the male character, the undermining of the foundation of "masculinity" in the family and in society'.[45] The possibility that Soviet writers in this field before the dawning of *glasnost'* were expected to toe a certain line would explain why Kon's more traditional statements fit so uncomfortably with those inspired by Western theories.

It might also explain the otherwise anomalous fact that at a time of evident interest in sex differences in personality, the publication of Kon's own weighty tome, *Vvedenie v seksologiya* (Introduction to Sexology), was delayed for almost a decade. Based on a series of lectures which he gave to medical students in Leningrad in 1977 and 1978,[46] the book finally appeared in print in the Russian language in 1988. Hungarian and Estonian versions appeared some years earlier, no doubt due to the fact that these are the languages of two of the more liberal enclaves within the Eastern bloc.[47]

MORE RECENT WORK

With the publication of his book, Kon's academic status is now firmly rooted in sexology. However, he retains a commitment to the interdisciplinary approach. Sexology is itself defined as an interdisciplinary subject,

> an equilateral triangle that has biomedical research on one side, sociological and cultural research on the second, and psychological research on the third. None of these approaches can make a full contribution to our understanding of sex and sexuality in isolation from the other two.[48]

Sexology is concerned with sexual behaviour in the broadest sense. Hence as well as looking at the physical aspects of sexual relations, it also charts the development of psychological sex differences and the learning of sex roles.

The more open climate which now prevails in the Soviet Union does find reflection in Kon's work. This is particularly clear in an interview with him on homosexuality, conducted by O. Moroz and published in the March 1989 issue of *Literaturnaya Gazeta*.[49] With homosexuality still illegal in the Soviet Union, and with intensified homophobic attitudes finding voice in the press in response to the threat of AIDS, Kon urges an understanding attitude to the phenomenon which within the Soviet context is almost revolutionary. People have different ways of expressing their sexuality, he argues, and the Soviet Union, in line with 'the overwhelming majority of countries', has to recognize this right. Yet when pressed by Moroz, Kon does concede that there are precautions parents can take to avoid the development of homosexuality in their sons. He links homosexuality with excessive guardianship, particularly on the part of mothers, which can lead to sons being overly dependent. Again, this suggests that boys and girls should be subject to variations in upbringing. Kon evidently still sees his work as a tool in the struggle to prop up the ailing family by improving heterosexual relations. This is clear in the introduction to one of two articles about the 'myths and reality' of the 'real' man and woman which appeared in *Nedelya* in April 1989, in which Kon argues that strengthening the family and harmonizing conjugal life are essential prerequisites for solving such problems as the increase in divorce, the fall in the birth-rate, and the threat of AIDS.[50]

These articles are mainly concerned with male and female sexuality. However, they also address the social understandings of appropriate male and female behaviour which have influenced sexual attitudes. In the first article, Kon argues that rigid stereotypes of masculinity have distorted male sexual behaviour. Learning from earliest childhood that he must be strong, brave and competitive, the boy tries to hide everything that he assumes to be a sign of weakness in himself. This is positive in the sense that it 'really helps to form the male character'. However, it also disfigures him by making him one-sided.[51] The boy puts on a parody of masculine strength and courage, turning these into bravado, coarseness and cruelty.[52] Ultimately this has a negative effect on male and female relationships. 'If it is necessary to be strong in front of male friends, it is even more shameful to appear weak in front of a girl!' So aggression and lack of tenderness become strong elements in male sexuality. Hence rape is not an act which is only committed by men with severe psychological problems; it is primarily an indication of the difference in male and female sexual attitudes.[53]

All the same, Kon does not promote the disappearance of the 'strong masculine man', and reassures male readers that man is still 'the instrumental leader, the master of many blessings'. He would just like to see a weakening of the stereotyped ideal of masculinity, which is an exaggeration of masculine traits and is devoid of humanity. 'In order to become a real person, the man must be not only strong and brave, but also learn a whole range of traditionally "female" traits. He must also learn to be tender, loving, understanding, and many others.'[54] This is not so different from the position expressed in the earlier writings, which could be summarized as the promotion of the continuation of traditional and distinct male and female personality types, but with a blurring of the edges. Perhaps the encouragement of 'female' traits in the male psyche could be seen as one step further.

In his article on women, Kon makes a scarcely veiled criticism of the government's pro-family movement. He begins by innocuously suggesting that the attempt to combine male and female traits in the female personality has gone too far:

> We expect every woman to be an active worker and at the same time an ideal wife and mother. We expect her not to lag behind man in intellect etc., and then at the same time to willingly darn his socks!

However, he continues, when contradictions inevitably emerge, a solution is imposed on women instead of them being given the means to decide how to organize their lives: 'instead of granting women themselves a choice based on their individual characteristics, we press on them an obligatory solution which they themselves are meant to prefer. No free choice, no right to individuality!'[55]

Evidently, then, Kon advocates granting women a choice as to whether they will prioritize work or family. As we shall see in subsequent chapters, this idea is becoming prominent within the Soviet literature. It does seem to mark a departure from Kon's earlier directive, to 'train, and train again', girls and boys into appropriate adult roles. However, it will become clear that the choice may not be as free as is initially supposed.

5 Sex-change in the USSR: A. I. Belkin's Theory of Gender Development and his Treatment of Hermaphrodites

A. I. Belkin, head of the laboratory of neuro-endocrinology at Moscow's Research Institute of Psychiatry, is primarily an endocrinologist. His work with hermaphrodites is a side-line (or, as he described it to me in a personal interview, his 'hobby'!)[1] Much has been written on the treatment of hermaphrodites in the West, and a brief review of the Western approach will provide a context for Belkin's work.

HERMAPHRODITISM AND TRANSSEXUALISM: THE WESTERN APPROACH

Hermaphroditism is, to quote John Money and Anke Ehrhardt, 'a congenital condition of ambiguity of the reproductive structures so that the sex of the individual is not clearly defined as exclusively male or female. The condition is named for Hermes and Aphrodite, the Greek god and goddess of love'.[2] There are six ways in which sex is defined. The first is anatomical sex, i.e. the appearance of the external genitalia. This is generally decided as soon as the baby is born. On its basis the second definition is made, that of legal sex. At this stage little thought is given to three other definitions – chromosomal sex (the XX pattern of the female and the XY pattern of the male), gonadal sex (the presence of either ovaries or testes) and hormonal sex (whether there is a preponderance of oestrogen or androgen). If the anatomical sex is unambiguous, it is assumed that these all match. Their combination is expected to produce the appropriate psychological sex, or gender. This encompasses the characteristics, traits, behaviour and sex-identification of a person.[3]

Yet it can happen that the various definitions of sex do not accord. This is the case with hermaphroditism. There are two ways in which such a condition can develop. The first is that an abnormality of the genitals in a person who is otherwise a biologically normal male or female results in the wrong label being attached at birth, which leads to a mistaken assignment of legal sex, and will have far-reaching consequences for the development of psychological sex. The genital abnormality may, on the other hand, be an indication of a chromosomal, gonadal or hormonal problem, which renders the person biologically neutral.

A clash between different definitions of sex is also present in transsexuals. Here it is not the biological sex and gender assignment which do not match, but the gender identity on the one hand and all the other definitions of sex on the other. Hence transsexuals feel themselves to be trapped in the body of the wrong sex.

Despite their differences, hermaphroditism and transsexualism do have a number of things in common. Firstly, they both show how distinct male and female gender identities can develop in contradiction to the biological sex of a person. As Janice Raymond has put it, 'we have the stereotypes of masculinity and femininity on stage, so to speak, for all to see in an *alien* body'.[4] They are also generally treated by the same method – the surgical and/or hormonal adaptation of the anatomical sex to match the gender identity. The reason for this is that gender identity is generally thought to be firmly established very early in life (according to Money, as early as 18 months), and that trying to change it beyond this age will result in severe trauma. This should only be attempted if a child has a weak gender identity. The most common reason for this is that the child's genital abnormality left the parents uncertain about the true sex of their child, and they involuntarily transferred this doubt to the child.[5]

BELKIN'S APPROACH: HORMONES AND SEX DIFFERENCES

At first glance, Belkin's work appears to be a complete repudiation of this basic premise. Although he uses the term 'sex-change' to describe his treatment of hermaphrodites, it is, in fact, a process of gender transformation. In a ten-year period he claims to have changed the gender identities of several hundred hermaphroditic patients from the ages of 17 to 27, with almost universal success. He reports no incidence of trauma. The only failure he has referred to is the case of a Moslem from a small Central Asian village, who insisted on returning home after a gender reassignment from female to male. His fellow villagers beat him for having defied the will of Allah, which had ordained that he be a women.[6] Although Belkin felt that this case could not be described as a success, its failure relates not to the patient's own reactions to the sex-change but to the reactions of others.

Consistent with Belkin's background as an endocrinologist, he places a greater emphasis on the biological and hormonal basis of personality and sex differences than is found in the Western material. In this description of the interaction of biological and social factors, the role of biology is paramount:

> Not withstanding the great significance and power of measures of pedagogical upbringing, they are not of ultimate importance. The absence or underdevelopment of some or other structures of the biological basis of sex will sooner or later bring the individual into conflict with the sex-role prescribed to him by society.[7]

This lies beneath his refusal to change a patient's anatomical sex to match his or her gender identity, even if this is what the patient fervently desires; he will only adapt the gender identity to match the person's biological sex. However, he is not always consistent in the level of control he grants biology. Elsewhere he describes the biological influence as a mere 'Principle of Facility', which makes the appropriate sex-role come more easily to a child.[8] Social factors, in the form of role-models and reinforcement, are essential in letting the child know what role options there are. Hence 'the ease with which the individual can accept his role depends on a biological disposition, further reinforced by the disposition of the social environment'.[9] This seems little different from the position held by Money and Erhardt, that there is a biological 'imprimatur' on personality but that personality is basically the result of an interaction between biology and social influences.[10]

Hormones play the primary role in Belkin's theory. He credits them with a profound influence on both animal and human behaviour, though their function is not the same in both cases. In animals, particularly those at the lower end of the evolutionary ladder, the influence of hormones, and of the instincts connected with them, is absolute. The more highly developed animals, however, especially those which have been domesticated, have developed a limited freedom from hormonal control. This accounts for certain behavioural reactions which seem to go against instincts. Humans, by their ability to think, have developed a still greater freedom from hormonal influence. If this freedom did not exist, social evolution would have been virtually impossible. None the less, hormones still exert a strong influence over a variety of mental processes and personality traits such as learning, memory, motivation, aggression, level of tolerance towards stress, etc.[11]

Hormones are, in turn, influenced by the mental state of the human individual. Belkin gives an account of a patient who underwent a successful gender change from male to female at the age of 23, and later married, but was unable to have children. She decided to adopt a child, and (presumably to convince friends and neighbours that the child was her own) pretended to be pregnant for several months before the adoption took place. During this period, not only did the patient's body experience certain changes which occur with a genuine pregnancy – enlargement of the breasts, darkening of the nipples, cessation of menstruation – but she also underwent the corresponding hormonal changes of a pregnant woman. Belkin concludes that just as the patient successfully played the role of a woman until her female identity was fully formed, now she was playing the role of pregnant woman, and that the organism could not remain indifferent to this play activity. 'In due course the endocrine system was also included in this process, producing corresponding changes in the organism.'[12]

According to this view, there is, then, a reciprocal relationship between hormones and the workings of the brain. The brain is influenced by hormones but, in turn, is capable of stimulating the activity of the endocrine glands. Since the brain is responsible for thought, which is largely influenced by the social environment, it follows that hormonal secretions can be influenced by a particular social situation.

The idea that hormones can be influenced by the social environment is not unique to Belkin. Janice Raymond cites a study which indicates a degree of social influence even on the degree of animal hormone levels: 'When dominant male monkeys who secrete testosterone in excess are placed in a social environment where their dominance is not recognized, they become inferior members of the group and their testosterone output lessens considerably.'[13]

The hormone levels of humans have similarly been found to fluctuate according to social circumstances, which has influenced their personality traits. In Raymond's view, this challenges attempts to explain sex differences in personality in terms of hormones, since the effects of hormones are outweighed by environmental factors.[14]

Belkin, however, puts his understanding of social influences over hormonal levels to a rather different use. During the early stages of gender assignment, his patients undergo play therapy in which they act out their new gender roles. This, according to Belkin, stimulates the hormonal secretions appropriate to their sex, which in turn augment and facilitate the process of psychological adjustment to this sex by triggering-off sex-typed behaviour and traits. He cites patients who, having changed from a male to a female sex-identity, soon began wanting children. He takes this as evidence of the stimulation of their female hormones.[15] Hence a 'maternal instinct' is, to Belkin, a natural, hormonal phenomenon.

THE PROCESS OF GENDER REASSIGNMENT

The majority of Belkin's patients come from small rural towns and villages. Urban parents, especially from Moscow and Leningrad, are likely to seek medical help if they perceive any signs of abnormality in their children, and an early gender reassignment can then be accomplished with comparative ease. In rural areas, however, people are more ruled by tradition, and more fearful of the attitude of others towards any deviations from the norm. Parents of hermaphroditic children are likely to hide any sign of abnormality, suppress their own worries, and continue to rear the child as a member of the assigned sex. In such cases the problems only comes to light with the onset of puberty, with the arrival of secondary sex characteristics which fail to correspond to the sex of rearing. Belkin's patients have often undergone a period of extreme emotional torment before seeking treatment, during which time they have watched with horror the unexpected changes in their bodies and attempted to conceal them from the world. Some have also been rejected by their families.[16] Given that the Soviet Union is a society which places great importance on familial relations and permits few deviations from the cultural norm, one might expect the sense of dislocation and isolation to be particularly acute. According to Belkin, most see sex-change as the only solution. Belkin thus sees it as 'a highly humanitarian act, which helps not only to deliver the person from a hopeless situation which sometimes leads to suicidal actions, but also to find his or her place in society.'[17]

One such case is that of the patient 'Yu'. Assigned a female gender at birth, at puberty she began to take on a decidedly masculine appearance. Her parents told her to leave home so as not to 'disgrace the family'. Yu. found a place in a women's hostel, but her appearance became too masculine to permit her to stay. She could not find a place in a men's hostel because her internal passport declared her to be female. After an unsuccessful suicide attempt she was brought to Belkin's attention. She was then 26 years old, and desperate for a solution to the problem of her 'indeterminate' sex. An examination found an absence of female internal organs, and external genitalia of both sexes in an undeveloped form – the opening of a vagina (1.5 cm long), a small penis, and inguinally-placed testicles. A change to male gender was advised, and agreed to by the patient. In addition to the necessary psychological readjustment, surgical alterations were made to further masculinize the patient's genitals. From Belkin's follow-up contact with Yu., we learn that he has married, become a specialist, and feels himself to be a full member of society.[18]

However, not all patients are happy at the beginning with Belkin's proposed solutions. 'K', a 22-year-old biological male, had been wrongly assigned female gender at birth because of a genital abnormality. K's parents were aware soon after the birth that all was not well, but continued to rear her as a girl, dress her in appropriate clothes, and teach her 'the habits essential for a women'. From puberty the mistake became increasingly obvious. According to Belkin, K was aware that she was really male, but her fear of rejection by friends and colleagues was greater than the problem of disguising her maleness. She felt her entire personality was bound up with her gender identity. She removed her facial hair daily, and took up sport to account for her masculine physique. When she came to Belkin, it was with a request for surgery to make her physical appearance match her gender; she did not want a change of gender and begged Belkin 'not to crush her psyche'. Belkin persuaded her to try living as a man for ten days, in a male hotel where no one would know of her history. If adjustment to the new gender proved impossible, Belkin agreed to grant her request (though given his strong views on the subject, it seems unlikely that he would have done so). Despite an initial period of depression, K did begin to adapt to a male gender. She asked for the experiment to be extended, and then finally agreed to a permanent gender reassignment.[19]

Some people have still greater problems in coming to terms with the reality of their biological sex. Many of these are still teenagers, aged 14 to 16, and Belkin feels that they have not yet grasped the full horror of their situation. When they do so, they will agree to a sex-change. 'In some cases it is more expedient to wait, until new life situations themselves lead the patient to understand the necessity of a sex-change.'[20] Hopefully he does not lose too many patients through the 'suicidal actions' referred to earlier. The special treatment in clinical conditions which such patients require provides the bonus of a particularly clear example of the process of gender development: 'With particular distinctness one can follow the most essential stages in the disintegration of one sexual identification and the genesis of another'.[21]

Approximately equal numbers of male-to-female and female-to-male transformations are performed. Male-to-female transformations tend to be more problematic. Belkin suggests that this is because women in Soviet Union have harder and hence less attractive lives than men. (In an interview with him, I suggested that women also derive considerably less status than men, making a male-to-female change a 'demotion'; but Belkin disagreed with this.) There are also specifically female rituals with no male equivalents, such as the application of make-up, which must be learned. Belkin's description of the process of sex-change makes it clear that the genders of male-to-female patients are reformed in accordance with a stereotype of female personality and behaviour, the content and parameters of which are defined by the doctor.

Unfortunately Belkin does not address in any detail the physical aspects of sex-change, although we do learn that since a disorder of the external genitalia is the usual cause of the original error in gender assignment, surgery is generally needed to correct the appearance of the genitals. The Western literature on sex-change operations makes it clear that while the fashioning of a functioning vagina is possible, the surgical construction of a functioning penis is not. Might this not offset the benefits to a female-to-male patient of gaining an easier life and higher status?

Belkin concedes that the task of changing a person's sex is generally not an easy one. In order to gain a deeper understanding of the inner world of an often disturbed person, the doctor must first develop a relationship of absolute trust with him or her. Patients are encouraged to discuss the smallest and most intimate details of their lives preceding and during the sex-change. They are asked to keep a diary in which they record every thought and feeling about the changes they are undergoing, every success and failure in the mastery of new forms of behaviour and speech. These are then discussed and analysed with the doctor. Patients are also filmed at various stages of their transformation, and the film sequences are later viewed and discussed. Patients are encouraged to ask a multitude of questions about the process they are undergoing, which help provide the doctor with an understanding of their thoughts, levels of conformity, and extent of willingness to re-evaluate former standards and stereotypes (as well as probably giving the doctor an opportunity to expound his own standards and stereotypes). Use is also made of fictional literature in order to judge (and influence?) the patient's attitudes towards the characteristics of male and female characters. Many patients live for a time in the clinic, and then in a hostel with members of their own sex, who remain unaware that the newcomer is anything but normal. For a while, contact is broken between patients and old friends and family. Such a break is sometimes, but not always, permanent.[22]

A sex-change is normally accomplished within six months. It takes place in three stages.[23] The first step is termed 'adjustment', and begins from the moment of awareness that the change is necessary. The patient is encouraged to create an 'ideal' model of masculinity and femininity, which is based on the behaviour of a real person or persons. This does not have to be someone from the patient's immediate sphere of social or familial relations; it might be a political or cultural figure, or a character from a novel. For girls, Valentina Tereshkova, the first women cosmonaut, has been a particularly popular model.[24]

The second stage is 'imitation'. The patient plays at being a member of the new sex, imitating as closely as possible the behaviour of the chosen model. The adoption of clothes appropriate for the new sex is particularly important and often acts as the turning point in the process, after which patients begin to really think of themselves as members of their new sex. In Belkin's view, this shows the extent to which clothes, external appearance, names and behaviour are all intertwined in gender identification. Once appropriately attired, patients begin to notice fine details of male or female behaviour: 'For example, subjects changing from male to female sex immediately turn their attention to how women hold a comb, a mirror; to cosmetics; to how they hold their elbows, to the positioning of their knees . . .'[25]

A Russian undergoing a change of sex has a problem which an English speaker would be spared, in that the Russian language is heavily differentiated according to the sex of the speaker. Belkin notes that speech which was rich and colourful may become dull, monotonous and slow, as if under tight conscious control. 'It is as if the patient lets out each word through a filter of a controlling consciousness, he is scared to make a mistake in the choice of appropriate pronouns for his role.'[26] However, soon patients

> notice with joy that in conversation with others they do not get confused with grammatical constructions, although they are not thinking especially about their speech. 'As soon as I put women's clothes on', one of our patients explained, 'conversation began to arrive "by itself"'.[27]

(It would seem that Belkin's male-to-female patients are also required to dress in an overtly feminine manner – no jeans or moonboots for them, regardless of what fashions prevail in the streets outside!)

After a period of role-play, patients have to put their new guise into practice with other people. These people function as a mirror, through which patients can see how they are perceived by others. Initially they are very conscious of their actions and attempt to duplicate precisely the behaviour of the models they have chosen. However, sometimes they find themselves reproducing the behaviour of new people they have met. Their original model of behaviour gives way to a 'generalized model' which forms as they observe and categorize the behaviour of all the people with whom they now come into contact. The ability to form emotional empathy with members of their new sex develops during this stage.

The third and final stage is 'transformation'. The behaviour of patients ceases to be an exact imitation of that of their chosen model and takes on more personal, individual features. Patients may become ambivalent or even hostile to aspects of their former model's behaviour.

Towards the end of the 'imitation' stage patients begin to actively distance themselves from their former sex. Seeing photographs or films of themselves in their previous sexual identities produces exclamations of surprise and disgust. They become increasingly negative to members of their previous sex, especially those of their own age. One female-to-male patient had initially expressed horror at the thought of having to identify with 'those coarse, callous creatures who can't even understand the tears of another person', but when the change was well underway he wrote in his diary that, 'I don't want to spend time with women any more. I'm opposed to their conventions . . . they cry so easily, they aren't able to stand up for themselves, they are too talkative and naive'.[28] Belkin makes no attempt to challenge such negative and stereotyped ideas about the opposite sex, seeing them as a natural part of the process of identifying with one's own sex – and in any case, a temporary phenomenon which will soon be replaced by sexual interest.

Social factors are evidently granted the major influence over sexual orientation. In a discussion on the sexual orientation of hermaphrodites (a subject rendered particularly complex in the Soviet Union because of the social and legal pressures against homosexuality), Belkin decides, after some deliberation, that a biological woman who was reared as a male and subsequently married a woman would not be considered homosexual. 'The sexual orientation of the hermaphrodite is formed under the influence of upbringing.... For the hermaphrodite, homosexuality, in its usual legal sense, evidently cannot exist.'[29]

Sexual morality appears to be an exclusively female trait, and one which Belkin's male-to-female patients need to acquire. Explaining that patients adopt a new system of values along with their new sex identification, Belkin gives the example of 'Sh.', who changed from male to female at the age of 18. Soon afterwards she decided to move out of her aunt's house to a hostel:

> The only reason was that periodically 'men stayed overnight' with this relative. In a discussion it was explained that before, when she thought herself a member of the male sex, she was unconcerned about such behaviour. 'I did not see this as indecent, and it sometimes even amused me', said the patient. But from the moment she identified herself with the female sex, such 'loose' behaviour on the part of her aunt became to her 'internally' unpleasant: 'Where is her female pride, her respect for herself?'.[30]

According to Belkin, this shows how one's role in society influences the way one perceives, experiences and evaluates the same situation. Alternately, it could show that Belkin's patients have been conscientious pupils of his sex-typed notions of morality. Evidently the aunt's femaleness did not cause her to evaluate the situation in the same way; her response to her niece's new morality was, 'What, have you just woken up?'[31]

During this stage, Patients sometimes remember incidents from their childhood which they now interpret as promptings of their real, biological sex. One male-to-female patient recalled wanting to play with dolls, and being punished for trying on make-up. She decided that she had never felt herself to be fully male, although up to the time of the sex-change she insisted that she was happy as a boy and had always participated with enjoyment in male activities with her peers. Belkin sees as significant not the incidents themselves – many boys take an interest in aspects of female behaviour – but the fact that they were repressed until after the sex-change. He offers no explanation for this 'repression'. However, according to the Western literature, many patients of anatomically-ambiguous hermaphroditic children have doubts as to their real sex, and this is likely to make them particularly alert to any indication of sex-inappropriate behaviour. The severity with which the father reacted, in the case Belkin describes, backs this up – and might be enough in itself to make the child want to forget the event.

At the outset of this discussion, we suggested that Belkin's work seemed to repudiate the fundamental premise of his Western counterparts, that gender identity is irrevocably formed in the first 18 months of a child's life. However, although Belkin claims to conduct successful gender reassignments on people who would be considered far too old in the West, the seeming contradiction is superficial. From the above discussion we can gather that the majority, if not all, of Belkin's patients have problems with their original gender indentification. This stems partly from physical transformations they have undergone at puberty, although according to the Western literature, this is not in itself enough to dislocate a normal gender identity.[32] More crucial is the fact that from earliest childhood these children have reason to doubt their membership of the assigned sex. It seems that no surgery is performed on their genitals until the time of their sex change, although they generally have an ambiguous appearance. The patients, we are told, are often aware soon after birth that something is wrong (something which Western specialists consider to be the most important factor in the development of a weak gender identity). The severity of the patients' reaction to any sex-inappropriate behaviour might further alert the children to the fact that all is not as it should be. Finally, at the time of the pubertal changes the children often receive complete negation instead of parental support. Hence even if Belkin is as successful as he claims (which is unlikely), his work is not a complete disavowal of the views of his Western counterparts, since the majority of his patients are likely to have very confused gender identities by the time he commences treatment.

All the same, if Belkin really is able to establish strong gender identities in young adults, this indicates that personality remains more malleable in adulthood than Western researchers on sex differences would have us believe. Otherwise Belkin's patients would surely remain of indeterminate gender. As it is, he claims to produce in them distinct male and female personalities and sexually 'appropriate' traits and patterns of behaviour. This is compatible with Soviet psychology's approach to human personality, which sees it as highly flexible and amenable to the processes of training and self-training well beyond the years of early childhood.

BELKIN'S THEORY OF GENDER DEVELOPMENT

Belkin has derived from his work a general theory of gender and personality development which now informs his subsequent sex-change 'operations', with, he claims, even better results.[33] It centres on the notion (reminiscent of cognitive-development theory) that children actively seek to locate themselves within society, and having ascertained to which categories and groups they belong, they set out to acquire the characteristics and patterns of behaviour observed therein. Two processes are at work, that of 'identification' and 'distinction'.[34] This means simply that children identify with people who are perceived to be like themselves, and distinguish themselves from those who are not. Hence their definition of themselves is formed on the basis of their similarities to some people and their dissimilarities to others.

Having decided in which categories they belong, children construct a model or ideal type of behaviour, which acts as a guide to their own behaviour. The model may be based on real people drawn from their own lives, or (especially in the Soviet Union, where children are encouraged to adopt the behaviour of certain notable heroes) on famous people, such as historical, political or cultural figures.[35] Identification involves the adoption not only of a certain type of behaviour, but also of a series of psychological traits, such as kindness, sympathy and aggression, which the child internalizes. (This suggests that aggression is at least partly learned, and not an innately male characteristic.) Children also empathize emotionally with the model and with other people who have similar traits.[36]

Identification involves not just the adoption of a model, but also of a reference group of 'one's own'.

> In the recognition of the group with whom the individual feels himself connected most closely and from which he draws the norms, values and aims of his behaviour, one can see a distinctive type of

social control over the ability of the subject to construct norms of behaviour and cultural and emotional stereotypes. The individual proves to be 'one of them' if he adopts the standards accepted by his social environment as essential.[37]

The process of distinction is less complex than that of identification since it does not require the construction of an ideal type, the mastery of stereotypes and conventions, or the ability to empathize emotionally with other people. For this reason, although they occur simultaneously in the process of normal child development, patients undergoing sex change accomplish distinction earlier than identification. That is, patients start by delineating themselves from members of their former sex and only later begin to define themselves according to their new sex role. (Distinction takes place not only in the sphere of sex roles but also, for example, in that of occupational roles; a member of the intelligentsia partly defines him or herself in relation to how he or she differs from a manual worker.)[38]

Distinction is always somewhat negative, particularly in its early stages.

In identifying with the cultural values, rituals, rites and ideals of one group, the subject simultaneously disparages the achievements and traditions of other groups.... Distinction includes the unconscious prejudice towards everything which is regarded as not immediately belonging to the sphere of values taken on by the subject.[39]

One could deduce from this that racism would be seen as an inevitable characteristic of children in a multi-racial society, since they would disparage each other's cultures and traditions in the process of identifying with their own. However, when questioned about this, Belkin said (after a pause) that a positive attitude on the part of parents and teachers could prevent this. None the less, in general – and in particular in the sphere of sex differences – Belkin grants the negative aspects of distinction a positive function, in that they facilitate identification. In making negative decisions about certain values and ideas, we make positive decisions about others. Hence: 'In the example of identification and distinction one can see the dialectical law of the unity of opposites.'[40]

One would be wrong, then, to think that changing the psychological sex of a person would be easier if male and female personalities were not so strongly differentiated. According to Belkin's theory, the process of distancing themselves from the traits and psychological peculiarities of their former sex will help propel patients towards an identification with, and mastery of, those connected with their new sex. For this distancing to be possible, the traits and psychological characteristics of the two sexes need to be quite different. Such reasoning justifies Belkin's encouragement of cultural stereotypes of masculinity and femininity in his patients. In fact, he would like such stereotypes to be inculcated more successfully in all children. In an article which does not mention his work with hermaphrodites, he suggests that patients should exhibit more differentiated sex roles and that children's literature should reflect such differentiation. At present, 'in most modern poems, stories and songs for children the conduct of heroes and heroines is often indistinguishable . . .'.[41] (Incidentally, this is not the conclusion reached by M. S. Rosenhan, whose study of Soviet children's books shows that the conduct of men and women is extremely sex-typed.)[42]

BELKIN AND WESTERN WRITINGS ON GENDER

Belkin's theory of personality and gender development accords with many of the principles of Kohlberg's cognitive-developmental approach to sex differences in personality. Kohlberg also sees children as active agents in their own sex-role socialization, seeking to imitate characteristics considered appropriate to them as members of one or other sex, and to reject or even disparage those which are not. However, Belkin grants reinforcement and modelling a more prominent role. He argues that parents have a particular responsibility for presenting to children dichotomized models of masculinity and femininity; their failure to do so will hinder the process of identification and distinction. The blurring of roles between parents confuses children and renders them incapable of deciding which to adopt as a model. Failure on the part of parents to encourage and reinforce sexually appropriate behaviour in their children has disastrous results:

> Research shows that mothers who never play with dolls during childhood often lack motherly feelings and maternal skills, while boys who have been pampered grow up physically weak, cowardly, and dependent. When they reach adulthood, such children often prove incapable of fulfilling the role which society requires of them.[43]

Since being 'pampered' evidently means being treated like a girl, one might wonder why girls do not grow up physically weak, cowardly and dependent – which Soviet women certainly are not – or, indeed, why Belkin does not find such negative traits equally abhorrent in women. That children should be primarily a female concern is an obvious assumption in Belkin's work; there is no mention of fatherly feelings and parental skills being useful male attributes.

Insufficiently differentiated male and female roles will lead to severe psychological disturbances in children. They have a 'deep need to set up an ideal of masculinity and femininity'; if they fail to do so they experience a sense of 'depersonalization' and lack of belonging.

> This intolerable feeling of 'sexlessness' expresses itself in anti-social behaviour such as alcoholism, drug-taking and homosexuality. This in turn creates bitterness and emotional instability that are sometimes responsible for crime and for unhappy, broken homes that not infrequently end in suicide.[44]

Despite the fundamental differences between Belkin's treatment of hermaphrodites and that of his Western counterparts (namely, that Belkin transforms the psychological sex of his patients to match their bodies, while in the West bodies are matched to minds) it can be argued that both approaches countenance the moulding of patients into psychological stereotypes of masculinity and femininity. Janice Raymond has accused Western doctors in this field of 'perpetuating, judging, and reinforcing the cultural stereotypes';[45] in Belkin's case an adherence to cultural stereotypes is quite explicit. He expresses deep concern at the increasing feminization of men and masculinization of women, and lists a number of dire consequences of this trend. He suggests that we rectify the situation by bringing all possible means of cultivating sex-role stereotypes to bear on the upbringing of children.[46] While his writings on sex-change do not state that he consciously constructs the new gender identities of his patients in accordance with his own stereotypes (he suggests, in fact, that much of the process is autonomous, with patients themselves seeking to acquire characteristics they consider appropriate and to shed those they do not), it is evident that Belkin becomes the arbitrator of appropriate male and female behaviour. His accounts of individual cases also suggests that his patients, like transsexuals in the West, tend to delineate personalities which are more in line with the stereotypes than are those of the population at large.

It is worth recalling Belkin's observation that there are specifically female rituals which have no male equivalent. These seem generally to relate to physical appearance; he mentions make-up, combs, mirrors, 'the positioning of the knees' in a lady-like manner. An interest in physical appearance is evidently an exclusively female phenomenon. Perhaps the absence in Belkin's discussion of typically 'male' behaviour which his female-to-male patients must acquire indicates that the high level of female employment – in jobs which often contradict traditional notions of femininity – has broken the male monopoly on certain qualities and characteristics, so that female-to-male patients already possess the essential 'masculine' characteristics before the sex-change commences. As we shall see in a later chapter, sociologists such as Yankova note that women's roles in Soviet society have widened the range of their psychological characteristics to include independence, self-confidence, responsibility, etc. At the same time, women are expected and encouraged to retain their traditional 'feminine' traits alongside these new psychological endowments.

BELKIN AND THE PRO-FAMILY ETHOS

Soviet society places a great emphasis on the social duties and obligations of the individual, which is reflected in Belkin's writings. We can perceive a continual stress on the obligations of the individual regarding marriage, rearing children, and holding down a responsible job. He argues that, 'every social role which an individual takes upon himself burdens him with a heavy responsibility towards society, which calls for considerable effort on his part if he is to fulfil that role succesfully.[47] It is evident that many of these remain sex-defined, despite the official rhetoric about women's equality and the very real participation of women in the hitherto male world of the economy.

> It may be true that those who vociferously demand a single 'identity' for the sexes, or who call for a 'sexual revolution' and for freedom from daily routine are merely demonstrating a selfish and irresponsible desire to escape from the role which nature and society assign to every individual.[48]

This emphasis on a person's duty to society, including that of raising the next generation of workers, soldiers and mothers, explains how Belkin feels able to put homosexuality on a par with drug-taking and alcoholism. All three, seen in the Soviet context, prevent the citizen from fulfilling certain of his or her social obligations. This has provided

Belkin with another interest – that of 'curing' homosexuals.[49] Both this, and his efforts to resolve the sexual ambiguity of hermaphroditic patients, are ways of reinstating some of society's misfits into the established, sexually-defined pattern of duties and obligations.

To be fair to Belkin, it should be noted that the social context within which he has had to operate has given him little choice of approach. A somewhat more liberal understanding of gender stereotypes may be permitted, even in the Brezhnev era, in a theoretical writer such as Kon (although we have noted that this was not always received with enthusiasm); but that funding would have been provided for practical work which challenged gender stereotypes in real human beings would have been unthinkable in the Soviet Union. In any case, in a society which does lay so much stress on gender differences, the extreme psychological discomfort that Belkin's patients experience as a consequence of their gender ambiguity is unlikely to be mitigated by anything less than the establishment within them of unequivocal gender identities. Hence Belkin's claim that changing the sex of his patients is highly humanitarian has validity. Similarly, he has argued that his treatment of homosexuals is undertaken at their request, following their acknowledgement that a successful and happy life in Soviet society is possible only within the confines of accepted social and familial relations.[50]

If Belkin's work and writings can be seen as a mirror of prevailing Soviet opinion and mores concerning sex differences, they are a mirror which highlights the warts and blemishes of its subject. It is a particular irony that his views on the desirability of dichotomized male and female roles are expounded in an issue of the *UNESCO Courier* which (despite Belkin's insistence that alarm over the feminization of men and the masculinization of women is universal) sets out to challenge traditional male and female roles. Other articles are concerned, for example, with a new law in Cuba which forces husbands to do housework; a Norwegian experiment in 'conjugal work sharing', in which both parents work part-time and take equal turns at parenting; and how to eliminate sexism from French textbooks. From the Soviet Union, the first country in the world to declare the equality of women, comes the only article which espouses the binding of women to a range of traditional roles and personality traits. Belkin does not see this as incompatible with equality, however, 'Equality of the sexes should not lead to the blurring of the psychological boundaries between them, to "asexual" behaviour.'[51] Again, equality does not mean identity.

BELKIN AND SOVIET PSYCHOLOGY

To what extent does Belkin's work accord with the Soviet approach to personality development which we looked at earlier? Although he makes no explicit reference to the work of Soviet psychologists, we can perceive some links or overtones. His use of stages is, of course, reminiscent of Vygotskii; so too is the importance he places on role play, and on the construction of an ideal behaviour from a chosen model or models. When Belkin talks of the behaviour of his patients ultimately becoming intuitive, we are reminded of the 'internalization' of moral norms discussed by Vygotskii, Makarenko and Subbotskii. Belkin's insistence that some patients live for a while in a single-sex hostel is also compatible with the importance placed by Soviet psychologists on the peer group and collective at a certain point in the socialization process of the child. The stress on the duties and obligations of the individual towards socialist society are also far from new; they were a particularly prominent feature, for example, of the work of Makarenko.

However, Belkin's ideas on male and female differences are evidently in sharp discord with certain aspects of mainstream Soviet psychology. According to the premise we argued earlier, Soviet psychology should see sharply dichotomized male and female personalities as neither inevitable nor desirable. Belkin, on the other hand, evidently sees them as both. (Like many of the writers discussed in this section, however, he is often contradictory, urging parents and teachers to concentrate all efforts on inculcating in children the traits which elsewhere he describes as natural and spontaneous.) The development of an all-round personality, so important in Soviet psychology, must to Belkin be contained within very strict confines, determined by 'nature and society' – which have a single, harmonious idea of what the individual's role should be. Although Belkin admits that women have a harder role in Soviet society, he opposes any attempt at a more even distribution of functions, on the grounds that women's lot is determined by society and nature.

The root of the discrepancy is that despite the Soviet assurance that under socialism the interests of the individual and of society are identical, for women this has not always proved to be the case. Men wield the power and decide on the priorities and needs of society. The needs of women, and the development of all-round personalities, are subordinate to the perceived social requirements of a high birth-rate and a cheap source of domestic labour. While the banner of women's equality is still in official rhetoric, this seems to have more to do with expedience than ideological commitment. The aim of women's equality has been used to justify the exploitation of their work potential, while references to nature and social duty ensure their continued service in the home and family.

6 Sociological and Demographic Approaches to Sex Differences

Given that the granting of a separate chapter to the work of I. S. Kon was justified at least partly on the grounds of the difficulty of placing him in one academic pigeon-hole, then another explanation is required for including in a single chapter the approaches of two separate disciplines, sociology and demography. There are, in fact, a number of reasons for doing so.

The interests of sociology and demography do converge to a considerable extent in this field. Both disciplines are concerned with the negative consequences of women's 'equality'. Demographic attention is focused on one of these, the drop in the birth-rate; but this is also the main concern of some sociologists, such as Igor Bestuzhev-Lada. It is also not unusual for demographers to borrow sociological arguments to back up their call for an increase in the birth-rate. To give just one example, in a round-table discussion organized by *Nedelya* on the future of the family, which was attended by both sociologists and demographers, the demographer A. G. Volkov suggests that it is not enough to ask how many children are necessary from a demographic point of view, but also what the optimum number is for the people concerned, including children themselves. (His conclusion is that four is the ideal number, so that a child of either sex will have both a brother and sister.[1] He fails to mention the fact that nature is not always so obliging.) Reference to sociological issues can also be a response on the part of demographers to the charge that they are engaged in a heartless manipulation of people on the basis of statistics. Answering just such an accusation in an interview in *Novoe Vremya*, A. Vishnevskii defends his profession with the claim that demography has lately become much more concerned about individual people, their behaviour and interests.[2] The Soviet sociologist now living in the USA, Vladimir Shlapentokh, notes a similarity between the views of demographer Perevedentsev (and, for that matter, of Kon) with American functionalist sociology.[3] Finally, it should be noted that the journal

Sotsiologicheskie Issledovaniya (*Sociological Studies*) frequently carries a section on demography.

Evidently, then, there is considerable overlap in both subject matter and approach. O. A. Voronina suggests, in an article in *Sotsiologicheskie Issledovaniya*, that the representatives of the different disciplines 'look at the problem each from his own belltower, . . . based on the idea of some special predestination of the female sex'.[4] We will begin this chapter by looking at the view which is best seen from the sociological belltower – i.e., the content of male and female personality – and then turn to the ground which lies between the two.

MALE AND FEMALE PERSONALITY IN SOCIALIST SOCIETY

Sociology was the first social science in the Soviet Union to voice a cautious acknowledgement that women had yet to achieve equality with men, regardless of how one defines this equality. The woman question, which was officially 'solved' by the early 1930s with the professed achievement of socialism, became a topic of debate once more when sociology re-emerged in the intellectual thaw of the 1960s. The post-war deficit of men led to labour shortages both in the present and the future (given the inevitable decrease in the birth-rate); hence women, and their dual function as workers and as the bearers of future workers, became the focus of sociological attention.[5] More recently, the instability of marriage, as epitomized by the high divorce rate, has become a major concern.

Soviet sociologists are more concerned with the difference in male and female roles in the family and the work-place than they are in the development of sex differences in personality. However, reference is made to certain 'psycho-physiological' differences between the sexes. These correspond to traditional notions of masculinity and femininity. In women, for example, they include emotionality, sensitivity, tenderness, and concern for others. A. G. Kharchev notes that differences in male and female personality are evident even in early childhood:

> The feeling of belonging to a certain sex appears already in preschool children's games. Male or female character begins to be seen in children also comparatively early. In other words, a range of human characteristics in the individual, which are called forth by

one's sex, appear long before sexual maturation, and correspondingly before the formation of sex urges.[6]

These differences are usually taken as self-evident fact, as something rooted in nature. In any case, any analysis of their origins would be the task of psychologists rather than sociologists. Kharchev makes this clear after claiming that women have a stronger need than men for love and romance. It is not important for sociologists to understand the reasons for this need, he asserts; they should merely be aware that the need exists, since it may be a partial explanation of the failure of marriage. 'For us, it is enough to note that . . . a certain "deficit of attention" on the part of a husband towards his wife can aggravate the contradictions engendered by other factors.'[7]

One of the claims which appears frequently in the sociological literature is that female personality has undergone some considerable changes with the onset of socialism, and that for the most part these have been positive. Zoya Yankova is a prominent exponent of this view.

Unlike many of the Soviet writers whose work we look at, Yankova does not fail to see the relevance for women of psychology's professed plan for the all-round development of the personality. She suggests that, 'At the present stage of the building of communism, when the formation of all-round developed personality has become an immediate practical aim, resolving the problem of the equality of women and men demands particular urgency.'[8] The full potential of the female personality can only be realized in the conditions of socialism, she claims, since it depends to a large extent on assistance from the state, from society, from the woman's husband, and from other members of the family.

The woman's involvement in the economy and in public life have contributed to the 'harmonious development' of her personality by expanding the range of her traits and abilities. Yankova cites studies in which women acknowledge the positive benefits they have derived from working outside the home. They list (in addition to the economic factor) the joy of doing something socially useful, taking part in a collective, experiencing independence, and taking initiative. This 'bears witness to the fact that professional activity gradually turns into one of the important determinants of the development of a woman's personality qualities.'[9]

The opportunities which socialism has opened up to women have inevitably had an impact on the hopes, expectations, and indeed the personalities of young girls. An interesting, if rather implausible, study by R. Gurova compares the questionnaire responses of Soviet schoolgirls in 1969 about their ambitions, interests, and views on marriage and the family, with those of their predecessors in the immediate pre-revolutionary years.[10]

The earlier studies found that girls were self-centred in their aims and bitter about their options. They saw marriage and full-time motherhood as inevitable, because of family pressures and the absence of educational and career opportunities, and were pessimistic about how much happiness they could expect from these. The 1969 girls, in contrast, were patriotic and public spirited. The vast increase in educational and professional opportunities had resulted in greater optimism about their futures and a high level of confidence about their worth and abilities. Socialism had imbued them with a greater social conscience, an awareness of the needs of people beyond themselves and their immediate sphere of relations. They still saw marriage as inevitable, but for positive rather than negative reasons – because of the need for love, and to have a true friend in life.

This study can hardly be taken at face value. The responses of the post-revolutionary girls are too good to be true, and Gurova's research methodology is of dubious accuracy and objectivity. However, though it may say little about the actual changes in female personality under socialism, it does indicate what sociologists feel those changes should be. The socialist woman should still have a strong commitment to marriage and the family, but should also expect to play an important role in economic and social life and have a strongly developed sense of the greater social need.

Hence socialism does not actually transform women's personalities. It merely grafts new qualities on to the old ones. Women are still the bearers and upbringers of children, and so still require the personality traits which reflect these roles. Although women's work activities have developed in their personalities some qualities formerly associated with men – for example, independence, initiative, and self-confidence – the continuing differences in male and female reproductive roles ensures that their personalities will never become identical. As Yankova writes, 'The function of motherhood has formed and will continue to form in women such character traits as tenderness, attentiveness, concern, softness, emotionality . . .'.[11] These traits are typically female. Emotion, for example, is characteristic of women and 'forms an indispensable element of the understanding of femininity'.[12]

The assumption that such traits are natural is seldom questioned. N. D. Shimin, however, seems to anticipate a challenge, and to respond with some irritation:

> It is hardly necessary to point out that the mother, with her individual traits of femininity and her special emotional relationship with the child, has a real possibility to successfully direct the upbringing of his feelings, and to form in him a correct emotional relationship to the world.[13]

The 'harmoniously developed personality' of the socialist woman, then, constitutes an amalgam of 'feminine' qualities and those formerly thought of as masculine. Together they promote the successful combination of maternal duties and professional work.

Some sociologists applaud the development and enrichment of the female personality under socialism not so much because of the benefits it brings to women themselves, but because of the benefits it engenders in them. While the all-round development of male personality is seen as a good thing in itself, the development of the female personality is a good thing because it turns women into better child-rearers.

Shimin, for example, talks of women as the primary upbringers, but it is obvious that he also sees them primarily as upbringers. He does not deny women other roles in society, but supports these only because they improve women's performance as mothers. The richer a woman's personality becomes in spiritual matters, and the more developed she is as an individual, the more effective will be her influence over her children:

> Therefore we consider that the participation of the woman-mother in socially productive work, the widening of her social connections and the enriching of her personality, has a beneficial influence on the fulfilment of the mother's important function – the socialization of children.[14]

Yet ultimately, femininity is still her main attribute. Shimin also claims that the more feminine a woman is, the more worthy.

E. Danilova similarly promotes the development of female personality on the grounds that it will improve her role as mother and upbringer. It 'has as its consequence the protection of her health and the development of the future generation'.[15] Like Shimin, she sees the woman as the natural upbringer, especially in the early period of the child's life, when the personality is formed. A woman with a highly developed personality has a huge, even decisive influence on the formation of the new person. 'Considering the specific social role of the woman-mother in the formation of the rising generation, a socialist society interests itself in the creation of the conditions essential for the development of a free, educated, high-level personality in the woman-mother.'[16]

Not only do the woman's new characteristics make a valuable contribution in the performance of her traditional roles; her traditional qualities also have a powerful impact in her new professional role, and enhance the lives of the other members of her work collective. The feminine woman can understand the moods and qualities of her colleagues, and has the desire to help and support them. In addition, her femininity has a positive effect on all around her, be they children, teenagers, men, or other women.[17] The combination of femininity with the new qualities emerging from the woman's professional roles produce the socialist woman, 'characterized above all by a high level of citizenship, selflessness, steadfastness, responsibility, and confidence in the correctness of her actions, but . . . also suffused with spiritual softness, emotion, an urge to help, to ease, to take care of others, to support'.[18]

The balance between old and new personality traits is very important. There is a danger that women will go too far in their acquisition of the personality traits appropriate to their professional lives, and become 'masculinized'. This will be detrimental to their domestic and maternal duties.

Some writers argue that this is already happening. However, there is some dispute on the subject. In Yankova's view, this is a mistaken notion based on the desire to restrict female personality to traits reflecting just one of her roles. Even if this is the most important, 'history shows that the process of personality formation is deformed if restricted only to the domestic role of women'.[19] She cites a study in which women were themselves asked to define femininity. Only 20 per cent listed such traits as softness, emotionality, concern for others, attentiveness, tenderness and tact. Approximately 15 per cent mentioned elegance, physical attractiveness, charm, and the ability to please. The overwhelming majority ignored such qualities completely. To these women, femininity can only be understood in terms of the whole developed personality of woman. It only has meaning if the woman is independent, confident in herself, and possesses a strong feeling of her own dignity and humanity. Yankova concludes that supposedly male and female traits should not be seen as opposites, but as complementary components of the same personality.[20]

Elsewhere, however, Yankova argues that there is indeed a danger of women becoming over masculinized. The problem develops when

> equality is understood as identity – women begin to perform work which is difficult and dangerous to their organism, to become coarse, and to take on masculine patterns of behaviour, patterns which lead to family conflicts. They lose their taste for domestic behaviour and interpersonal intimacy verified by the centuries. The weakening of femininity inevitably has an adverse affect on the psychological climate of the family, and often leads to complex collisions and frustrations in the work collective. Femininity is therefore an important mechanism for stabilising and strengthening the family, protecting and deepening in it a pleasant emotional and spiritual atmosphere, and is an important characteristic of a socialist female personality.[21]

The solution is to ensure that a psychological balance is maintained between the new and traditional personality traits of women, which reflect the balance between their professional and domestic functions.

The question of female personality has generated more interest amongst sociologists than male personality. The mass entry of women into the work-force and the more prominent role they play in the family make them a more obvious focus of attention. Hence there is no parallel discussion of the changes which socialism effects in men's personalities. The 'demands of developed socialism' are said to have produced a range of hitherto 'masculine' qualities in women, but there is no suggestion that it will result in hitherto 'feminine' qualities in men, even though these qualities prove so valuable in both the family and work-place. Any domestic work men perform apparently remains external to them; it does not enter into their personalities in the form of corresponding traits and habits, as women's professional work does. Few Soviet sociologists contemplate the possibility of men in whom the 'feminine' aspects of personality – the caring, nurturant, supportive qualities – have been strongly developed.

What discussion there is on the effects of socialism on male personality is far from optimistic. Kharchev expresses concern about men's loss of status as a consequence of women's emancipation. This has made it difficult for them to fulfil their historical role as the 'strong sex'. The problem can be partially solved by men marrying women a few years younger than them. This is because the role of the 'strong sex' encompasses 'the sphere of knowledge, intellect, tastes, etc. – i.e., everything that to a large extent stems from life experience and, accordingly, from age'. So if the man has an advantage over his female partner in age, this will help offset the loss of the advantage he once had merely on the grounds of sex.[22]

Women's 'emancipation' should not challenge male superiority, then. While Kharchev claims to support the development of women's knowledge, intellect and tastes, he evidently feels that this should take place under the spiritual leadership of men. If men lose the role of leader, this can result in them developing such ailments as 'feminization, infantilism, and a lack of independence'.[23]

Kharchev claims support from Karl Marx for the perpetuance of distinct male and female personalities. He refers to the questionnaire in which Marx described his favourite male quality as strength and his favourite female quality as weakness, and argues that these characteristics are complementary and form the basis of successful marriage. Harmony does not stem from a 'banal similarity' but from 'a mutual compliment and contrast . . . Marx's answer, of course, is a joke, but there is great significance in it. Femininity is funny in a man, while it is one of the attractive qualities of a woman. A person above all values and seeks in another what he does not have himself'.[24]

The demise of masculinity also has an effect on femininity. While the 'moral substance of masculinity' has historically been defined on the basis of the man shouldering the major responsibility for the fate of his family, femininity is defined not according to the woman's performance of her roles, but her partner's performance of his. 'Female responsibility, and indeed femininity itself, usually depended to a large extent on how the man she was close to understood and realised his moral position in love and marriage.'[25] It is not in the woman's interests, then, to challenge male hegemony. Kharchev explains that 'a woman experiences humiliation and disappointment not when a man tries to be morally stronger and more responsible than her, but when he runs away from his traditional role in the family, trying to be equal to the woman – which in fact means to surpass her in weakness'.[26]

In conclusion, it would seem from the sociological literature that socialism has had a more decisive impact on women's lives than on those of men. For the most part this has been positive. It has released them from the confines of the family and opened up a range of educational and professional possibilities. This has led to a vast expansion of their personalities, with new qualities appearing in accordance with the demands of their new lives. It could be said, then, that the dual roles of work and family have enabled women to come closer to the ideal 'all-round personality' than men.

However, the psychological development of women is generally kept within strict boundaries. To begin with, it is curtailed by limits supposedly dictated by their biological sex. It should also take place under the leadership of men, and must not challenge at least the illusion of male superiority. It must take account of the inviolable fact that for women to be feminine, which is still seen as their most desirable trait, they must appear weak. Finally, many 'masculine' habits are inappropriate for women since they are incompatible with femininity and with women's traditional charm. The message which emerges most strongly from the sociological literature is, once more, that 'equality does not mean identity'.

It could, in fact, be argued that rather than being freed from a psychological straitjacket, women have been bound still tighter into social definitions of how they should think and feel. Just as the grafting of professional work on to their former domestic roles has resulted in a double work-load, the grafting of a range of hitherto 'masculine' psychological traits on to their traditional 'feminine' personalities has resulted in a psychological double burden. They now have to exhibit both 'feminine' and 'masculine' characteristics (to appropriate, socially-sanctioned levels) to qualify as real socialist women.

MALE AND FEMALE ROLES IN THE FAMILY

The discussion on male and female roles in the family is one of the areas in which sociologists and demographers overlap. Between them they offer a number of different approaches.

The first is based on a traditional idea of natural male and female functions. Although it is argued that men should take more of a role in traditional female activities in the family, it is felt that women will inevitably remain the more prominent family members. Although male participation in the upbringing of children is seen as particularly important, this does not mean that it should equal that of women. As Shimin explains, the female role is paramount because of the natural disposition of the woman and the greater closeness of her biological relationship to the child. The paternal duty is to provide a figure of authority as the children get older, since men's lack of involvement in the past is said to have resulted in an increase in anti-social and delinquent behaviour in children.[27] Men are also called on to take on a greater share of the domestic work-load than they do at present and so reduce the woman's 'double-burden'. However, it is assumed that housework, like child-care, will remain primarily a female activity. The suggestion has been made that there should be more acknowledgement of the domestic work women perform as mothers and housewives when assessing their contribution to society.[28] Although this may sound, on the surface, like a positive move, it endorses the notion that women will inevitably perform the greater share of housework, albeit with a bit more help from men.

The 'biarchy' theory provides an alternative model of family relations. It holds that the Soviet family is in a state of transition from the patriarchal institution of the past to a 'biarchy', in which men and women enjoy a more equal partnership. M. I. Matskovskii and T. Gurko, of the Academy of Sciences' Institute of Sociological Research, are among the most prominent exponents of this position. They explain the family's current problems as a temporary result of the process of change which it is undergoing. As with any organization in a state of transition, it is now an awkward mixture of old and new features which often stand in opposition to one another. The old and new are sometimes personified by husband and wife, with him clinging to his traditional patriarchal advantages and her demanding a more egalitarian distribution of roles.[29] The demographer Perevedentsev similarly notes that men do not readily relinquish power, and that since women will no longer concede to it, tensions inevitably arise.[30] Most of these will disappear when the transition is complete. The biarchal family represents a more complex organization of relationships than the simple patriarchy of the past. It requires greater understanding of the needs of the other partner, and the ability to adapt to them. However, it offers a much more rewarding form of relationship.[31]

It is not only women who will gain. A study by Matskovskii on children's participation in domestic life found that those who take little part in household responsibilities (and he implies that these are usually male) are accorded a low status within the family collective and are not treated as full members. They also face the prospect of an unsuccessful marriage in the future, since they will be equally excluded from the new family collective, and their wives will become discontented because of the lack of help they get. Matskovskii's message is that boys should learn to see domestic involvement in a positive light, almost as a right, through which they will gain full membership of the family collective.

Hence they should want to take part in it even if their future wives do not actually insist on this.[32]

Most of the writings on biarchy present an optimistic view of the possibility of more egalitarian family relations in the Soviet Union, and challenge the idea that differentiated sex roles are both inevitable and desirable. However, not all of biarchy's supposed supporters are as progressive as they first appear. Yu. B. Ryurikov, also of the Sociological Research Institute, is a prime example. At times his description of changing demographic patterns and family relations sounds almost like a feminist analysis of the drop in the birth-rate. He argues that this is an essential factor in the move from patriarchy to biarchy, the result of women seeking to establish control over their own lives. By limiting the size of their families they resist the excessive demands made on them, and reduce the tensions between their family and work roles.[33]

However, elsewhere Ryurikov puts the case for the perpetuance of distinct male and female roles and patterns of behaviour.[34] He is a frequent contributor to discussions on the 'demographic crisis', and a supporter of the pro-natal campaign in the European republics.[35] Hence it turns out that there are distinct limitations to his support of women's right to choose how many children they have. What he sanctions is a reduction from seven or eight children per family – which is seldom to be found now, in any case, outside of the Central Asian republics – to the two or three child family promoted by current demographic policy. 'Women could still realise the advantages of a moderate birth-rate if they had an average of two or three children', he argues; they would only have to devote three or four years to child-care instead of the fifteen or so required in the past.[36] The pseudo-feminist approach turns out to be a novel way of persuading women to produce what has been decreed the demographic optimum under the guise of promoting women's rights. The 'biarchy' argument seems here to have been hijacked by a writer who clearly supports patriarchal family relations, with women firmly lodged in the domestic mould. Ryurikov's version of biarchy evidently means no more than the granting of additional status to women's traditional roles. As Ryurikov himself puts it, 'the mother of a suckling child is doing no less for society than the great discoverers and creators.'[37]

A third approach to family relations is based on the notion of individual choice. This has become increasingly popular within the sociological literature since the onset of *perestroika*. Bestuzhev-Lada was one of the earliest exponents of this view, and remains one of the most prominent. He suggests that the biarchal model of family relations is one of several possibilities, and that different people have different needs.[38] He delineates three different types of woman. The first is the exceptionally gifted career woman, for whom work is a paramount need. The husband of such a woman will inevitably end up taking on much of the house-work, but this is justified by the woman's talent. He warns men, however, of being tricked by 'the dishevelled, untidy woman in a soiled dressing-gown, a novel in her hand, whose husband whirls around her . . .'. It seems that an equal distribution of domestic responsibilities is only due to exceptional career women.

The majority of women have a dual orientation towards both work and family. This stems not from the dictates of their natures, but is the result of socialization. The tradition of working has produced in women over the years the feeling that they need to work. However, it results in an excessive work-load and nervous exhaustion. Evidently this is not a satisfactory situation.

Around 20 to 30 per cent of women are oriented exclusively towards the family. At present most of them also go out to work, but it would be better if they did not have to. However, their independence and equality should be safeguarded. They should receive a large enough state grant to ensure their economic independence, their work in the home should have the same status as that of a paid worker, and they should be able to return to the work-force when their children have grown up. Special clubs should also be set up to provide them with essential contact with other adults.

Despite Bestuzhev-Lada's suggestion that women should be able to choose which model of family and professional life suits them best, it is evident that unless they have an exceptionally strong career drive, he sees the family and children as their primary responsibility. Work should occupy a subsidiary role in their lives. By explaining the current dual-orientation of women towards work and family as the result of socialization, he implies that with some re-socialization they will follow the call of nature and place their children in the centre of their lives. This is his image of the woman of the 21st century, who 'I would like to think will be typical':

> She will have paid leave for six months before the birth, and will spend the whole of it in a sanitorium in order to give birth to a healthy child . . . . After birth comes another three years paid leave. There will be a Child Consultation Centre near her home (formerly a crèche), where she can leave her child from time to time with a

trained worker while she goes to the library, the theatre, a seminar (on the pedagogical role of a parent, perhaps), or just rests. Then for another seven years – until the child becomes a teenager – she will work part time, on full pay or perhaps half-pay, but in any case with enough to provide for the child properly and be economically independent, like a working woman.[39]

Of course, continues Bestuzhev-Lada, the mother of two or three children, who is away from work for many years, can hardly be expected to have a career in the same way as a childless woman or a woman with only one child. Yet, he asks, what does this matter? For too long women have been forced to accept a purely masculine understanding of 'career'. He reaffirms that those who still want to have careers will be able to make this choice. However, it is evident that in his ideal world only the exceptional woman would do so, the kind destined to be 'one of the "top people" – perhaps a director, perhaps a leading figure in politics, culture, science or art (leaving the child in a kindergarten or in the arms of a granny)'. All other women will be full-time housewives, but with their status raised to the level 'of a Candidate of pedagogical science . . . society will see her as a state director of her own "mini-collective", as a private assistant professor, or even, perhaps, as a corresponding member of the Academy of Pedagogical Sciences . . .'[40]

It is not easy to accord Bestuzhev-Lada's image of the future the serious attention which, judging by the general tone of the article, he evidently feels it deserves. The first obvious objection is that with the vast majority of women removed from public life and confined to the home, society will be an even stronger reflection of male interests and values than it is at present; hence it is laughable to think of the full-time housewife being granted such prestige. Secondly, the idea that women will have a free choice as to whether to prioritize career or family is a complete myth. N. Zakharova, A. Posadskaya and N. Rimashevskaya, of the Institute of Socio-economic Problems, argue that even if she has only one child, the woman who is orientated towards 'a career' often has to abandon her plans because of the pressures of her domestic life. Her 'choice' is hence determined not by her own inclinations but by social conditions. In any case, there is such a general lack of trust in the leadership abilities of women that they come to undervalue themselves and doubt their own abilities. Perhaps this is why many women choose jobs which fit in with the stereotyped ideas about appropriate female roles.[41] Voronina similarly notes that ideas about women's natural inclinations and capabilities have a strong influence on both male and female choice of profession. For example, girls who show potential at school in a 'masculine' subject such as maths will often refuse to study it because they do not want to lose their feminine 'face'. Most men, on the other hand, simply do not consider work with children. The low level of female achievement even in the professions in which they predominate has much to do with the notion that women are not able to achieve 'men's heights' at work, and that in any case work is not so important for them.[42] If this is the case even now, when almost all women work, the psychological pressures against women succeeding in a career will be still greater in a climate where the vast majority are full-time housewives.

We have already mentioned that the idea of women being able to choose whether to work or devote themselves to their families has gained particular credence in recent times. A clue as to why this should be can be found in an article by sociologist M. Malysheva. Although she begins by challenging the idea that women's place is in the home, we soon find her arguing that, 'The most important thing a woman can make is not several metres of road or kilogrammes of bread, it is children . . .', and then explaining that, 'Women's work at present is fairly ineffective, both economically and socially'. Although she advocates a choice for women, it is clear that she feels a tiny minority will continue to work outside the home. '(W)ork in social production will become the destiny of the really professionally active. This will guarantee its quality. For those women, who are more able and better educated and have shown a distinct preference for work in social production, new possibilities for advancement in work will open up.'[43] In other words, in the era of *khozraschet*, only those women who are really able to pull their weight should be allowed to take part.

7 The Pedagogical Approach to Sex Differences

In the previous chapters we looked at the ways in which psychology, endocrinology and sociology have dealt with sex differences in personality. However, as we discussed in the introduction, this has become the province primarily of pedagogy. The interest of educational theorists in the subject began in the 1960s, as a consequence of the debate on whether a form of sex education was advisable in Soviet schools. Yet although a sizeable trickle of articles and books appeared over the following decade, from the late 1970s this turned into a torrent. A. G. Khripkova and D. V. Kolesov, two of the most prolific of the later writers, implicitly suggest that the earlier material is without value when they remark, in 1979, that, 'In the available literature of the past 30 to 40 years, we have not encountered any scientific work on this subject'.[1] None the less, though the later writings are generally dressed up in a more academic style, the pedagogical understanding of sex differences in personality has not changed. To make this clear we will begin by looking at some of the earlier writings before turning to the glut of more recent literature.

THE EARLY PEDAGOGICAL WRITINGS ON SEX DIFFERENCES

Immediately noticeable in the work of the pedagogical writers of the 1960s is a fondness for the questionnaire responses of Karl Marx, in which he gave his favourite male quality as 'strength' and his favourite female quality as 'weakness'. Generally these responses are seen as problematic, or at least not entirely clear. However, there are some serious attempts to interpret and justify Marx's words, and to construct a model of masculinity and femininity on their basis. Iosif Dik, for example, writes that:

> In these words, in my opinion, is concentrated the romance of human life. Behind the word 'strength' I divine the deep implications

of masculinity and nobleness, the strength of masculine intelligence and the poetry of iron muscles. And behind the work 'weakness' I see not feebleness and an impractical approach to life, but femininity, beauty and charm.[2]

If Marx's favourite female qualities were femininity, beauty and charm, one might wonder why he chose not to list these directly, rather than conceal them behind the concept 'weakness'. Dik is not given to such musings, however.

The basic drift of Dik's chatty, anecdotal book on the parental role in the upbringing of boys is that the qualities we seek in men – that they be 'intelligent, ideologically sound, educated, strong, keen-witted, of great endurance, big-hearted, kind . . .'[3] – do not come about by themselves, but only through careful and continual cultivation. He quotes approvingly from a poem by Mikhael L'vov:

> In order to become a man
> It is not enough to be born one
> Just as to become iron
> It is not enough to be ore.
> You must be smelted, be smashed,
> And, like ore, sacrifice yourself.[4]

The process by which parents can 'smelt' their sons in indicated by an anecdote from Dik's own past. The passage leading to his family's flat was very dark and frightened him. One day when he arrived home from school his father refused to interrupt a telephone call to let him in. The son begged and pleaded, his knees shaking with fear, but the father's response was only to send him off for firewood. Dik's mother admonished her husband and said she would let the boy in herself before he had a heart attack, but she was ordered not to on the grounds that 'a man must grow up in this house!'.[5]

L. A. Levshin also pays considerable attention to Marx's questionnaire responses, although he, unlike Dik, notices that they were written in a 'half-joking manner'.[6] None the less, he makes a serious attempt to come to terms with them.

> What did Marx have in mind when he answered that he valued strength in a man but weakness in a woman? Of course not physical strength; such an opinion would be too primitive and platitudinous. But evidently it could not mean spiritual strength either, nor creative strength, nor strength of character, otherwise one could reach the conclusion that Marx denies the presence of such strength in

woman. This would contradict the real opinions of the great revolutionary on woman and the reason for her subordinate position in bourgeois society. Undoubtedly, Marx had in mind something entirely different. And above all, the beauty of those vital relations between man and woman which flow from the difference in their sexes. For woman it is natural to lean on the help, the support, and the protection of man, in order to give life to a new creature, rear him and make him independent. And it is equally natural for the man to support, protect and defend the woman in order that she is able to fulfill the mission entrusted to her by nature.

These natural relations, enriched by all the achievements of human culture and morality, led to the formation of that quality in man which we call masculinity, and that quality in woman which we call femininity. These qualities are profoundly different, because the beauty of humanity in each of these is organically fused with the beauty of the sex. Marx had in mind precisely this when he talked about strength in man and weakness in woman.[7]

Having accepted, then, that 'strength' epitomizes masculinity and 'weakness' femininity, Levshin goes on to urge parents to let 'all boys know, from the years of childhood, that they are "men", and, consequently, are called on to support, defend and protect their mothers and sisters'.[8] Addressing a meeting of schoolboys, he attempts to inspire in them respect for girls by (surely a paradox) stressing the weakness of the latter. 'Girls are weaker than boys, their organism is more delicate and fragile, and at the same time more complex, since, after all, the girl is the future mother . . . we, boys, must in every way possible defend girls, not push them around but help them, look after them.'[9] He applauds a class of 'noisy mischievous' boys who all the same let the girls enter the classroom first, and do all the physical tasks such as lifting desks and carrying water while the girls look after the flowers and do the cleaning.[10]

Levshin, like Dik, seeks the support of poetry. He recounts a poem which is set on a farm in the Caucasus, where 13 milkmaids live. They are all frightened at night, so when a young boy comes to the farm they are delighted: 'Although he's a boy, all the same there is now a man amongst us!' They make up a comfortable bed for him, but he throws his cloak on the ground and sleeps by the embers of the fire. 'This is the masculine way!', Levshin exclaims approvingly. Another anecdote tells of a boy who walks into a dark room of which his sisters are afraid, declaring that 'father and I are not afraid of anything!'.[11]

Unlike other writers, Levshin does show an awareness that the 'superior strength' of men could in fact be turned against women – though the only example he offers of this is a tendency among naughty school-boys to pull girls' plaits! In any case, he feels that this possibility will be avoided by correct upbringing.[12] In general, parents and teachers are exhorted to kindle 'a real desire in boys to manifest their "masculinity", their physical superiority'.[13]

Although this is not made explicit, Levshin's writings imply that he sees masculine and feminine traits as natural inclinations, and that the task of upbringing is to enhance and direct them. He talks in particular of inherent nurturant qualities in women: 'The love of a mother towards her child is deeply instinctive in origin, it lies in the very nature of woman. The mighty instinct of maternal love appears already in the games of the girl, the endearments, caresses and concern with which she looks after her dolls.'[14] He also posits a natural origin for the age-old and unchanging relationship between boys and girls which prompts boys to show off their masculinity to girls, 'their strength, originality and heroism', while 'our little girls, intuitively as well as comically, try to win masculine favour with feminine tenderness and helplessness, through their weakness'.[15]

This leads Levshin to a sharp criticism of school-teachers who, because of their failure to appreciate the male psyche and the complexities of adolescent needs, put girls in positions of prominence in school and Komsomol committees. Girls seem to them more appropriate for the posts because they are more obedient and conscientious, and because boys, in an effort to preserve their masculine independence, seem to prefer to stand on the sidelines. However, if teachers allow this situation to continue boys become increasingly passive and indisciplined. Positive effort on the part of teachers can steer boys into more active and responsible patterns of behaviour, and away from anti-social modes of displaying their masculinity.[16]

Levshin does not advocate a complete division of labour into 'masculine' and 'feminine' functions. He does, however, see housework as a predominantly female activity (though he calls on the state to make greater efforts to ease women's domestic burden, and on men to give their wives some help). Domestic skills should thus be taught primarily to girls. However, boys need some domestic knowledge in their army years, when they will need to peel potatoes and to make minor repairs to their uniforms. He quotes from a young soldier's letter to a magazine: 'Housework, which I considered the lot of girls, is the very thing with which every boy entering the army comes into collision!'[17] Domestic skills are also useful for men in certain professions which require travel away from home. All the same, when their wives are there to do it, the housework rightly falls mainly on their shoulders, although 'masculine virtue and a caring attitude towards the wife . . . manifests itself in a readiness and an ability to help her as far as one is able in domestic work'.[18]

The late E. G. Kostyashkin was one of the most eminent of the early writers, a member of the Academy of Pedagogical Sciences in the Scientific Research Institute of the Theory and History of Pedagogy. He too makes a reference to the questionnaire responses of Marx, if a rather oblique one. Unlike Dik and Levshin, he evidently feels no need to justify them or render them more palatable. The notion that women should be weak and men should be strong is the starting point for his promotion of a severely sex-typed programme of child-upbringing.

> The strength of man, to which Marx gave such significance, does not arrive suddenly and is not an inevitable consequence of age and sexual development. It must be developed from earliest childhood. Strength is one of the basic traits of man; on its basis are developed more easily nobleness, restraint, generosity, and moral purity. A weak body, a cowardly and timid character, and frailty of spirit are the most negative results of bad upbringing of the boy.[19]

How is strength to be developed in the boy? This is the programme Kostyashkin advises a 'sensible family' to adopt:

> the attitude towards the boy is stricter, demands on his physical strength and endurance and on a display of bravery are decisively higher, and defeats and failures are criticised more sharply. Even the food of the boy begins, from around the age of 14 or earlier, to be distinguished by fewer sweets and porridge, and a larger portion of meat. The boy's bed is harder, the mother's caresses are more restrained, the look of the father is more stern and punishment is stricter. And especially important is the continuous increase in the physical load, especially the work load.[20]

Despite the strictness of the regime Kostyashkin advocates in order to produce these traits, he seems to see differentiated male and female personalities as natural. He talks, for example, of the autonomous manifestation of femininity in adolescent girls in accordance with the physical changes taking place in them. This takes the form of a

> revival of the desire to play with toys, to take part in cooking and cleaning, and to look after small children. Girls in this period demand more individual attention and affection, and a warm attitude towards them on the part of adults. In their relations with boys, girls become more tolerant towards their pranks, and love to look after a particular boy; the rationality and logical analysis clearly expressed in girls in the 4th and 5th class [i.e. age 10 to 12] turns into a more emotional attitude towards the world around them.[21]

Adolescent boys similarly undergo changes, becoming more concerned about their physical strength, about competition, and about their appearance. They are particularly concerned to show off their strength and masculinity to girls.[22]

Masculinity and femininity and the traits they encompass appear, then, to be natural, but in the form of potentialities. Their development into full-blown characteristics requires conscious cultivation. If this is a correct reading of Kostyashkin's rather ambiguous writings, upbringing has a different function for him than for Levshin. It serves for Levshin merely to channel natural characteristics into positive directions; to Kostyashkin, it is essential in actually developing those characteristics. Social influences thus perform something of the role granted them by psychologists of personality development. However, the aim of developing all-round personalities is not to be found in Kostyashkin's work. Parents and teachers are, in fact, exhorted to concentrate their efforts on moulding their children's personalities more successfully to traditional stereotypes.

Kostyashkin, like Levshin, is very critical of teachers who defy nature by placing girls in top school and Komsomol posts.

> Instead of helping to develop and affirm the commanding masculine position at the time of the clearest 'cock-dance' of boys, they put girls in command, who do not need this. Girls aged 15 to 16 like to command some 'assistants', but not a group or a detachment; and in no event do they become accustomed to the role of commander over boys . . . . Rarely will a girl in this period be offended if a boy is nominated president of the Soviet of the detachment, or field-team leader. Girls are fully satisfied with a secondary role, and in fact quietly get on with practically any job.[23]

In any case, Kostyashkin adds, the wiser girls will realize that they are the real powers behind the throne, even if boys have the appearance of control, and that this covert use of power does not 'knock against the overly sensitive pride of the boys'.[24]

Little new is to be found in the other pedagogical tracts on sex differences. Indeed, sometimes we find the same exhortations, word for word, in the texts of different writers. For example, Kostyashkin's description of the 'sensible' family's differential upbringing of sons and daughters is found again a decade later in an article by V. A. Grigorova, and four years after that in L. N. Timoshchenko's book on family upbringing.[25] The following advice also appears in two different texts, one by V. Aleshina in 1964 and the other by Khripkova in 1969:

> Even from the first class it is important to demand of boys that they defend girls, giving up their places to them, letting them go first, not allowing them to do heavy physical work. The understanding 'You are a boy', or 'You are a man', which strengthens these actions, will inculcate a chivalrous attitude towards girls.[26]

Kolbanovskii also writes, in very similar terms, that:

> From the boy's earliest years, from the moment when he begins to speak, it is necessary to instil in him a feeling of respect and regard for girls. In as much as boys are physically stronger than girls, it is important to explain to them that man has been given his strength in order to protect the weak.[27]

As we noted earlier, there is something contradictory about attempting to instil respect in boys for girls by stressing girls' inherent weakness. It is interesting to note that Kolbanovskii comes close to admitting that the greater physical strength of boys is not entirely natural, when he suggests that the more active, strength-building sports are inappropriate for girls 'not only because of biological considerations, but also for aesthetic reasons'.[28] The contradiction is compounded with a sense of pride connected with masculinity and maleness which is absent from discussions concerning femininity. Dik, for example, virtually congratulates the parents of sons with these words: 'When a boy is born in your family, and the responsibility for his upbringing lies on you, always remember: "In our house a man is growing!"'[29]

The authority of Makarenko is frequently invoked. We learn from Aleshina that he was supremely chivalrous, always opening doors for his female pupils, and in this way giving his male pupils a practical lesson in masculine attentiveness. The girl on the receiving end of his chivalry 'walks past, skirt rustling, feeling like a princess; and of course, the feeling of feminine dignity is raised in her'.[30]

CONFLICTING OPINIONS WITHIN THE EARLY WRITINGS

The material we have looked at thus far suggests that there was a virtual consensus of views on sex differences in personality within Soviet pedagogy of the 1960s. This is not entirely the case, however. The journal *Sem'ya i Shkola* makes this particularly clear by publishing two articles side by side representing vastly different viewpoints.

The first of these, by B. Ryabinin, puts forward an extreme version of the familiar position.[31] He argues that the chief role of woman is that of wife and mother: 'Is it possible to deny that every normal woman has the inherent desire to please and be loving, the inherent craving for a husband, a family, her own nest . . ?' Whatever new paths open up before her in Soviet society, whatever profession she chooses, 'this is in her blood – without it her life is not full, her existence is impoverished'. Yet evidently some women do not see things in the same light. Ryabinin goes on to blame them for the problems which have emerged in child upbringing, on the grounds that they have forgotten they are mothers and neglected their maternal duties. To rectify this position, he seeks to rekindle respect in the term 'housewife'; after all, 'the woman giving to the world the greatest of people – Lenin – was a housewife!'.

Ryabinin insists that he does not wish to return women to the kitchen, or put an end to their social and professional activities. His concern is to help them combine their two roles. To this end he recommends the opening of hairdressing salons, mobile shops and nurseries in factories, and a system whereby women can place advance orders during their lunch-breaks and pick up the ready-prepared items as they leave work. He also suggests that married men be given a salary increment to free their wives from financial pressures! He is sure that when it is able, the state will grant women a shorter working day with no salary reduction. Although Ryabinin does not completely deny a paternal role in the family, he evidently sees this as very minor, especially when the children are small. He asserts that, 'The feeling of motherhood is above all a feeling of great responsibility towards society and the child, a responsibility which can be transferred to nobody else. Nobody.'

The views expounded by E. Andreeva are the complete antithesis of those by Ryabinin and other pedagogical writers. They would, in fact, not appear amiss in a Western feminist journal. It is not Western feminism which provides her with a theoretical framework, however, but the ideas propounded and enacted in the Soviet Union in the years immediately following the Revolution, when Andreeva was herself a schoolgirl.[32]

Andreeva begins by arguing that men and women may be equal before the law in the Soviet Union, but they are not equal in reality. Lenin himself thought that changes in the law were not an end to the problem, and that intense upbringing work amongst men was also needed; but this ceased to take place beyond the early years of the Revolution. The articles which currently appear in the Soviet press about the upbringing of boys and girls are suffused with a patriarchal ideology which holds that women are weak creatures in need of chivalrous protection. This view is not only false but also hypocritical, in that the supposed 'weaker sex' has a work-load which is incomparably greater than that of the 'stronger sex'. Also hypocritical is the notion of chivalry. On the one hand, we know from history that the knights from whom it stems had no genuine respect or concern for their wives; on the other, while training modern Soviet boys to perform such 'chivalrous' acts as holding out girls' coats for them, schools neglect to teach them any domestic habits, so that 'at home, the gallant knights do nothing'. Chivalry creates an illusion of respect, or serves as a feeble compensation to women for their lack of genuine equality. 'It is not difficult to put on a coat', Andreeva points out. 'A woman can easily do this herself. If she is pleased with such a pitiful compensation for her subordinate position, then one can only pity that woman.' The greatest hypocrisy of all is the suggestion that woman's burden could be lightened by reducing the number of hours she works per day outside the home to give her more time to spend on housework and child-care: 'This would just legalize her subordinate position.'

Like other pedagogical writers, Andreeva draws support from the heroes and pedagogues of the Revolutionary era. However, the ideas she attributes to them are quite different, and indicate how selective use of quotations can justify virtually any position. Makarenko, she tells us, granted men an equal role in child-upbringing when he referred to it as the task of the entire family, the whole range of human relations, and work in general. Men evidently cannot breast-feed their offspring, adds Andreeva, but they can do absolutely everything else. Krupskaya also wrote about the need to teach domestic skills to boys and girls alike. In an article in 1910 she declared, 'It is essential that both boys and girls are taught identically to do all necessary domestic work, and not to consider this work to be somehow beneath their dignity.' Even in Tsarist Russia, progressive pedagogues like Krupskaya were organizing co-educational schools where supposedly male and female skills were taught to all children, irrespective of sex. In the Soviet Union this no longer happens. Andreeva muses:

> Sometimes the discussion arises: can one teach boys to do domestic work as well as girls? These authors must be young, otherwise they would know from personal experience that straight after the establishment of the Soviet state we didn't ask this question – we just did it.

She describes her own childhood pleasure in learning manual skills: 'My friends and I considered these studies incomparably more interesting than lessons on sewing and house-keeping. They demanded physical effort, which is always enjoyable (and very useful) to any child, absolutely regardless of sex.' Andreeva sees the demise of such tuition as the legacy, to a large extent, of the years of single-sex education, an innovation of the Stalinist period, which lasted from 1943 to 1954.

The differential upbringing of boys and girls produces the range of differences we observe in adult men and women, including even the difference in muscular strength. Girls are not given sufficient physical training to develop their muscles; 'while the boys are playing football, the girls are washing dishes'. In addition they are told from earliest childhood that they are weak, and the power of suggestion has a profound effect. Because of traditional ideas about appropriate female behaviour, they also do not engage in the childhood battles which are common amongst boys, and through which boys gain an understanding of their physical abilities. The upbringing of boys is no better. Because they are spared most domestic obligations, they do not develop a concern for other people and an awareness of their duty to them. They learn to please themselves, to do only that which interests them. Hence they are brought up to be egotists and exploiters. This is responsible for their low performance and bad behaviour in school.

Such differentiated upbringing is useless for communist society. It precludes the development of comradeship and friendship between men and women, and hence the possibility of marriage between equals.

Relations between the sexes are distorted by false and patriarchal notions of masculine strength and female weakness.

In order to believe in his strength, the modern man requires weakness in his female partner, and in order to believe in his intelligence he needs her to be stupid. This need for self-affirmation through the abasement of another person is, in fact, weakness.

Femininity, as currently defined in the Soviet literature,

is not needed by a friend or a comrade, but by a man who seeks to subordinate a woman to himself in order to protect his 'masculinity'. . . .

A man who is free and strong will not be able to love a weak, obsequious, fearful and sly creature. Nor will a free and strong woman disengage from the struggles of life on the grounds that her 'femininity' makes her weak and fearful.

Only such men and women will create a family which will become the cell of genuine communist relations, of respect and great spiritual closeness. Such a family will also rear different children, with new opinions and habits.

Andreeva's article makes it clear that the pedagogical writers we have discussed above cannot be ignorant of alternative ideas about the nature of men and women and the feasibility and advisability of creating new types of male and female personality. While the ideas of Western feminism (which are cited disapprovingly by a later generation of Soviet writers on sex differences) were scarcely developed or disseminated at that time, Andreeva finds such alternatives in the theories and practice of the Revolution, in the work of the very writers who are also invoked to support the modern pedagogical approach which she rejects.

The articles by Ryabinin and Andreeva produced a considerable response in subsequent issues of *Sem'ya i Shkola*. While many of the participants begin by saying that neither view is entirely correct, the majority side more with Ryabinin. V. Mikhailova is an exception. She is touched by Ryabinin's 'beautiful' descriptions of women's maternal feeling, but concerned about the cost to the state of educating women to be specialists only to lose them to full-time child-care. She applauds Ryabinin's call to raise the status of housework, but does not agree that it should then fall to the lot of women. The suggestion that married men be paid more in order to free their wives from material worries also misses the point that women do not work solely for money but also for moral satisfaction; she is doubtful that housework will provide this. She also agrees with Andreeva that a shorter working day for women will reinforce the idea that housework is exclusively their business. However, she is not in full accord with Andreeva either. In particular she rejects her view, rooted in the 1920s, that the concepts of masculinity and femininity serve to oppress women. However, she then relates a discussion she had with friends about the articles which makes it clear that women certainly are oppressed by notions of what is innately male and female. The men agreed wholeheartedly with 'comrade Ryabinin'; they claimed that house-work is in women's blood, and that since they perform other types of work with less creativity and dedication than men, there was no reason for them not to devote themselves to it. The women asked with annoyance how the men knew what was in their blood, and pointed out that since they had all the housework to do as well as their paid work they had little time to develop their creativity.[33]

A. Burenkova claims to be in broad agreement with Andreeva, though with reservations. She supports women working outside the home and boys learning to wash dishes. However, she is disturbed at the thought of girls playing football, and goes on to assert that, 'Of course women are weaker than men, there can be no argument about it'. She evidently means this in a mental as much as a physical sense; 'whenever there is a need for great physical or intellectual force', she adds, one finds mostly men in action.[34]

Many find nothing of credit in Andreeva's article. S. Gazaryan is 'bewildered' by her views. They threaten the destruction of love, he argues, since it is based not only on sexual difference and a unity of opinions, but above all on 'femininity in women and chivalry in men'.[35] Yu. Shilov argues that if Andreeva's ideas were taken to their logical conclusion, a man who offered his seat to a woman, or helped her with her baggage, could be accused of placing her in a position of subordination.[36] Levshin refers briefly to the articles by Ryabinin and Andreeva in his book, and after telling us that neither author is completely right he goes on to express a viewpoint which supports that of Ryabinin.[37]

Andreeva's support for the ideas of the Revolution evidently made her something of a dissident within the pedagogical community of her day. Yet despite the general rejection of her views, the discussion which they initiated was more lively and contentious than those found in similar journals a decade later. In this later material, views like

Andreeva's are simply not to be found. This suggests that the voice of dissent within the discipline had effectively been stifled. In the literary press, most notably *Literaturnaya Gazeta*, views similar to Andreeva's could be found, but here too they appeared in a much milder form. This has changed in the more open climate of the Gorbachev era. As we shall see, Andreeva's views are finding voice again, although not in the pedagogical press.

THE RECENT WRITINGS

As we have mentioned, pedagogical interest in the subject of sex differences in personality showed a marked increase towards the end of the 1970s. In 1979, Khripkova and Kolesov were established as the principal exponents of the pedagogical approach with the publication of their book *Devochka-podrostok-devushka*, about the psychology of girls and their specific upbringing needs. This was serialized in the journal *Sem'ya i Shkola*, and followed by a sequel on the psychology and upbringing of boys. In addition to the numerous books and articles they have written themselves, both together and individually, their views have also been widely disseminated through published interviews, comments summing up articles by other authors, and frequent references to their work in the popular, pedagogical and medical press. It is therefore necessary to look at their work in some detail.

Unlike the earlier writers, Khripkova and Kolesov offer a lengthy description of male and female psychological differences. They see these as radical and immediate. By the age of five months, a child can tell men and women apart and generally shows a strong preference for one or the other sex. Even very small children are aware of normal and abnormal sex characteristics; kindergarten children have been seen to mock and show hostility towards children whose sexual identity appears ambiguous.[38]

From a very early age girls are coquettish in their behaviour, to attract the attention of men; this is so normal that it fails to provoke a reaction in adults. It stems from the fact that 'every normal woman feels an urge to please, to be noticed'; and since women are more passive than men, they cannot attract attention through their activity. This also explains why men's fashions are more restrained than women's.[39] Female passivity and a female urge to please are presented as entirely natural; there is no mention of modelling, or parental and social reinforcement of what are seen as accepted forms of behaviour.

The different reproductive roles of men and women are placed firmly at the centre of their psychological differences. Khripkova and Kolesov note that

> girls are inclined towards caring activities – looking after people, nursing, showing concern, and so on. They are more inclined to criticise, admonish and teach their smaller brothers, than boys are with their younger sisters. This inclination may be seen as a manifestation appropriate to their age of the maternal instinct.[40]

They then go on to produce a comprehensive list of male and female personality differences, most of which have no apparent link with reproduction.[41]

Girls, we learn, are much more concerned with their immediate environment – with human relationships, consumer goods, clothes, utensils, and the home. They are better at spatial and colour perception than boys, but worse in perception of time. They are less inclined towards investigative behaviour than boys. They may learn to use an object efficiently, but they remain indifferent to its structure. Accordingly, they are less inventive and innovative than boys when playing with toys, using them for their direct purpose rather than adapting them to different uses. While boys tend to break their toys as a result of their investigative behaviour, girls' toys are broken by pure accident.

Girls are more impulsive, industrious, impressionable, and subjective than boys. They are less decisive in their action, and less factual. This means that they are less capable of explaining a sequence of events, becoming more involved in the personal aspects of the story and less attentive to the facts. They are more sensitive to personal relations, and take these more into account in their activities. They are more aware and responsive to the norms of their social group, and more sensitive to the violation of those norms. Girls are more inclined than boys to appeal to someone older in the event of a conflict or difficulty. Girls of all ages are more emotional than boys, taking praise and censure more to heart. They are more concerned about their appearance, which can turn into a pathological conviction of physical inadequacy. They are more easily moved than boys, more inclined to both laugh and cry. Their greater emotionality and compulsiveness make 'difficult' girls more of a problem than 'difficult' boys, although boys are noisier.

Boys are more mobile and restless than girls. They are braver, so raise their hands more often in class since they are less afraid of giving the wrong answer. They have a wider range of interests than girls, and, correspondingly, a larger vocabulary with which to deal with them. None the less, girls are more fluent in their statements and write better essays. Boys' speech contains more words communicating action – i.e. verbs and exclamations – while girls are more inclined towards subject appraisal and use more nouns, adjectives, negatives and affirmatives. When telling stories, boys are more concise and keep more to the point; girls, on the other hand, are more detailed and inclined to digress.

Girls are more precise, accurate, neat, and conscientious than boys. They are also more patient. When unsure of what they should be doing in class, they will more often wait for the teacher to explain. Boys, on the other hand, are likely to propose their own ideas to the teacher.

Girls are better than boys at understanding simple and commonplace ideas, but worse regarding specialized concepts. They prefer more organized and less varied free-time activities. Beyond the boundaries of the home they are more quickly lost, and have difficulty finding something with which to occupy themselves. (Khripkova and Kolesov seem in some confusion here, as elsewhere in the same text they tell us that girls are more adaptable than boys and more able to find their feet in new situations.) Different school subjects attract girls and boys. Girls tend towards arts subjects such as history and literature, especially poetry, and dislike physics, biology and maths. Boys, on the other hand, are more interested in handcrafts and sport.

The characteristics offered above differ little from those which Maccoby and Jacklin described as 'myths' about sex differences in Western society – the majority of which were dismissed on analysis of the actual behaviour of boys and girls. Particularly interesting is the assertion made by Khripkova and Kolesov that boys are better than girls at spatial and colour perception, when one of the few sex differences Maccoby and Jacklin found any evidence for is a male advantage in visual and spatial ability. At times Khripkova and Kolesov also contradict themselves, as with the differential adaptability of boys and girls to unknown situations.

They fail to tell us how they arrive at their list of sex differences. After insisting that 'the study of the psychological differences between men and women is an important scientific and practical question, no less important than the further study of their biological and physiological peculiarities'[42] they offer a completely unscientific description of psychological sex differences, validated by nothing more than the phrase 'it is well known that . . .' (*izvestno, chto* . . .), which no Western undergraduate, let alone scientist, could get away with. They do once acknowledge the possibility of environmental influences in moulding such traits, when they suggest that the lesser ability of boys to perform domestic duties is 'to a large extent . . . connected with the lack of constant chores around the house; but the chief thing, all the same, is the fact that it is more difficult to train boys to do them than it is to train girls'.[43] Ultimately, they insist, a child's upbringing merely 'promotes . . . that which the child already possessed from the moment of birth'.[44]

These features are not only natural, but are exactly what we wish to find in men and women. Khripkova goes on to describe the features which men and women find attractive in one another. Men are keen on shyness and modesty in a woman, while modesty in a man would be taken as 'a sign of sexual weakness'.[45] Men also go for 'a lively facial expression, pleasant gestures, emotionality, a melodic voice, and the sensitivity which is peculiar to women'.[46] They are not impressed by a woman who adopts 'masculine' habits and characteristics – 'a cigarette between the lips, a harsh voice, a too-free, rather coarse way of conducting herself, an intentionally masculine turn of phrase . . .'[47] Women value most in men their propensity for logical and abstract thought, seeing these as an indication of masculine strength.

The description of male and female differences in personality sounds rather like a blueprint for self-training. This is due mainly to the authors' concern about the increase in divorce. Their proposed solution (a strange one, given that it is women rather than men who initiate the majority of divorces) is for girls to cultivate more successfully in themselves the characteristics which most appeal to men. Not only will this attract men to them; it will also rekindle the flagging masculinity of their partners. They quote journalist Ada Baskina's description of the positive benefits femininity has on a man: 'Marriage with a really feminine girl instils in a man two things. On the one hand, he becomes more masculine from the need to protect and defend her, and on the other hand, sharp traits in his character soften; gradually he becomes more tender and kind.'[48] Rejecting the idea which abounded in the early years of the Revolution that communist marriage should be based on equality and friendship, Khripkova and Kolesov criticize women who do not learn enough about the male psyche to know that friendship is not the same as love, and that the qualities which allow them to develop a rapport with men as friends are not those which will make a successful marriage. 'Of course, femininity is a natural gift', they add; 'however, it is possible to develop it or suppress it in oneself'.[49] They are, then, urging women to play at being weak and helpless in order to give men someone to protect – as they put it, 'there is great strength in women's "weakness".'[50]

Khripkova and Kolesov do not disavow the role of the environment in the development of male and female personalities. In fact, despite their detailed discussion of 'natural' sex differences, it is given a large role, especially in the form of training and self-training. It is probable that assertions about the 'naturalness' of dichotomized male and female personalities are intended to justify the promotion of a programme of training and self-training designed to emphasize sex differences, on the grounds that it does not attempt to mould men and women to cultural stereotypes, but merely to assist nature. To this end, as Khripkova declares emphatically in an article in *Rabotnitsa*, 'boys and girls need a differentiated upbringing. Pedagogy must not be sexless. That is why it is important to study the interaction of biological and social laws of sex development'.[51] In the West, an understanding of the 'social laws' of sex development has been used by feminists to challenge the traditional roles of men and women. In the Soviet Union it has the opposite function of reinforcing them.

The writings Kolesov has produced independent of Khripkova give the initial impression of a more flexible understanding of the development of sex differences in personality. He still talks of natural personality differences between men and women which are independent of history, culture and upbringing, but he also acknowledges a 'second aspect' of sex identity which is linked to the norms and ideas of a given society in a given historical setting. References to masculinization and feminization to explain an interest or aptitude for occupations traditionally linked to the other sex are dismissed as unscientific: 'In actual fact . . . what is happening is a modification of traditional ideas about the content of male and female social roles, of the nature of traditionally male and female professions.[52] However, such modifications turn out to be slight. Even when men engage in 'female' occupations, we are assured that they perform them in a 'masculine way' – i.e., with more inventiveness and initiative, but less care and thoroughness.[53] Kolesov's conclusions turn out to be the usual ones. Sex differences are natural and useful to society, and children should be brought up to understand this and to respect these differences. The assumption throughout his writings is that this is universally accepted. The question is how to develop the differences more successfully, and in accordance with the varied demands, professional and domestic, which are placed on Soviet women.

Kolesov evidently has some awareness of Soviet psychology. He writes, for example, that 'a child develops himself as a personality in the process of activity'.[54] He also talks of the two philosophical (for which one could substitute psychological) approaches to the person – that which sees him or her as initially a 'biological' creature, and that which sees the child as social from the moment of birth. According to the first of these, the demands of society are external; people are forced to adapt to them and serve society only because they are controlled by its norms. The second position, that held by Soviet theorists, sees no such conflict between society and its members. Instead of suppressing people, society helps them to develop their full potential. Although Kolesov does not mention him, the idea that the child is initially a biological creature who only gradually becomes socialized is particularly associated with Piaget, and provides the main focus for Soviet criticism of his work. The conflict between the individual and society is also one of the tenets of Freudianism which Soviet psychologists have persistently attacked.

Kolesov goes on to discuss Freud's work in some detail. He praises Freud's role in attracting attention to the unconscious, and his influence on all spheres of social science. However, he ultimately rejects psychoanalysis for its biologism and for its supposition that people's behaviour is motivated mainly by 'the unconscious, which consists largely of the sex urge and the instinct of aggression'.[55] Freud found particular favour in his life-time, he explains, with those who attributed the negative aspects of bourgeois society not

> to an unjust social system, but according to basic peculiarities in human nature. Recognising the correctness of Freud's views and allowing him to appear at times as a critic of the hypocrisy of bourgeois morality, promoted an understanding of the naturalness of everything that happens in bourgeois society – and of the stability of this society, since any changes in it would seem to contradict the very nature of the person, and would thus be both impossible and undesirable.[56]

The same critique, with minor modifications, could surely be made of Khripkova and Kolesov's views on sex differences in personality. They too promote an understanding of the naturalness of these differences, and of their stability, since any changes in them (at least, of a more than cosmetic nature) would seem to contradict the very nature of men and women and would thus be both impossible and undesirable.

Kolesov pays considerable attention to the history of women's oppression, and to the Soviet Union's efforts to eradicate it. He is dismissive of the equality achieved in the 1920s, arguing that it rested on a disrespect for women since men were always taken as the standard of appropriate behaviour. 'If a woman in granted the "right" (which in fact means she is forced) to do work unusual for her, this is also inequality.'[57] In contrast, women in the Soviet Union of the present day are not equal because they are identical to men, but because they are members of a new and free society.

Kolesov agrees to some extent with the suggestion that no spheres of work should now be seen as exclusively male or female, or incompatible with masculinity or femininity. This is because increased mechanization and automation reduces the physical hardship of work. None the less, he argues that there is a natural male or female disposition for certain jobs. The only evidence he offers is that certain professional spheres in the Soviet Union continue to be dominated by men or women. Citing the small numbers of women electric drillers, timber workers, steel foundry workers and blacksmiths, he concludes that 'there *is* special male work! The natural differences between men and women *do* influence their division of labour!'[58] Evidently the reasoning behind this is that Soviet women have complete equality of opportunity, and so any discrepancies in male and female employment must be due to natural differences. One is reminded of Efimov's attack, in 1931, on an attempt to explain the relative underachievement of Chuvash children in terms of their specific socio-economic conditions. Since these conditions were by then the creation of the Soviet state, they were beyond criticism.

Kolesov admits that child-care complicates the notion of full professional equality for women. However, when evaluating the work contribution of men and women, 'the demographic, social and ethical' consequences of women's work must be taken into account, and the complex interaction between family and work and the penetration of each into the other.[59] This throws new light on the Soviet concept of women's equality. In this context it appears to mean not so much that women are entitled to equal rights and opportunities, but to make an equal *contribution* to society.

Lyudmila Timoshchenko is another prominent voice in the pedagogical literature on sex differences. Like Khripkova and Kolesov, she offers a comprehensive list of male and female personality differences, using the 'maternal instinct' as her starting-point.[60] Since her list differs little from theirs, we need only mention a few points. Again, girls are portrayed as excessively sensitive and emotional. This results in a tendency towards emotional scarring and neurosis. Girls are more diligent, honest, perseverent, and passive than boys. Their passivity is reflected in an attraction for the gentler sports, those requiring 'flexibility and beauty of movement', while boys prefer those which stress action, such as football, volleyball and ice-hockey. This active/passive dichotomy is also reflected in reading preferences; boys look for action in books, while girls are more interested in the psychology of the heroes. Hence boys read detective and adventure stories, while girls prefer lyrical poetry.[61]

At times these characteristics are presented as fact; at others, as the personal and often contradictory opinions of teachers.[62] However, Timoshchenko is evidently aware that social factors do play at least some role in the behaviour of boys and girls, since she talks of the importance of role models:

> Consciously or unconsciously, boys and girls learn forms of behaviour which are considered typical for their sex. Boys, beginning from an early age, imitate primarily men. Girls imitate their mothers, from whom they learn about female psychology, with the emotional-altruistic tint which is characteristic to them.[63]

It is not unknown for girls to adopt male models, she adds, though very rare for boys to choose women.[64] She offers no explanation for this, however.

In one article she suggests that nature and socialization have become inextricably fused in a long-term process of socialization of the species, in that 'natural' male and female personality traits – which she refers to as the 'eternally masculine' and 'eternally feminine' – are 'defined by nature' but have 'taken shape in the course of many centuries, in relation to the social position of women'.[65] Surely, then, the establishment of socialism and the transformation of the former social position of women would begin to erode the 'eternally' masculine and feminine? Timoshchenko does not go into this. It becomes clear that she is less concerned about what lies behind them than that they continue to be reproduced in successive generations of children.

She is more anxious about the demise of femininity than masculinity. She bemoans the fact that girls no longer learn how to look after young children as they did in large families of the past, that they underrate such qualities as diligence, thrift and femininity, and declare a lack of interest in housework. Their professional activities are responsible for this: 'Many girls in the final year at school cannot imagine themselves in the role of wife and mother. The majority of them connect their future lives only with study and work.'[66] To rectify this collapse in family orientation, Timoshchenko advocates the combined efforts of teachers and parents to stimulate domesticity and a correct psychological outlook. Mothers, as the 'natural upbringers', are given detailed instructions on the characteristics they should inculcate in their daughters. The enormous list includes kindness, carefulness, thrift, unselfishness, politeness, generosity, delicacy, femininity, modesty, compassion, tactfulness, diligence, honest, sensitivity, an awareness of the importance of chastity, and a serious and responsible attitude towards marriage and the choice of a partner. She should not be wilful, obstinate or egotistical, since these characteristics 'may lead to a reluctance to consider others. It is difficult for such a girl to become a good wife, mother and homemaker'. Timoshchenko also suggests that girls should be strong and brave, but she evidently feels that these qualities should be covert since she adds that they can exist inside girls who appear, on the surface, to be the frailest, quietest and most tender creatures.[67]

Mothers should also teach their daughters about other aspects of their future roles as Soviet citizens, as well as the purely maternal. However, these are evidently of secondary importance. They should make clear to their daughters the fact that despite their official equality 'there are still big differences between men and women', and that because of this, 'the desire to prove oneself in adulthood, or be the same as boys ("This is the age of equality!") might end badly . . .'.[68]

Timoshchenko acknowledges that women have a hard time coping with their various functions. She cites a 1972 time-budget study which shows that they spend twice as much time on housework as men (29 hours per week compared with 15). Her proposed solution is to increase the availability of domestic services, and to distribute the household duties more justly. However, this does not mean an even distribution; 'Each should participate in housework to the best of their ability.'[69] Given her advocation of the development of domestic abilities in girls but not in boys, it is difficult to see how this advice will improve the position of women.

Men are expected to play some part in the upbringing of their children, but this is not the same as that of women. The fact that the mother is so affectionate and compassionate tends to make her insufficiently strict, and the father's masculine approach is needed to bring balance and harmony to upbringing. The nature of these different male and female roles are thus happily complementary. 'The husband is the head, and the wife – the heart of the whole family organization.' These roles are, of course, natural and inevitable; 'the basic natural function of the woman is motherhood', and of the man, 'to be the head of the family, its guardian'.[70] If a woman attempts to take on the man's role, this leads to disaster. She becomes 'demanding and categorical' like a man, and leaves the family bereft of warmth and kindness. The children form an image of the mother as the independent, decisive, and energetic parent, the one who goes to parents' meetings, arranges the passes for the pioneer camp, does the scolding for misdemeanours, and so on. This combines with the image of women in control as upbringers in the kindergarten and teachers in the school. This has a bad effect on both boys and girls. Boys develop the idea that men are not independent and require looking after by women, which affects their own development. Girls also fail to develop an understanding of men as respected and needed members of society.[71] To avoid this, sex-roles in the family must be different and inflexible.

Again, the authority of Marx is invoked to justify the stress on a domestic upbringing for girls. Timoshchenko informs readers that,

> Marx and Jenny gave much attention to the participation of their daughters in housework. By the time she was a teenager, Laura, who showed genuine talent in such matters, was able to cook tasty pies and tarts, and to prepare unusual sauces. The daughters sewed their own sheets and dresses, embroidered and knitted.

Marx did not, of course, neglect other aspects of his daughters' education. All three went to business school, we learn – and became their father's 'secretaries'.[72]

A SUMMARY OF THE PEDAGOGICAL WRITINGS

The views outlined above are repeated, with few variations, in the rest of the pedagogical literature on sex differences. The relative emphasis placed on the roles of biology and on social and cultural factors in producing differentiated male and female personalities does vary from writer to writer, but this is a minor difference of degree. On the whole, the following pattern emerges with consistency.

Biological inheritance is seen as the foundation of male and female differences in personality. These differences relate primarily to the different reproductive roles of men and women, which have engendered a range of psychological peculiarities relating to the woman's need to create a nest for her offspring, and the man's need to protect this nest.[73] The range of differences offered by Soviet writers are at times contradictory, but generally coincide with the popular myths about male and female personality in the West, which the study by Maccoby and Jacklin effectively debunked. (One interesting exception is the widespread assumption that men are naturally more aggressive than women. Maccoby and Jacklin did find some evidence to support this; however, in the Soviet pedagogical literature we come across the argument that aggression is one male characteristic which does not have a biological basis, being instead a resilient legacy from the bourgeois ideology of the past!)[74]

While biology has an important role to play, it is not a deterministic one. It leaves a sufficiently strong imprint on the personality to preclude the possibility of an absolute psychological identity of men and women; however, in order to successfully develop the tendencies contained in this imprint, biology needs the assistance of parental and pedagogical forces of socialization. With the exception of the article by Andreeva, there is no real attempt within the pedagogical literature to challenge the idea that these differences are healthy and necessary. The general view is that though fashions may change, the ideal male and female qualities are timeless.[75] This view is reflected in the general consistency between the pedagogical writings of the 1960s and the 1980s. The obscure poem cited by Dik in 1966 even makes an appearance in a book by V. Vasil'ev sixteen years later, urging teenage boys to develop in themselves the qualities of masculinity: 'In order to become a man, it is not enough to be born one . . .'[76]

The role of the environment *per se* in developing psychological sex differences is virtually ignored, no doubt because, as Kolesov makes clear, the environment is considered to treat men and women as equals and to offer the same life chances to each.

Self-training is granted a considerable role in both children and teenagers. In children it takes the form of a natural inclination to adopt models as standards of behaviour, and to adapt their own behaviour in accordance with that of these models. Self-training is particularly important in the period of adolescence, from around 14 to 17, when children, fully aware now of the characteristics associated with their own sex and of their importance, make positive efforts to reproduce them in themselves, to become truly 'masculine' or 'feminine'. However, it does not end with the years of adolescence. According to V. Vasil'ev, it should continue 'till the last breath . . .'[77] As we have seen, Khripkova and Kolesov also exhort women to work at developing their femininity throughout their adult lives.

The largest role of all in the development of sex-typed personalities is accorded to training by parents and teachers. This training is not seen as an attempt to push male and female personalities down culturally-constructed paths, but rather as a means of assisting nature and enhancing natural inclinations and propensities. Many of the recommendations are reminiscent of social learning theory and Soviet psychology of personality development. For example, parents are urged to make active use of the child's natural urge to imitate chosen models. As Gudkovich and Kondratov explain, 'From the early years it is necessary to form in the child an ideal of personality which he will imitate, and, unconsciously and then consciously, model his "ego" on – masculine for the boy, feminine for the girl.'[78] Despite the fact that a number of writers talk approvingly of women's high representation in professions such as teaching, since these supposedly reflect their natural urge to nurture, the inadequate supply of role models available to boys has led to the call for an increase in the number of male teachers. It is hoped that this will encourage a more active involvement in school life, the lack of which is currently evident from their absence from school and Komsomol *aktiv*.

Reinforcement of appropriate behaviour is also essential. Parents should 'scold a boy for tearfulness ("You burst into tears, just like a girl!") and a girl for being naughty ("You are playing pranks, like a boy!")'[79] Elsewhere the same authors are still blunter: 'it is necessary to programme the son into definite traits of behaviour of "a boy", the daughter of "a girl".'[80] Play, which was stressed in psychological writings as an important factor in personality development, is also harnessed to the service of developing male and female differences. Karakovskii, for example, talks of the importance of war games to develop a boy's courage, self-control and patriotism, while 'Girls, as is appropriate for them, fulfil the role of hospital attendants and doctors. They gasp, they grieve . . .'[81]

Children's failure to delineate strong male and female personalities is held to account for the instability of marriage and the rising divorce rate. According to Gudkovich and Kondratov, it results in a tragic condition which (reminiscent of Belkin) is known as 'incorrect sexual orientation'. They write:

If the girl does not play with dolls, she frequently discovers, when she has become a mother, that her maternal feeling is weak; the child seems to her a burden and not a joy. In addition, she has few maternal habits. Boys, brought up by molly coddling, become cowardly, delicate, weak and dependent. They want to play only with girls. And having grown up, they reap the sad fruit of such an upbringing, for the demands made on them are those made on men, and no-one will make allowances for 'feminine upbringing'.[82]

Yet as Andreeva noted, the suggestion that fewer demands are made on women than on men is rather hypocritical, since Soviet women – as revealed in a multitude of time-budget studies – have considerably heavier work-loads than men.

In short, then, the pedagogical literature of the late 1970s and early 1980s is no more scientific than the earlier contributions. It offers little more than a description of psychological sex differences, with the implicit suggestion that these are biologically determined. Yet just in case social influences start to interfere, a programme of training is recommended, designed to nurture these differences and thus produce healthy, dichotomized male and female personalties. The association of prominent pedagogical writers with the subject seems like little more than an attempt to give weight to popular ideological assumptions, to imbue them with academic prestige.

PEDAGOGY AND PSYCHOLOGY

Despite the strong connection between psychology and pedagogy in the past, the pedagogical approach to sex differences stands in stark contrast to the psychological approach to personality. Although it can be said to fit roughly within the framework of the four-factor theory of personality development (though with the environment given a minimal role), the relative emphasis placed on these is very different. While psychologists have granted biology a very minor role in personality development and consider what input it does have to be amenable to social influence and transformation, pedagogues elevate it to a major position in the creation of sex-typed personality. It is ultimately impervious to social influence; as Khripkova and Kolesov explain, whatever new roles men and women assume in socialist society, the character of the activity or profession does not smooth out the specifically sexual differences and ... with an attentive and unbiased scrutiny it is always possible to bring these to light. Therefore any changes in the nature of the activities of members of the male and female sex will never lead to a smoothing-out of the psychological differences between them.[83]

When pedagogical writers do acknowledge environmental influences, they appear in the form of a negative force, threatening social collapse by perverting the natural order of feminine women and masculine men unless we can succeed in controlling them. In this they differ from the relatively liberal Kon and Yankova, who grant social influences a relatively minor function in comparison with mainstream Soviet psychologists, but still a positive one – that of modifying out-dated features of the stereotypes of masculinity and femininity.

On the other hand, the roles of training and self-training are maximized in pedagogical writings. It is held that although sex differences in personality are natural and inevitable, they can wither away as the result of incorrect upbringing. Parents and teachers are thus exhorted to inculcate in their children those 'natural' male and female traits and patterns of behaviour, and, through stimulating awareness in their children of their importance in their future adult lives, to encourage a simultaneous process of self-training.

The natural urge of children to select models and construct ideal types of behaviour, as well as role-practice through play, also make an appearance in the pedagogical writings. As we have seen, these are also prominent in psychological accounts of personality development. However, this apparent adherence to certain tenets of the psychological approach is probably accidental. The references to modelling, play etc. are random; they do not appear as part of a coherent application of psychology to the development of male and female personality. Nowhere to be found, for example, is an application of Vygotskii's stage theory of personality and the utilization of leading activities to the development of sex-differentiated personalities. This might just be the result of a gap between theory and practice. Alternately, it could reflect a realization that a genuine attempt to apply Soviet psychology to the development of male and female differences would expose the contradictions between the psychological understanding of human personality and the pedagogical framework of assumptions about male and female differences.

PEDAGOGY AND THE MEDICAL PROFESSION

Despite the golden partnership of the post-revolutionary years, then, psychology and pedagogy have become estranged in the area of sex differences in personality. Pedagogy is now more inclined to parade on the arm of the medical profession. Indeed, a number of pedagogical theorists themselves straddle the two disciplines. Khripkova and Kolesov, for example, have successively headed the Institute of Scientific Research of the Physiology of Children and Teenagers, which is part of the Academy of Pedagogical Sciences. Their writings include discussions of physical health and hygiene as well as psychological sex differences. This makes the biological emphasis in their work on psychological sex differences less surprising. However, at the same time they attempt to place work on sex differences within the orbit of psychology (evidently acknowledging no contradiction between the approaches of the two disciplines) when they attribute its existence to the new maturity of psychology as a discipline, enabling it to divide into specialized fields.[84]

Reference to medical experts is often made to affirm the view that psychological sex differences have a natural, biological basis. The partnership of pedagogy and medicine is particularly pronounced in the realm of sexuality and sex education. In the era of *glasnost'*, there have been calls for a more frank and honest approach to sex education; however, this is a very recent phenomenon. Khripkova's report on sex education in Sweden epitomizes the more usual position. She condemned it as 'sex enlightenment' for children, which served to focus their attention on sex for its own sake.[85] In the Soviet Union, children must learn that sex takes place only between married people who love each other; lessons about the technical aspects of sex should take place within wider discussions on the family and children's roles within it, both at present and in their adulthood. Given that these roles are still (and, in the view of pedagogical theorists, should remain) largely sex-typed, the medical discussions on sex have generally been intertwined with pedagogical discussions on sex differences in personality. Hence many articles on the subject in the popular pedagogical journal *Sem'ya i Shkola* are almost indistinguishable from those in the popular health journal *Zdorov'e*. The focus may differ, with pedagogical writers concentrating more on sex differences in personality and medical writers on sexuality and sex education, but the ideas espoused are identical, and both make frequent references to the work of the other.

Zdorov'e is one of the most widely read of Soviet journals, with a distribution of over sixteen million and an actual readership which is far larger. (The '*knizhnii golod*', or hunger for reading material, far outstrips the availability of books and journals – at least, those which are not of an overtly political nature. Popular journals thus tend to be passed from friend to friend, or throughout the members of a work collective.) The inclusion in *Zdorov'e* of such articles, whose link with health issues is often far from obvious, thus ensures (whether intentionally or accidentally) a particularly wide dissemination of these views. We will take a brief look at a few such articles, which appeared in *Zdorov'e* in the early 1980s.

N. N. Kuindzhi, a Candidate of Science in medicine, begins with a reference to the 'scientific work' of Kolesov. The main concern of his article is sex-education and the need to prevent premature sexual awakening in children, but he also makes a familiar exhortation to parents to inculcate appropriate male and female personality characteristics in their children. As soon as the child is aware of his or her sex identity, 'it is necessary to take advantage of this, and to inculcate in him the corresponding behaviour: "you are a boy, you must protect the weak": or "you are a girl, you must always be neat and tidy . . .".'[86]

V. A. Sysenko tells us that men and women are 'made for each other', on the grounds both of their complementary roles in procreation and their complementary personalities. 'Male resoluteness and an inclination towards risk counterbalances female caution; male sharpness counterbalances female gentleness; and male neglect of the details of everyday life counterbalances the greater aesthetic demands of women.'[87] Sysenko attributes these differences in personality partly to nature, but mainly to the division of labour which has existed between men and women throughout history. In terms once again reminiscent of functionalist sociology, he talks of a male orientation towards the external world, requiring traits of bravery and resoluteness, and a female orientation towards the inner world of the family, requiring gentle and nurturant qualities and the development of intuition about the moods of others.

If such personality differences are the product of history, should they not be amenable to change? Surely the break-up of the old sexual division of labour would produce corresponding changes in male and female personality? Sysenko seems not to agree. He talks approvingly of the professional achievements of women in the Soviet Union, but sees these as no threat to traditional femininity since the types of jobs they do are generally linked to their female proclivities. The high level of female employment in more delicate areas of machine assemblage, for example, reflects 'female accurateness, precise movements, and attentiveness . . .', which have proved particularly valuable to such branches of industry.

However, Sysenko is prone to the usual contradiction. He goes on to suggest that there is indeed an erosion of masculine and feminine stereotypes, not only in the Soviet Union but throughout the world, and that this is having dangerous consequences. Despite their new independence and prestige, women are still physically weaker and more emotional than men. Hence they need to lean on male support, understanding and strength. Women who do not enjoy male protection do not have happy marriages. Similarly, a strong, practical and independent woman challenges and erodes a man's masculinity. Men who turn to alcohol are very often those who have lost their role as head of the family. 'This is a very serious signal to women: be wise!' Again, it would seem that women are being encouraged to play at being weak in order to preserve the illusion of male strength.

An article by A. N. Obozova and V. I. Shtil'bans is concerned with upbringing by parents, and reproduces the views found in the pedagogical press. Parents are urged to inculcate in their sons responsibility for 'masculine' activities around the home, such as repairing domestic appliances and doing any heavy lifting, and are warned about the negative consequences of the feminization of men and masculinization of women. The authors do suggest that boys be taught to help with certain 'feminine' occupations since there are now so many fewer which are specifically masculine, but this help has distinct limits: 'All these matters which require softness and tenderness have from time immemorial been the work of women, because these qualities are peculiar to her from nature.'[88]

An article by I. V. Dorno, 'Men over thirty', is of particular interest.[89] The article is concerned with the dire consequences which befall men who fail to marry and have children before they reach the age of 30. The death-rate of single men is twice that of married men of the same age because men deprived of a warm and secure 'home front' are unable to organize their lives and are often ill. The article contains, as well as a number of dubious medical assertions, a series of assumptions about male and female sexuality and personality.

Women, inevitably, are to blame for men's failure to marry, since they allow them to enjoy a sex life without doing so. Male and female behaviour patterns should balance each other; if women were sufficiently modest and tender, this would make men more protective and 'correct' in their behaviour. They would then consider 'intimacy without conjugal obligations, without responsibility for the good name and well-being of the woman, to be dishonourable'. Again, women are cast as the custodians of morality.

Dorno then claims that a man of 30 has little time left for creating a family, partly because a prolonged single life has told on his health, and partly because late paternity increases the risk of the child not being normal. As usual, these statements are not backed up by any references to scientific study. The impression one gets is that *Zdorov'e* is being used to promote certain desired patterns of behaviour – i.e. marriage and parenthood – with pseudo-scientific arguments adding muscle.

Similar articles can be found in other journals and newspapers. An absurd tale appeared in *Moskovskaya Pravda* in 1985, about a child whose mother was over-protective. Instead of playing with other boys of his age, whose primary interests were football and fighting, he had to spend all his time with his mother and her female friends, who apparently talked about nothing but cake-making and house-keeping. So the boy developed habits and inclinations more appropriate for a woman, which in adulthood led to psychiatric and even cardiovascular disorders. The author of the article, a physician, concludes that he can be cured, but it will take a long time – it is no easy task to undo decades of feminized upbringing. He warns women readers not to make the same mistake, and to remember that 'A man should be raised as a man'.[90]

WARNINGS AGAINST THE ENCOURAGEMENT OF EXCESSIVE SEX-DIFFERENTIATION IN PERSONALITY

Occasionally there is a cautious warning in the pedagogical and medical literature that training for sex-differences may go too far and produce excessively masculine and feminine personalities. Koryakina tells of one boy who was brought up by his parents to be a 'real man', but turned out to be a creature devoid of love or any other human sentiment, who subsequently subjected his own wife and child to a life of misery. In another family, the parents concentrated all efforts on their son's scientific education but, again, forgot to inculcate in him any sense of concern for others. Koryakina concludes that certain qualities are essential in children of both sexes: 'sympathy and kindness, sensitivity and a feeling of gratitude for any good thing which is done for them...'. Children of neither sex should be ashamed to cry; a person who cannot show emotion in a situation of supreme grief 'is worse than dirt'. None the less, she goes on to argue that training in masculinity is still essential for boys, and chastises parents who are too afraid for their sons' safety to develop their courage and bravery.[91]

In similar vein, Mikaberidze tells of a girl whose parents were determined to protect her from any hardship or effort.[92] They dissuaded her from taking part in any active children's games or even tasks requiring serious effort, and

> restricted her life purely to women's interests and cultivated female helplessness in her, as though firmly convinced that all her life somebody's trustworthy hands would protect Natasha from all worries and difficulties.

Yet the man she married was an ordinary, fallible human-being, who was not able to give this level of support. Natasha became increasingly resentful of her husband's imperfections and disappointed in her life, until finally she was reduced to 'a slovenly, plump, unattractive, and, one could see at once, unhappy woman'. Like Koryakina, Mikaberidze concludes that certain qualities are important for both men and women, such as 'the ability to overcome difficulties and to defend one's ideas and opinions, the ability to work, self-restraint, and the ability to operate in a collective'. At the same time, parents should encourage the development of an essential femininity – 'a desire to help, to look after others, to sympathise, to forgive, and to concede'. This combination will provide the girl with an appropriate personality.

SUMMARY OF THE PEDAGOGICAL AND MEDICAL APPROACH

From the lists of male and female characteristics offered by Soviet pedagogical writers, we can see that women in the Soviet Union of the present day are dealt almost as raw a deal as they were by Freud. They tend towards over-emotionality, a characteristic of which Vygotskii disapproved and sought to control in children, and which pedagogical writers themselves feel renders women prone to neurosis. The peculiarly female interest in appearance can turn into a pathological conviction of physical inadequacy. Women are shy and impulsive, both of which were considered by the psychologist Kovalev to be qualities leading to undesirable behaviour in school-children, which should be inhibited by training. It is never suggested by the pedagogical writers that methods of training be designed to reduce and control these undesirable, even dangerous, traits in women. On the contrary, they urge parents and teachers to assist nature and help to develop these very traits.

The pedagogical stress on women's weakness and male strength is not reflected in reality. Pedagogical writers are not blind to the changes which have taken place in women's lives, but see them as a largely negative phenomenon.

Many of them support the fact that women are most often found in the service industries, claiming that this is evidence of the unchangeability of feminine qualities, since these jobs reflect their supposedly natural capacity for nurturing and caring.[93] It would be no great leap in consciousness to also attribute women's under-representation in politics, heavy industry, and the higher echelons even of the spheres in which they do predominate, to their natural inclinations. Soviet pedagogy fails to address factors such as unequal professional opportunities, the resilience and continued propagation of traditional ideas about appropriate male and female careers, differential training in schools (for example, the 'Trud' class, which is aimed at developing a love of work and appropriate work skills in young people, is strongly sex-differentiated in urban schools), and the blow which child-rearing deals to women's chances of promotion. Instead we find an insistence that the Soviet Union has provided complete equality of opportunity for men and women, so different choices of profession or position must be due to nature. The insistence on the naturalness of dichotomized personalities seems to be intended as a justification for a staunchly sex-differentiated upbringing, and the perpetuance of traditional differences in male and female activity.

8 The Popular Press

Anatolii Strelyanyi recalls that in 1976 the journal *Literaturnaya Gazeta* ventured to suggest, for the first time since the Revolution, that there were certain 'negative aspects to the independence of the female sex'.[1] In fact, as we have seen, pedagogical writers had been arguing the same point for more than a decade. In the mid-1970s, the themes which had long held an important place within the pedagogical literature – the need to resurrect traditional ideals of masculinity and femininity, to revise the definition of equality between the sexes, and to praise (though seemingly not reward) women's demographic contribution to society as highly as men's work contribution – entered the pages of the general press.

The main forum for such discussions have been the literary and discussion newspapers such as *Nedelya* and *Literaturnaya Gazeta*, women's magazines like *Rabotnitsa*, and newspapers and journals directed at young people, such as *Yunost'* and *Komsomol'skaya Pravda*. However, the weightier newspapers like *Pravda* have also taken part. We would suggest that such discussions have been aimed, to a large extent, at mobilizing the population in the European republics to greater reproductive efforts, and propagandizing a more domestic lifestyle for women. The strong ideological function of the Soviet press has been acknowledged by Soviet as well as Western commentators; it has been described as 'the strongest ideological weapon of the Party',[2] placing a certain 'model of the world in people's consciousness'.[3] The arrival of *glasnost'* may have knocked chinks in the monolithic presentation of a single model, but the role of the press in propagandizing Party policy is far from over. Angus Roxburgh makes this point in his recent analysis of *Pravda*. He suggests that while the boundaries of what information can be presented to the public have been removed, they still remain within the control of the Party, and that 'the media, when it comes to it, are to "try harder" at the same old methods of mobilising the population'.[4]

One of the functions of the popular press has been to popularize and disseminate the views of the specialists whose work we looked at earlier. A common format is to begin with a general discussion by a journalist about possible determinants of sex differences in personalities, and then invite an expert to decide the matter. Another is to begin with a letter from a reader (for example, a women complaining about the difficulty of combining work and family duties, or a man about his wife's poor domestic orientation), invite other readers to give their views on the subject, and then again conclude with the views of one or more experts.

Contributions from readers have played a particularly prominent role. Although there are exceptions, the majority of letters which have appeared in print have fit into a similar overall pattern. They have called for a cleaner demarcation of male and female personalities and roles, and a stronger maternal orientation in women. It is possible that such letters have been selected for publication as 'evidence' of popular support for a move towards reducing women's contribution to the economy and increasing their family commitment. This would accord with Mark Hopkins's observation in his study of the Soviet media, that despite a professed commitment to readers' participation, the Soviet press does not function as 'an unregulated channel of public opinion'. Letters to the editor undergo a rigourous selection process which generally limits publication to those the Party agrees with or wishes to act upon. They are also subject to 'extensive rewriting or even ghostwriting of what are supposedly the raw outpourings of the Soviet citizen'.[5]

Most of the articles on this subject which appeared in the general press in the late 1970s and early 1980s reflect the arguments presented in the previous chapters. It is said that nature made the personalities of men and women different to match their different roles in procreation, but that the erosion of distinctly male and female roles in other spheres of life has resulted in a feminization of male personality and a masculinization of female personality. This has had disastrous consequences for family, health and happiness. It is not necessary to look at the writings which virtually repeat the pedagogical position on male and female personality differences. We will concentrate instead on those which could be said to complement or develop this position.

THE CAUSES OF THE MASCULINIZATION OF WOMEN AND THE FEMINIZATION OF MEN

The question of the masculinization of female personality and the feminization of male personality is one on which journalists have been particularly eloquent. This is said to have developed for a number of reasons. The main reason is the relatively new role women have as workers in production, as well as in the home. This has not merely given them new qualities, but has destroyed some of the old ones. As G. Belskaya cautions, 'When cultivating in the woman the characteristics so useful in the sphere of business, such as firmness, steadfastness, intolerance [sic], rationality, and a grasp of business, we must be clearly aware that we are certainly reconstructing her emotional balance and contracting her purely maternal qualities.'[6]

The fact that women have too few children has also contributed to their loss of femininity. Making a particularly vivid link between demographic policy and the writings on sex differences, one writer suggests that for a women to be really feminine she must have no fewer than three children.[7]

The masculinity of men has been damaged by the fact that many of the tasks which once fell to them have been taken over by the state or by women. As a result, their sense of self-value has crumbled, and they are both idle and demoralized. For example 'The title of family breadwinner – an honourable and responsible title – has always helped the man to realize his significance and his essentialness to the people closest to him. Without this role the very earth slips from beneath his feet'.[8] Women have exacerbated the situation because of their false understanding of equality, which has led them to demand kindness, tact and sensitivity from their men instead of masculinity.[9]

The curious suggestion has also been made that biology has responded to social factors and has contributed further to the feminization of men. To ensure the successful continuation of the species, nature seeks to maintain a certain level of nurturant qualities in the population. As women lose these, nature injects them into men.[10] Hence as women's professional work effects changes in their personalities, this in turn alters the personalities of men.

> But the traits which added to women's quality have the opposite effect in men. Softness becomes spinelessness, attention to detail becomes pettiness, maternal prudence becomes cowardice.... Flabbiness and passivity, prolonged vacillation and the inability to make decisions, the hoisting onto women's shoulders of the most nerve-wracking burdens of the partnership – all this has been instilled into men's psychology with the spread of an epidemic.[11]

Journalists are also inclined to point their finger at their own profession, making obvious their role as propagandists of a desired model of the world. The popular press, it is said, has long held up the career woman as the ideal model for women to follow, and has been too profuse in its praises of women's contribution to society. Tamara Afanas'eva argues that *Rabotnitsa* has encouraged the last two generations of women to demand complete equality with men and to see family responsibilities as unfashionable. She quotes a letter from a reader who left her husband because he disapproved of her working outside the home, and under the magazine's influence, became 'a modern women – and that means a strong individual, able to step over her own feelings and those of the man she loves for the sake of the triumph of "principle"'.[12] Too late, she came to regret her decision, and blamed *Rabotnitsa* on the grounds that 'You always wrote that women shouldn't give in on anything to the stronger sex . . .'.[13]

Komsomol'skaya Pravda has also been accused of promoting a notion of equality which is now seen as false. After publishing a letter from a man who divorced his wife on grounds of neglect since she was more interested in her dissertation and her female colleagues than in him and their daughter, the editors invited two sociologists to give their responses. Yu. Kovalev sympathized with the husband, described the woman's prioritization of her profession as 'sexual disorientation', and linked it with bad upbringing. E. Anisimov, on the other hand, argued that the woman had a right to work outside the home, and that this was vital both to herself and to the economy. Afanas'eva accuses *Komsomol'skaya Pravda* of endorsing Anisimov's 'economic fetishism' by printing his article last and so giving him the final word.[14]

Grant Bagrazyan charges journalists with 'praising women to the hilt, almost singing hymns to their honour, and letting fathers slip to the periphery of our consciousness'. Encouraged by such praise, women have undervalued men and vied with them for leadership of the family. This has resulted in quarrels and confusion, incorrect upbringing of children, divorce, and a moral distortion in life.[15]

Nobody benefits from the reversal of traditional roles. Leonid Zhukovitskii argues in *Literaturnaya Gazeta* that a man hates his wife to be stronger than him since it wounds his self-esteem, but a woman is equally resentful of her weak husband since she 'finds her own supremacy an unnatural deviation from the rule. She wants to be weak! Hence the ideal pattern of family relations is a strong husband and a weak wife . . .'.[16] Bagrazyan similarly suggests that the happiest marriages are those in which women voluntarily surrender leadership to their husbands. He describes one woman's experience of her husband's feminization with particular pathos:

He was washing the dishes. I saw him wearing an apron, red in the face, sweating, and my heart broke. I went up to him, I wanted to spare him, caress him. And he, the poor thing, answered me with a wet hand on my hair, and said weakly, 'it's going slowly. I'm tired.' I saw how my husband had changed – even his voice . . . . Suddenly it was as if someone took me on one side and said: what are you doing? What are you turning your husband into? Do you want a husband or a girlfriend at home? 'Take off your apron', I said to him. 'In the future there'll be neither the kitchen nor the washing up for you. Be a man!'[17]

The press has also published letters from women who see themselves as 'masculinized', and bitterly regret it. They appeal for help in restoring their lost femininity.[18]

Health as well as happiness suffers from the disintegration of male and female roles. L. Tarkhova urges women to follow the advice of psychologists and 'transfer family power into the hands of the husband' on the grounds that he may otherwise turn to alcohol, will be prone to early senility, and will have a shorter life expectancy.[19] Larisa Proshina also links male health with the role of leader of the family. When men lose responsibility for their families they feel they have no reason to remain healthy, and so drink, lie in front of the TV for hours, and neglect their children.[20]

There are, of course, also the demographic consequences. Proshina points out that women's urge 'to write theses' and 'engage in business' results not only in 'flabbiness' in their husbands and hardness and cruelty in themselves, but also the disintegration of marriage and a drop in the birth-rate.[21] The congruence of the needs of society and its citizens is presented as purely coincidental.

The solution is to resurrect distinct male and female roles and, accordingly, personalities. Again there is much talk about the need to train girls and boys to have the right personality traits, and for adult men and women to train themselves. Afanas'eva also urges the setting up of public workshops in apartment blocks, where 'fathers and sons can grind, plane, solder, saw and paint together . . .'. Women should stop rebuking their husbands for being idle, she continues, and work on restoring their shattered egos.[22] Pressing idle men into service as domestic helpers and nursemaids is not a valid option. For one thing, it would not work; few of them have the appropriate skills and patience which women have developed over thousands of years. For another, it would reinforce men's feminization.[23]

THE TENSIONS BETWEEN WOMEN'S WORK AND FAMILY ROLES

Another subject which now receives considerable coverage in the press is the tension which exists between women's two roles – that of mother and housewife, and member of the work-force. The image of the Soviet woman which was consistently portrayed in the past, who excels in her chosen career as well as being a devoted wife and mother, is now said to be seldom found in reality. The attempt to combine these roles has actually had negative consequences. It has given women an excessive work-load, has contributed to their loss of femininity, and has led to neglect of their families.

The wisdom of past efforts to free women from full-time child-care is also challenged. The creation of crèches is said to have rested on false convictions: that women should be able to return to work as soon as possible after the birth of a child, and that child-care in public institutions is more beneficial than upbringing at home. A high price has been paid, which includes the drop in the birth-rate, poor emotional development in children, juvenile delinquency, and a weakening of family ties, especially those of marriage. The new recognition of the need for constant emotional contact between mother and child lies behind the plans to increase post-maternity leave to three years.[24]

In 1985 *Rabotnitsa* held a 'discussion club' on the subject of women's two roles. This was prompted by a letter from a reader, Elena T., in which she recounted her own hopeless attempt to combine them. The contrast between the media image and the reality of women's lives is again exposed in Elena's cynical comment that there must be women who can cope – 'I've met them in the pages of journals and newspapers . . .'.[25] This point is made again by another reader, who compares her own life with that of a woman in an article. Both wanted to be pilots and have families, but while the woman in the story succeeded, her own attempt collapsed under the pressure of housework and child-care.[26]

The solution which, as we saw earlier, is increasingly popular amongst sociologists and demographers, also finds expression in *Rabotnitsa's* discussion club. This is that women have to make a choice between putting work or family first. Yet once again, the family is presented as the only really morally valid choice. Hence most participants in the discussion call for better socialization in schools and family so that girls will grow up seeing their future primarily in terms of the family. 'What has happened to us sweet women?', asks one. 'Why have we changed, forgotten to rejoice in our main predestination – motherhood?'[27] Another complains: 'If you turn on the TV or pick up a newspaper, you see and hear above all about women tractor drivers, welders and pilots. Even in school they glorify only the so-called businesswoman. Perhaps we have gone too far?'[28] A third suggests that women's education and intelligence is useless anyway unless it is used for the good of the family.[29]

Women will not suffer if they give up work. Readers who reluctantly abandoned careers for their children tell how they now realize that their true happiness and fulfilment lies in child-care. Women can still achieve their professional aspirations through their male children.[30] In any case, their contribution was exaggerated; 'men can achieve progress in science without us'.[31]

The discussion club was concluded with the contributions of four family experts. A. G. Alekseeva is a philosopher who specializes in ethics. She sees Elena's decision to place career before family as a denial of femininity. She offers the familiar adage, endorsed now by Marx: 'Marxism says that equality does not mean, and more important cannot mean, identity. The physical characteristics produced by a person's sex predetermine differences both in the physical traits of the organism, and in the psyche.'[32]

I. A. Golubeva is a member of the committee on work and social problems. She does not think that women should actually give up work, and expresses concern that they are being encouraged to do so; this will merely result in men having to work longer hours to make up the financial loss, and so will effectively deprive families of fathers. A better solution is for women to work from home. The problem of women's double work-load can therefore be solved by placing the two jobs in one location and having women perform them concurrently.[33]

Sociologist I. V. Bestuzhev-Lada, whose views we examined at some length in Chapter 6, is *Rabotnitsa's* third expert. To recap briefly, he suggests that different solutions are needed for different women, and that those with a strong career motivation should be able to follow this path. However, his ideal situation for the vast majority of women is for them to leave work six months before the birth of a child and then have a further three years at home after the birth. This would be followed by part-time work at least until the child reaches the age of ten. Work outside the home would thus play a very small role in the lives of most women. The envisaged increase in the efficiency and productivity of Soviet industry under *perestroika* would make such a situation feasible.[34]

The last expert is I. Stolin, whose work on family problems we discuss in the next chapter. He argues that women who attempt to divide themselves between work and family place themselves in an intolerable psychological position. They are convinced that they are neglecting both, so suffer perpetual guilt. He too thinks they should make a choice and prioritize either work or family – but his hints about the fate of the family make it clear which choice he backs.[35]

The main conclusion which can be drawn from *Rabotnitsa*'s discussion club is that the model of the Soviet woman which was formerly presented in the press, as successful worker and mother who finds equal fulfilment in both, has been transformed. The combination of work and family is now said to lead to an overloading of the woman and the neglect of both her roles. The solution which is commonly put forward is a choice between the roles. Yet in most cases this will mean prioritizing the family and putting work in second place, or even giving it up completely for a lengthy period.

PROPAGANDIZING THE MULTI-CHILD FAMILY

The pro-family drive for Soviet women is particularly clear in the press promotion of the 'multi-child family'. That with three children is said to be the optimum. Readers are assured that the hardships involved are greatly exaggerated, and the benefits enormous. The three-child family is portrayed as a happy collective, which promotes the physical and psychological health of all its members.

The mother, for example, undergoes a 'physical blossoming' after the first and second births, which makes her stronger and better prepared for those that follow. The pregnancies are easier, the births are faster and less painful, and the babies are healthier and happier. The very healthiest are the products of third and fourth pregnancies, but the health of the first-born is also improved by the arrival of siblings.[36]

Children of large families are not prone to the egoism and consumerism common amongst only children. They have a greater love of work, a more communal outlook, and a more responsible and caring attitude towards other people.[37] Their willingness to help ensures that the work-load of a large family is not as great as people imagine. In any case, the amount of work a large family generates is in itself no bad thing, since 'Research shows that alcoholism is extremely rare in the multi-child family. This is because there are too many things occupying the mind, hands and heart'.[38] The third child also generally looks more like the parents than the first or second, is more affectionate, and more inclined to care for its parents when they are old.[39]

Finally, the demographic situation is also improved, and the reproduction of the population guaranteed. As Kozhevnikov and Vinogradov point out, 'it turns out that the third child is essential both for the family and the state!'[40] The supposed congruence between the interests of the citizens and those of society is again presented as coincidental.

Yet as we have seen, even the mother of one child finds it difficult to combine work and family responsibilities. How is the mother of three to manage? Stories do occasionally appear in the press about women who have successfully combined multiple maternity with full-time work,[41] but it is generally acknowledged that this is rare. The prevailing message is that the rewards of having a family outweigh those of an abandoned career.

PROMOTING THE FULL-TIME HOUSEWIFE

The possibility of women becoming full-time housewives has accordingly been taken up by the press. Tamara Afanas'eva has long urged the press to stop encouraging a negative attitude in women towards housework, and disparaging those who choose to make a career of it.[42] Her call has been answered. Women who give up their careers to have children are now lauded for having got their priorities right,[43] and letters like these now appear quite commonly. Alla Moiseikova tells *Rabotnitsa* readers that she used to have no interest in domestic work and devoted herself to her studies. Then she met her husband, and now finds complete fulfilment in being a wife and a mother of three children. 'Now I can stand for hours in the kitchen, and I don't begrudge the lost time. I feel that this is right – to cook a lunch which my husband praises, to painstakingly iron a shirt for him.'[44] V. Lavrentsova writes in *Pravda* that she is proud to describe herself as a housewife, and that more women should be encouraged to stay at home with their children. She suggests that a new magazine be introduced to raise the status of full-time motherhood, called 'Domokhozyaika' – 'The Housewife'.[45]

A glorification of full-time motherhood is also found in the film 'One day 20 years later' (*Odnazhdy dvadtsat' let spustya*), and in the enthusiastic appraisals it has received in the press. The heroine, Nadya Kruglova, is a housewife with ten children. She hosts a reunion of her old school-friends, many of whom now have successful careers. 'At first glance she has nothing to boast about', writes I. Langueva in *Komsomol'skaya Pravda*, but when her children walk into the room, 'her classmates realize that hers, Nadya's, is the highest prize after all'.[46] O. Dmitrieva, in the same newspaper, congratulates the film for levelling out the achievements of career women and those who are simply mothers, and so 'rehabilitating' women whose basic orientation is towards the home and children.[47]

WRITINGS IN THE POPULAR PRESS WHICH OPPOSE THE RESURRECTION OF TRADITIONAL SEX ROLES

There have always been some voices in the press which oppose the resurrection of traditional sex roles. One of the most persistent has been that of Larisa Kuznetsova. Through numerous journal articles and a book, *Zhenshchina na Rabote i Doma*, she has put forward ideas which clash with the more mainstream approach to the subject. At times she comes close to a Western feminist perspective; one Western commentator even claims that she promotes a 'transcendence of sex as the basis for allocating social roles'.[48] However, at others she reproduces some very traditional ideas about sex roles.

Female personality, argues Kuznetsova, 'gets 50 kopecks from nature and a rouble from upbringing'.[49] At first glance, however, nature's 50 kopecks seems to buy very little. Kuznetsova tells us that sex differences in personality are 'learned like a multiplication table', and that nature is defenceless against the power of upbringing and the social environment. Women's success in the professional world has defied the stereotypes of female behaviour. Yet not all people's attitudes have changed at the same pace as their lives. Many still cling to the idea that there are distinct spheres of male and female competence, and that the absence of clear gender differences result in confusion and unhappiness. In their many letters to the press, men lament the demise of femininity – that 'tender attention with which my wife follows the trajectory of my first trial spoon from the bowl of soup', the ability to 'decorate the family hearth, like flowers decorate a field . . .' – and insist that although a man may be happy to talk for hours with an emancipated women over a shared packet of cigarettes, this is no basis for marriage.[50]

Kuznetsova responds to such views by suggesting that there are two different ways of looking at the changes in female personality. One is that they are a defiance of nature; the other is that they are a development of nature, an enhancement of women's natural strengths. In contrast to most of the writings we looked at earlier, Kuznetsova's have a distinct Marxist ring to them, an acknowledgement of dialectics and materialism:

> the history of mankind looks like a play, in the course of which various personality features of the woman become extinct because of the strength of socio-historical conditions . . . . [This evolution] has not been completed. It is a process which finds itself in motion, in a state of development . . . it always depends not only on nature but also on the concrete historical conditions, places and periods in which it is manifested.[51]

Inevitably this leads to some contradiction and absence of harmony. Yet 'where there is no contradiction, there is no progress'.[52]

These changes have generally been positive. Not only have women gained valuable new qualities through their work and lost some of their outmoded old ones, such as a proneness to 'swoons and hysterics',[53] but men have also changed for the better. They have developed closer relationships with their children and proved themselves capable of being kind and attentive fathers. Unlike those writers who express fear of male feminization, Kuznetsova is optimistic about the prospect of a new male role as women's partner in the family. In a democratic society there is no need for a head of the family, she argues. If one person does take on the role, it should be on the basis of personal qualities rather than sex.

However, Kuznetsova goes on to argue that male and female roles will never merge completely, and women will never wander too far from their psychological 'village'.[54] There is a natural and inevitable basis for such female traits as kindness and maternal love, for example, which are essential for healthy child development. Kuznetsova makes uncritical reference to John Bowlby's theory of maternal deprivation, seemingly unaware of its contribution to the creation of a reactionary, child-centred era for British women in the 1950s. (One of Bowlby's dictates was that women with young children 'should not be free to earn'.)[55]

She then makes the still more surprising claim that women have the right to be weak, and to bask in the guardianship which this stimulates in men. 'We are not ready for such psychological upheavals as men competing with women in weakness', she argues; 'tradition is strong with us.'[56] The 'old-fashioned gallantries' are essential for the creation of a moral atmosphere in which women's kindness, warmth and tenderness can grow, and women can enjoy them now without having to pay the heavy price exacted from them under capitalism – i.e., the lack of educational and professional opportunities. Kuznetsova criticizes both men who do not offer their seats to women, and women who refuse to accept them. She even advocates signs on public transport declaring that 'here seats are given to women', which she likens to plans mooted in other countries to provide separate carriages for women so that they will not be jostled during rush-hours.[57] (It evidently does not occur to her that such schemes may be intended to protect women from rather more than being jostled.)

Rather than promoting a transcendence of sex roles, then, Kuznetsova's position at times seems little different to that of Kon and Yankova; a hankering for certain old-fashioned, idealized notions of masculinity and femininity, but in a modified form to accommodate women's new role in the work-place and men's new role in the family. In an interview with lawyer Nina Sergeeva on the subject of divorce, she even comes close to declaring women over-emancipated. 'Two thirds of all divorces are initiated by women under the age of 25', she notes; 'is this not evidence of flippancy?' When Sergeeva reminds her that Lenin saw easy access to divorce as an essential prerequisite of women's emancipation, Kuznetsova replies that, 'Women can now in no way be called oppressed – more like the opposite'.[58]

It might be that such apparent contradictions are at least partly due, as we have suggested in the case of Kon, to the political climate in which she was initially writing. One of the aims of a writer is to be published, and in the pre-*glasnost'* days this inevitably required some self-censorship. However, although there have been changes in Kuznetsova's approach to the subject, she still could not be said to promote transcendence of sex roles.

The more recent articles express a far greater anger about women's lot in Soviet society. In an article in *Novoe Vremya* entitled 'In defence of women's careers' ('*V zashchitu zhenskoi kar'ery*'), she makes a vehement attack on the patriarchal view often presented in the press, that women's place is in the home rather than in high-powered jobs. The same divorce statistics are now given a rather different meaning: if women are naturally so suited to family life, why is that they initiate 70 to 80 per cent of divorces, and are much less inclined than men to risk marriage a second time? She talks of the 'artful rumour' put about to influence public opinion, backed up with 'semi-literate psychological twaddle', that the particular features of women's psyche make them naturally unfit for high-powered careers. The slogan 'women do not want to be leaders', she claims, is merely a camouflage for the view that 'a woman leader is not a good thing'.[59]

Subsequent articles have been still more vitriolic. In the same journal a year later, Kuznetsova argues that women have been turned into a 'third sex' – a hybrid containing all the features and the functions of the other two, and loaded down with all the tasks rejected by men. Specifically female roles and characteristics are degraded, and female needs ignored. Yet this supposedly sexless being 'sometimes gets pregnant. And sometimes gives birth'. Given the high abortion figures, 'More often gets pregnant than gives birth . . .'.[60] Although women are portrayed as the weaker sex, they are put through the physical torture of abortion and childbirth often without anaesthetic. They are saddled with almost all domestic work ('all queues consist of women, except the queue for vodka'),[61] and are at the same time employed in some of the harshest occupations. (They form, for example, a third of all itinerant workers doing heavy manual labour.) They are then pushed aside from the top jobs and decision-making positions on the grounds that they are less capable than men.

Perestroika expects the support of women, but it will have to do something for them if it is to win this support. On the one hand, Kuznetsova wants to see women's faces amongst those of decision makers. On the other hand, she wants returned to them 'the face they once had in a long lost era'.[62] What she seems to mean is that women should be allowed to become women again, to be entitled to the male gallantries she talked about in her earlier writings.

Against this background, Kuznetsova's views on the introduction of beauty contests in the Soviet Union comes as less of a surprise than might otherwise have been the case. (They are said to have caused considerable confusion when she announced them to the Plenum of the Committee of Soviet Women in October 1988, however.)[63] Women have a right to be beautiful, she argues, a right they have long been denied in the Soviet Union by the harshness of their lives and the paucity of beauty aids. Such contests can serve a positive purpose, since they can make society aware that it has an obligation to women, and that their ability to be beautiful is an index of its level of culture and prosperity. They can also help to unify people, since ordinary women can identify with the winners. Kuznetsova's main criticism is not that such contests demean women, but that in the Soviet Union they may merely serve to highlight the appalling contrast between ordinary women's live and those of the contestants, with their Western cosmetics and designer clothes, which are totally unavailable in Soviet shops.[64]

In short, then, although Kuznetsova wants equal opportunities for women at work and a real say in decision making, she also insists on their right to be 'real' women. This is a far from uncommon response to the hardships women have endured with their supposed equality. Kuznetsova herself quotes a letter which appeared in *Pravda*, from a women extremely anxious about her daughter's future. She is a machinist in a pumping station, and a hero worker; yet she has been treated as 'a cart horse, both at work and at home.' She now believes that 'It would be better for our daughters to be women and mamas, not machinists and tractor drivers.'[65]

The idea that women have an innate femininity is not universal, however. Irma Marmaladse has made a particularly vehement attack on the traditional notion of femininity. She argues that the 'real, feminine woman' is an outmoded concept, and that a new kind of relationship between men and women is required. For the first time in history women have had the opportunity to fulfil themselves through a profession, and inevitably this has led to changes in their personalities. Men may hanker after the woman of the past, but they themselves have made her demise essential:

> In a society of equal opportunities, a women doesn't like being self-sacrificing, tractable and gentle. Gentleness makes her uncompetitive. After all, if she weakens just a little, she is instantly pushed aside by the strong shoulder of some seeker of the Eternal Feminine. So women take their traditional virtues and 'throw them off the steamship of modern life', to a nostalgic chorus of idle men . . .[66]

Some women do still try to retain their femininity in their private lives, but this seems to do little to endear them to men.

> (H)ere is the paradox: those who, one might think, should be most highly valued by men find life harder than anyone else. They experience the bitterest family tragedies. Men who have become

rather adept in relations with the more 'modern' woman (and, it cannot be denied, have been burned by such women more than once) abuse their devotion, their gentleness and their constant willingness to help.[67]

That the urge to resurrect traditional femininity poses a threat to women's careers has been mentioned by a number of Soviet women writers. Kuznetsova's alarm, which we noted earlier, is echoed in an article by Ninel' Maslova and El'vira Novikova. After reminding readers of Lenin's conviction than neither democracy nor socialism could succeed until women were freed from the kitchen and drawn into productive work, they ask, 'is it not strange to hear now, in the course of some polemic or other, the judgement that it is necessary for women to 'return home', in order to strengthen the family and become feminine again?' Work outside the home is essential for women, not only from an economic point of view, but also as a means of self-realization and spiritual development. It is also beneficial, rather than harmful, to the family; without such experience of the world, women will not be able to bring up their children properly. Maslova and Novikova call for an end to the present outdated image of femininity, and its replacement with one which is more suited to the reality of the times.[68]

All the same, Maslova and Novikova also favour the possibility of women working part-time, and suggest that more of them would choose to do so if managers were not so inflexible and obstructive.[69] This rejection of strongly differentiated sex roles on the one hand, and support of part-time work for women on the other, appears quite frequently in the more recent Soviet literature. The seeming contradiction is probably the result of a realistic appraisal of the situation in the Soviet Union of the present day. Whether they like it or not, the sexual division of labour is not about to end; it is, then, understandable that for many women, the immediate task is to ensure that a lesser share of this labour falls on their shoulders than is presently the case.

However, as was the case with Ryurikov's embrace of the 'biarchy' theory (discussed in Chapter 6), it sometimes seems that the contradiction might stem from an attempt to present a traditional view of sex roles under the guise of a commitment to women's equality. An interview with legal expert Tamara Abova, which appeared in the journal *Sovetskaya Zhenshchina*, is a good example.[70] The interviewer talks of the problems women have in trying to combine their family duties with work outside the home, and asks for Abova's opinion on the solution which the press and various government bodies now frequently put forward – that women should choose between the two. Abova responds with a vehement rejection of the idea that women should give their all to the family. The question should not be whether it is best to free women totally or partially from social production so that she can give more attention to the family, but why the family is seen as an exclusively female concern. 'Why should the upbringing of children fall primarily to women?', she asks. 'Two people take part in love, and their duty towards the children should be the same.' She also attacks the idea that the kitchen is primarily a women's place, and criticizes the media for cultivating this idea by aiming advertisements and information about household products solely at women. However, during the course of the interview she contrives a complete about-turn. By the end, it transpires that the extent of women's past involvement in professional activities was a great mistake because it resulted in the current high rate of divorce. The solution is, after all, to increase the availability of part-time work for women, and to have them choose between career and family. Hence while Abova begins by opposing the resurrection of traditional sex roles, it turns out that she ultimately supports them. She does suggest that women who stay at home with their children should receive a salary and a pension as if they were still working, but this is still hardly consistent with her earlier statement, that the family should be the equal responsibility of both men and women.

However, articles can be found which are more consistent in promoting domestic equality and, accordingly, in opposing the spread of part-time work for women. One writer points out that while women's difficulties in combining family and work are continually discussed, men are not yet called on to combine anything.[71] Another wonders why 'any work the man performs in the home, in the service of all members of the family(including himself), has the status of "helping his wife" . . .'.[72] I. Zhuravskaya goes still further and asks, 'Why is it usually the mother who stays home with a sick child? And why is the 18 month post-natal leave only for women, and the father is not able to take it?'[73] In neighouring Bulgaria, recent legal changes have made it possible for men to apply for paternity leave. *Rabotnitsa* journalist Dalina Akivis went to investigate, and found that for those few fathers who try it, it is generally a very positive experience. They no longer see family life as if through the window of a passing train, and are able to develop tender and intimate relations with their children. They also discover that the 'special bond' which a mother supposedly has with her children is not something given by nature, but can be developed with a parent of either sex through continual contact with the child. Although few Bulgarian families are choosing to reverse traditional sex roles, Akivis implies that the mere possibility of doing so has begun to change social attitudes about men's role in the family. She suggests that sharing post-natal leave between mother and father may eventually become the norm.[74]

CONCLUDING REMARKS

We have seen during the course of this chapter how the general press, in the late 1970s, took on many of the issues which had begun to interest pedagogical writers a decade earlier. We have suggested that this was a response to the demographic crisis, and marked the start of a propaganda campaign to encourage a pro-natal and pro-family stance for women. This view is supported by E. Cherenakhova, who notes that society only stopped applauding women's professional achievements when 'it was revealed that we have steadily become fewer – that the family with few children has become typical in Russia, the Baltic republics, the Ukraine, and Byelorussia'.[75]

As the main ideological weapon of the Party, the press was an obvious vehicle through which to implement such resocialization. At times it has even come close to acknowledging that it has a definite role to play in tilting the balance of professional and family responsibilities in women's lives. For example, *Komsomol'skaya Pravda* preceded an article on strengthening the family with a quotation from a Komsomol Central Committee report which outlined the role of the press in the campaign against the demographic crisis:

> It is necessary to form a responsible attitude towards marriage, towards the upbringing of children, towards propagandizing more widely the ideals of fatherhood and motherhood, to inculcate in young people the habits of housework and looking after children...[76]

Pedagogical theorists concerned with strengthening the family have acknowledged the support the press can give them. L. S. Lomize, for example, has praised Lithuania for the series of articles on family themes which have appeared in its journals.[77]

In the late 1970s and early 1980s there was a definite preponderance of pro-family, pro-natal articles. However, there was never a complete consensus of views. This is increasingly the case. The articles promoting traditional male and female personality types, and the roles which reflect them, are now frequently challenged by others calling for more balanced sex roles. Indeed, a veritable battle is being fought in the pages of the press.

Yet many of the writers who are staunch defenders of women's participation in social production, such as Maslova and Novikova, still support the idea of more part-time work for women. The desire to ease their current double-burden has made many women receptive to a reduced participation in the work-force. Shifting the balance in women's lives in favour of the family may ultimately be achieved with the support of women themselves.

9 The Practical Application of Soviet Ideas on Sex Differences

We mentioned in the introduction that efforts have been made to tackle the demographic crisis on a practical as well as an ideological level. Yet improvements in material conditions do not automatically increase the birth-rate; indeed, Soviet demographers have shown that they can have the opposite effect.[1] They have, accordingly, argued that it is also necessary to convince people that they want more children – to form in them, as one writer put it, 'a thirst for fatherhood and motherhood'.[2]

The combined forces of schools, the mass media, adult education, family consultation centres, and even the Soviet version of Lonely Hearts columns, have been harnessed to this end. Family specialist Arkadii Egides describes them each as essential links in a whole system of psychological help for the family, with different links directed at different stages in a family's experience. The formation of a new family is the first stage, and help here includes preparing young people for family life, making sure that they have the correct family attitudes, and ensuring that they are able to find partners. The second stage is concerned with the consolidation of the family, and psychological help here is directed at helping families in trouble. The third stage – which should, of course, be avoided – is divorce. Psychological help is currently at its weakest in this stage, but should consist of psychologists and pedagogical experts attending court and deciding in consort with lawyers matters such as child custody.[3]

The various links in Egides's 'total system' which already exist were brought into being in the wake of concern about the demographic crisis; and, as we shall see, they involve a considerable amount of sex-role socialization. They could be described as a practical application of the writings on sex differences which we looked at in the previous chapters.

THE SCHOOL COURSE: 'THE ETHICS AND PSYCHOLOGY OF FAMILY LIFE'

We have already seen that the variety of opinions about sex roles which is now expressed in the general press is not to be found in the pedagogical literature. A more traditional approach to the subject is still prevalent there. It is no surprise to find that this has also entered into the school course on 'The Ethics and Psychology of Family Life'. The attitude can be summed up by educational researcher G. Belskaya's response to a husband's complaint in *Literaturnaya Gazeta*, about his wife's poor domestic orientation. 'I am a man', he points out, 'and my family responsibility is to work, not to potter about the kitchen and laundry room when I have a perfectly healthy wife . . .'

Belskaya evidently feels that he has a valid point, and explains that his problem derives at least partly from the Soviet education system: 'Our schools are to be praised for their success in bringing up girls to be good citizens, but it is time we paid more attention to making them more feminine and housewifely, more kindly, neat and gentle.'[4]

The introduction of the school course was no spontaneous move. For several years beforehand the aims and objectives of such a course were discussed in education journals and in the popular press. Since poor preparation for family life was seen as one of the main reasons for family tension and divorce, its functions would include the provision of a more thorough domestic training, an awareness of the kind of relationship which should exist between marriage partners, and a correct understanding of sex-roles, masculinity and femininity, and family morality.[5] It has been described as a distinct departure from the normal school curriculum; it is concerned not with education but with upbringing, not with the communication of knowledge but with the formation of moral qualities appropriate to future marriage partners.[6]

The course officially began in the academic year beginning in September 1984, although it was given a trial run in certain schools in the Russian and Baltic republics for up to five years before this. It takes place in the ninth and tenth grades, for two hours per week. Although it is said to run nation-wide, there is never any mention of its progress beyond the confines of the European republics. This is not surprising, since one of its professed aims is to boost the birth-rate where it is flagging, and it is not flagging outside of Europe. On a recent visit to Central Asia I found no one who had even heard of the course. Admittedly, I was not able to ask any secondary-school teachers; but in the European republics there is so much propaganda about the course that it would be hard to remain oblivious to its existence. In any case, presumably it would not apply to many Central Asian girls, especially in the rural areas, since a large number of them leave school before the 9th grade.[7]

A number of preparatory studies were conducted to determine boys and girls' attitudes to sex roles and the family before the course began. T. I. Yufereva, for example, analysed the essays of 265 children in the 6th and 9th grades of various Moscow schools on the subject 'How I see the men and women of today'. She was disappointed with the results. The children's ideas about the ideal qualities of men and women turned out to have more to do with comradeship than with male and female differences. Some of the children, not understanding the purpose of the study, even wrote about 'people' of unspecified sex, suggesting that they saw the role of men and women in Soviet society as broadly identical. Hence 'the ideal [masculinity and femininity] does not fulfil its regulatory function in the capacity of a model of behaviour'.[8] This is interesting, since it suggests that there is a clash between the new ideology, which is based on the separation of male and female roles and personality traits, and an operational ideology which assumes at least a theoretical equality and comradeship between the sexes.

The course is intended to solve this problem. As Yufereva explains,

> Up to now, school-children's ideas about the psychological differences of men and women have been formed by chance. With the introduction of the new school subject, teachers will be directed towards the upbringing of children according to the laws of personality development connected with their sex.[9]

This suggests that the course is, at least in part, a programme of overt sex-role socialization. This is reinforced by psychologist Tat'yana Snegireva's remark, that it will help children 'become aware of themselves and their special male and female roles'.[10]

THE COURSE OUTLINE

A recommended course outline has been designed by members of the Academy of Pedagogical Sciences and approved by the Ministry of Education.[11] This states that teachers should begin by impressing on children the importance of the family and the state's concern for it. They should make children aware that the family is the basic cell of socialist society, and has been 'taken under the protection of the State' (a reference to Article 53 of the 1977 Constitution). The laws and benefits concerning the family are then enumerated; the period of paid maternity leave, the moves to establish a shorter working day for mothers with small children, recent improvements in pre-school institutions and extended-day school facilities, domestic services, and the privileges and allowances granted to large families.

Next comes a series of lessons on 'the Personality, Society and the Family'. This is divided into three sub-sections: 'the personality and self-upbringing', 'the personality, work-collective and society', and 'the personality and the family'. The teacher begins by explaining that one of the basic aims of socialist society is the all-sided and harmonious development of the personality of each person. Pupils are told that Marxism sees personality as a social phenomenon, formed and transformed through interaction with society. However, they then learn that there are certain innate features in male and female personality.

This leads on to the most overt sex role socialization in the course, under the heading 'the moral basis of the mutual relations between boys and girls'. A week before the class, pupils are set the task of writing about their understanding of masculinity and femininity. They are asked to list the qualities they most value in men and women, which they would most like their future partners to possess. These essays provide a starting point for a lesson on the desired content of masculinity and femininity.

'The modern boy', pupils learn, has 'an understanding of masculinity, and of the duty to protect and preserve the virtue and honour of the girl.'[12] He should be honest, responsible, intelligent, brave, decisive, noble; he should possess self-control, a love of work, a readiness to defend the weak and take on himself the most difficult and demanding jobs. This is true in the domestic as well as the work situation, so 'helping' his wife with the housework – at least, certain types of housework – is not incompatible with his masculine pride. It is suggested that teachers read aloud in class some of the letters which appear in the popular press on women's perceptions of masculinity, such as, 'An intelligent man might not be a knight, but he understands that he must offer his seat to a woman. He might not be able to prepare a tasty meal, but he understands that he must help with the housework.'[13]

The appraisal of the 'modern girl' begins with an outline of the role of women in the family and society, and about the qualities which women should possess in order to manage this difficult combination. (No mention is made in the course outline of a combination of male roles, even if men are now expected to help more with the housework.) The changing status of women throughout history is analysed; the early matriarchal cultures, the male acquisition of power, the contradictions of the Renaissance period (when men idolized women and fought duels for them, but treated them as slaves and playthings), capitalism with its double oppression by husbands and employers, and finally the achievement of equality under socialism. This is contrasted with women's continuing oppression in the capitalist countries.

It is then explained to pupils that the achievement of equality has introduced a new problem. 'The new male and female roles in the family and society have entered into contradiction with traditional ideas about the kind of qualities men and women should possess.'[14] In shedding their dependence and subordination, women have sometimes also shed their femininity – their kindness, concern for others, softness, tenderness, thoughtfulness, and their willingness to give in. Men, on the other hand, have lost their former role of bread-winner, and sometimes, along with it, their masculinity. This has resulted in their becoming indecisive and weak of character. This collapse of traditional roles is a disaster for society, and must be reversed. This can be done without sacrificing women's equality with men since it is now known that 'equality does not mean identity'. Again, teachers are told to draw on letters in the popular press to illustrate the qualities essential in women. A debate in *Komsomol'skaya Pravda*, for example, established that 'the modern woman' should be kind, affable, able to understand other people, tender, sincere, natural, trusting, modest, sensitive, loyal, intelligent: she should possess a high level of morality, the ability to love, and the ability to be a housekeeper. She should also understand the value of 'maidenly honour' and 'female virtue'.[15]

The first year of the course ends with a discussion on 'Marriage and The Family'. This covers 'what being prepared for marriage means', 'the Soviet family and its functions', and 'special features of the young family'. Children are guided step by step through courtship and marriage, and are presented with a single model of family happiness. Apparently the opening line of *Anna Karenina* has been taken to heart: 'All happy families resemble one another . . .'. Teachers are advised to make pupils aware that a one-child family is not a real collective, and will result in over-anxious parents and egoistic children.[16]

In the tenth grade, the focus of the course shifts to the family's relationship with the external world. It begins with 'the Basic Values of the Family'. This looks at the family's ideological values, moral functions, its role as a collective, its promotion of an appropriate work ethic, its budget and economy, its domestic organization, and the social consequences of a breach in family relations. Pupils are taught that not only their future happiness, but also their physical health rests on their successful creation of a family; married people live longer than single people, and are less often ill.[17]

The course ends with a detailed discussion about children – society's concern for children, the family's role in their upbringing, its relationship to other upbringing institutions, and the different roles of mothers and fathers. Again, the benefits mothers and children have achieved under socialism are enumerated, and the new measures which have been introduced to help women combine their two roles (in other words, to have more children). Motherhood is eulogized. It is the highest social values, the woman's great mission.[18]

A television series of the same name, consisting of eight monthly programmes, was planned to supplement the school course. Bestuzhev-Lada described its main aims as encouraging more interest in the school course, and breaking down a possible barrier of hostility towards what teenagers could perceive as adult 'interference' in their lives. The programmes were to include interviews with parents and children, as well as snippets from feature films and documentaries.[19]

One term after the introduction of the course, the education journal *Vospitanie Shkol'nikov*, which had previously serialized the textbook, began another series of articles which offered further advice to teachers from experts. However, these articles add little new, and for the most part present a homogeneous view about the correctness of developing polarized sex roles in pupils.

Many of these articles discuss the correct distribution of family chores. These are often assumed to be exclusively the women's lot. L. Kovalenko, for example, talks at length about the girl's future roles as wife, mother and housekeeper, and only later concedes that she may also have a life outside the home.[20] I. Ovchinnikova relates an argument she overheard on a bus between a young married couple, in which the woman complained to her husband that he continually dirtied the kitchen floor with his boots, and he retorted that she always sent him out wearing crumpled shirts. Ovchinnikova does not comment on this assumption that floor-cleaning and shirt-ironing are the inevitable task of women, only on the pettiness of many family squabbles.[21]

'Who is now the head of the family?' is another favourite topic. According to questionnaire responses, we are told, even women think men should be, but they are forced to take on the role themselves because their husbands shirk responsibility. This is a disaster for marital relations because, as A. Kotlyar explains, 'a woman can only love a man who is stronger than her . . .'.[22]

In the midst of such opinions, it is strange to come across an article by Kuznetsova in this series. Inevitably she offers a rather different viewpoint. She advises teachers that work outside the home is no less essential for women than men, and that domestic work should also be equally divided between the sexes. Helping their parents with housework is the first work experience children have, and if boys are denied this it will be harder to develop in them an orientation towards any kind of work.[23] It is difficult to see how teachers could possibly combine this advice with that which has gone before it.

In conclusion, the course could be said to tackle the 'demographic crisis' simultaneously from two directions. On the one hand, it seeks to strengthen marriage and the family by changing people's attitudes to it. This involves the inculcation of a greater awareness of what conjugal life entails, the understanding that marriage is not just a private matter but has great social significance, and a stronger moral approach to sex, placing it firmly within the confines of marriage. It also publicizes recent changes in government policy on the family, including the extension of maternity leave and the introduction of part-time work for women. These are presented as positive moves for women, allowing them to spend more time on family matters.

At the same time, the course aims to re-socialize male and female personalities into traditional patterns of masculinity and femininity, which will fit better into family life. Pupils are told that equality between the sexes was misinterpreted in the past, and this led to the demise of essential male and female qualities. Now that the mistake has been rectified, masculinity and femininity can be reinstated in their rightful place in Soviet society. Girls are taught that a feminine women places her family and home in the forefront of her interests, and subordinates her professional interests to them. They are assured that women have an innate need to nurture, supposedly in the hope that this will encourage their own desire for maternity and the establishment of a cosy nest. Their rediscovered tenderness and ability to provide emotional support will rekindle men's masculinity, with the result that their future husbands will be more inclined to do things with and for their families. The desired result should be fewer divorces, more babies, and a stable environment in which to rear them.

There are mixed opinions about whether the course will achieve this result. Some teachers give the course an enthusiastic appraisal, and report keen interest on the part of their pupils.[24] However, others are less optimistic. The most common complaints are that teachers are inadequately prepared, and that there is a shortage of appropriate material for them to use on the course. The attention of pupils is said to be difficult to hold, partly because the course does not lead to an examination, but also because the idea of starting a family often seems remote from their present lives. This is especially the case with boys.[25] A teacher from Leningrad reported in *Vospitanie Shkol'nikov* that some of her pupils dismissed the course as 'utter boredom' and used the time to get on with other things.[26] Her experience does not seem uncommon.[27]

The basic approach of the course is also under some dispute. Egides argues that it will achieve nothing as long as it limits itself to teaching pupils a set of slogans along the lines of 'the family is the basic cell of society'. Instead it should concentrate on frank and serious discussion of issues which have real relevance to adolescent boys and girls and their relationships with each other. Not least of these is the subject of sexual relations, which the course currently ignores. Such discussions will result in the pupil's assimilation of basic ethical positions which will later be reflected in their own family lives. They will also gain a solid understanding of the institutions which now exist to guide ailing families through their problems, and willingness to turn to these whenever they themselves need help.[28]

The lifestyles of the teachers themselves have also come under attack. One prominent pedagogical theorist, L. S. Lomize, points with alarm at certain sociological studies which indicate that teachers have a particularly weak family orientation, and that this can have an adverse influence on their pupils. According to these studies, more teachers remain single than people in other professions, and those who do marry generally do so later than usual. They have a higher divorce rate, and a lower birth-rate than the population as a whole – most have only one child, and many remain childless. Lomize concludes that 'the personal marriage and familial orientation of the teacher clashes with the content of "the Ethics and Psychology of Family Life" course', and that students in pedagogical institutions need help themselves in developing a correct family orientation.[29] College rectors and the Komsomol committee should also work at encouraging student teachers to begin families. It these suggestions were adopted, it would be interesting to see if the teaching profession's current recruitment problems become still worse.

FAMILY CONSULTATION CENTRES

The first family consultation service was set up in Leningrad in 1970.[30] Similar organizations have now spread throughout Russia and the Baltic republics, i.e. those republics with a particularly low birth-rate. Like the school course, they tackle the problem from two directions. On the one hand, they give help to existing families which are under threat. On the other, they offer preventative treatment for future families by preparing them better for the duties and disillusionments of family life.

Concern about strengthening the family is evidently not the same thing as promoting the differences in male and female roles and personalities. The one need not necessarily include the other. Yet in the Soviet Union there is, in fact, considerable overlap between them. In other words, the organizations which have been set up to strengthen and encourage a family orientation in the European republics of the Soviet Union do carry out a considerable amount of sex role socialization in the adult population, just as the school course does amongst teenagers.

Cheslovas Grizitskas, head of the Latvian family consultation service, makes this clear when he argues that however useful these services are, they are essentially only a back-up to the school course because the school period is the best time to teach people about sex differences.[31] As we shall see, his own consultations promote the same ideology as that inherent in the school course. This is that men and women have innate psychological differences based on their different roles in reproduction, and that these form the basis of successful marriage.

The socializing function of family consultation services is also indicated by a particularly effusive report in *Pravda* on a centre in Shakhty, a town in the Rostov region of Russia. The writer, M. Bednyi, sees the main success of this centre as the creation of a new, pro-natal 'psychological climate' in the town:

> Hundreds of families which were on the verge of collapse have been saved, and thousands of newly-weds, as well as those about to get

married, have been given qualified advice on marital hygiene, [i.e. sex], health care, etc. But most important is the change in the psychological climate, in the mood of those who must actively participate in the strengthening of the family. A new psychological climate has become firmly established, directed at the strengthening of the conjugal bonds and the creation of a full-blooded, healthy family with two or three children.[32]

The services are run by a variety of organizations. Some are organized by City Soviet Executive Committees. The Moscow Soviet set up a network of Departments of the Family and Marriage in 1980. Each of the 32 boroughs of the city now has one, with a combined staff of 450 people.[33]

Others come under the public health sector. The Lithuanian family consultation services began in 1974 as 'departments of psycho-hygiene and family relations', attached to polyclinics throughout the republic.[34] The driving force behind the Latvian services, Cheslovas Grizitskas, is the head of neuropathology at the ministry of health care. Grizitskas explains the link between family services and the health sector by pointing out that if marriage is not harmonious it can be highly unhealthy. 'Insomnia, severe head-aches, sexual incompatibility, and sometimes more serious nervous conditions can result from family conflicts.' He even produces a 'scientific term' for the phenomenon – 'the neurosis of marriage'.[35] Others echo the argument put forward in the magazine *Zdorov'e*, that a person can damage his or her health merely by remaining single. Marriage and parenthood are seen as a medicine for poor health. As Bednyi puts it,

> the source of the 'ill health' of many men and women is frequently the conditions which they have chosen for themselves in their intimate, marital and family relations. Studies show, for example, that widowers and bachelors lead a less healthy way of life than their peers who have families. This in itself can lead to nervous and psychological disorders, to illness in general, and to alcohol abuse. Here our public health agencies must, in our opinion, more intently monitor and form correct opinions about the most medically advisable relations between the sexes, and views on marriage and the family.[36]

The family consultation centres are very broad-based, employing a range of specialists; lawyers, psychiatrists, psychologists, sexologists.

One Estonian centre even includes cosmetologists,[37] which is presumably aimed at helping women rescue their marriages by paying more attention to their personal appearance. As we have noted, the centres offer both an education service aimed at preventing marital breakdown by ensuring young couples are better prepared for married life, and advice and help to families undergoing crisis. Some of them also conduct research into the causes of family tension and disintegration.

The educational aspect of the service is similar to that of the school course. According to a report on the Leningrad services, young couples are invited to attend two three-hour lectures on family matters a month or two before they marry. The first lecture, given by a psychologist, is on the psychology of family relations. This includes the different roles of the partners in the family, the nature of love, relations with the two sets of parents, how to plan the family budget, and problems which may arise in the couple's relationship. The second, by a sexologist, is on 'sex hygiene', the Soviet euphemism for sex education, and is attended separately by the man and the woman.[38] Attendance is usually voluntary, but in Lithuania couples applying to get married are required by law to have a consultation with a doctor, and to attend a lecture series on psychological adjustment to marriage.[39] However, this system is not immune from corruption. Egides describes the 'gentleman's agreement' which sometimes takes place between the psychologist and the couple – 'We give you five roubles and you give us the certificate that says we've done what we need to . . .'. Himself a lecturer on some of these courses, he recounts turning up to one class and finding only ten students in attendance, although 150 tickets had been distributed through the marriage registration offices.[40]

Counselling sessions for families with problems also contain a fair amount of education on male and female differences in personalities and family roles. The work of Grizitskas is reported widely in the press. He describes in *Komsomol'skaya Pravda* how he rescued a marriage on the verge of collapse by encouraging the husband to be more attentive to his wife's feminine needs. He explained to the wife that her husband neglected her because he had been badly prepared for marriage, and that she should be patient for a while longer; in the meantime, he instructed the husband to ply her with flowers. He now brings her carnations every Wednesday, and relations between the couple have been transformed.[41] Grizitskas admits that not all floundering marriages are so easily rescued, but he feels that the philosophy behind this treatment is universally valid. This is that divorce is the result of men and women's inability to understand the mentality of the other sex.

> We talk a lot these days about the equality of men and women. They are equal in work, in study, in social life, and in marriage. But one ineradicable inequality exists – the bio-psychological. Each sex has its psychological peculiarities. The man is physically stronger, but the woman endures pain more stoically . . . . The woman loves flowers, and cannot understand why her educated husband lounges in front of the television watching hockey. When the young wife is expecting a child, she is especially touchy, quick-tempered and easily hurt . . .[42]

The sex differences which Grizitskas teaches his clients are a mixed bag of common sense, scientific fact and myth. Yet he implies that each of them is rooted in nature.

All the same, Grizitskas does not think that domestic matters should be an entirely female concern. Like the designers of the school course, he insists that men should take on a larger share than they have done in the past. This is especially the case with child-care. However, the role Grizitskas assigns to men has distinctly patriarchal overtones. The father 'brings up his successor, the heir of his ideas . . .'.[43] Child-care and housework do not come naturally to men, so their wives need to show tolerance: 'The woman must not forget that the man does not immediately get used to the family and to its duties. The wife must prepare him tactfully and gradually for the role of young partner.'[44]

Similar ideas inform the family consultations run by Aleksandr Poleev. He explains to *Rabotnitsa* readers that: 'The psychological climate in the family is mainly a female matter, for which nature provides you with intuition, the ability to understand and empathise with another person, and deep emotionality.'[45] One of his clients was upset at the lack of attention her husband showed to their new-born baby, but he assured her that a man should not be expected to 'act like a mother' and shower the baby with tender caresses. The role of a father is to provide for his family, 'to manifest love for his children not so much emotionally as practically . . .'.[46] Poleev goes on to offer a series of questions which women should ask themselves in order to find out how good their psychological rapport with their husbands is. Do they, for example, know how to cheer their husbands up if they come home from work tired and irritable? Or what to say to restore familial harmony after a row? Do they know what words to use to persuade their husbands to tackle some essential but not particularly pleasant job that needs doing at home? Most astounding of all, 'Can you tell from the way your husband dresses in the morning and ties his tie whether he has a difficult day ahead of him or just an ordinary one?'[47] Poleev's image of an average Soviet woman's life is at complete odds with reality. Far from having a full programme of her own to worry about, she seems to have nothing to do with her day apart from guess at, and minister to, her husband's needs.

Family Consultation Services also deal with such problems as confusion about who is the head of the family, jealousy, problems with in-laws, and disillusionment following the over-idealization of a partner before marriage.[48] In general, the treatment consists of trying to persuade clients that these are not sufficient reasons for divorce. This is particularly clear in an article by Natal'ya Dar'yalova in *Literaturnaya Gazeta*. Again, the example she offers comes from the case-book of Grizitskas. A client complains that her husband habitually comes home from work, feeds himself and their two children, and then leaves her with the washing up. Dar'yalova is surprised that she is so upset about what he fails to do rather than grateful for what he does, and it turns out that the dirty pans are not the real reason for her discontent. The fact is that they have stopped communicating. The treatment consists of convincing the woman that this lack of spiritual affinity is not so important, and that it only seems so in times of relative prosperity, when material difficulties are no longer the main concern.[49] Women should not expect so much from their husbands, and be less hasty in resorting to divorce. 'Of course, there are simple cases of heavy drunkenness, betrayal and cruelty', Dar'yalova concedes. 'But all the same, don't hurry to take the final step . . .'[50]

Unlike the marriage guidance councils of the West, whose name belies the fact that they have opened their doors to unmarried cohabiting couples, Soviet family consultation services are concerned only with married couples, or those about to marry. Family consultant I. V. Dorno makes the attitude towards unmarried couples clear in an article in *Zdorov'e*. They defend their relationships on the grounds that 'trial marriages' are fashionable in the West, and help determine whether the partners are compatible before they commit themselves. Yet in the United States trial marriages are very common, and the incidence of divorce has not decreased. Sexual and psychological compatibility need time to develop, Dorno explains, and so a brief trial marriage determines nothing. It can, on the other hand, destroy a potentially good relationship by judging it too soon.[51]

In addition to the usual family consultation services, Moscow has an additional Consultation Centre of Psychological Help for the Family. Set up in 1980, it is run jointly by the Faculty of Psychology at Moscow State University and the APN's research institute of general and pedagogical psychology, under the leadership of psychologists V. Stolin and A. A. Bodalev. It does both theoretical and practical work, conducting research into family problems and using psychotherapy to treat families in trouble.

It claims to have a somewhat different approach to family problems. It focuses on the psychology of family members rather than the social factors involved in marriage breakdown, and uses 'the theory of personality and interpersonal relations' to help individuals solve their own problems.[52] However, Stolin's description of particular issues dealt with by the centre suggest that it is still primarily concerned with clients' ideas about male and female roles and personality differences.

One of its main concerns is the stress people experience because of the contradictions they are forced to deal with in their lives. One example is the chasm between the ideas men and women have about the opposite sex, and the way in which they bring up their own sons and daughters. Letters to the press reveal that most men think that women should be brought up to have a particular awareness of the value of the family and of the predestination of their roles as mothers. However, they continue to encourage their own daughters to go on to higher education. Similarly, women have an ideal of their husbands as brave, strong and decisive, but they suppress initiative and leadership qualities in their own sons and encourage above all obedience. (This suggests a conflict, as we have noted before, between an 'official' ideology about sex differences and roles, and an operational ideology which most people live their lives by, even if they agree in principle with the official view.) Vital psychological energy is wasted in dealing with these contradictions. The implicit suggestion is that family psychotherapy aims to help mothers and fathers match their upbringing methods with the ideals of masculinity and femininity, so bringing their daughters up to be maternal and family-orientated and their sons to be strong and decisive.[53]

A second contradiction is unique to women. This arises when they seek to divide themselves equally between their work and their families. This places them in 'the worst psychological position'. Not only are they torn between their two lives, but they also suffer perpetual guilt because they feel they succeed in neither. Once again, the solution is to encourage women to prioritize either work or family – and as usual, there seems to be pressure on them to choose the latter. Stolin explains:

> If a woman has decided to achieve perfection in professional life, where does she draw the line below which she must not go in her role as house-keeper? .... We are talking about the family, and we must not forget that there are at least two people involved .... Rarely is the question asked, 'What choice did your partner make, and does your choice accord with his?'[54]

There is also a miscellany of other projects to strengthen the family and promote appropriate relations between its members. A network of 'Peoples' Universities' has been organized throughout Russia and the Baltic republics, offering lectures on family-related topics. Lithuania claims to have more than 100 of these, providing some 56 000 people with lectures, seminars, discussions and outings.[55] In the Latvian capital, Riga, such lectures are offered to young people at their workplaces.[56] The Moscow state organization of domestic service, 'Zarya', has also voiced a plan to offer courses 'for the young housewife'.[57]

Some institutions of higher education have followed the example of schools and started their own family life classes. An article in *Pravda* describes their efforts as particularly useful, since the period between the ages of 16 and 23 is critical. It is a time of rapid physical and mental maturation and considerable geographical mobility, which results in a weakening of family ties and parental control; but a timely intervention on the part of the college authorities can prevent a collapse in family orientation. Moscow's Institute of the Petrochemical and Gas Industry has set a glowing example. It holds regular courses on subjects such as interpersonal and family relations, nutrition, clothing and children's upbringing, and in 1983 it also started a club for young families. This meets twice monthly, when members are given lectures and practical advice by qualified specialists on family issues. The club also holds name-giving ceremonies for its members' infants, an attempt to inject some celebration and festivity into the family in the form of a secular alternative to baptism.[58]

It has also been suggested that an annual 'Holiday of the Soviet Family' be held throughout the country. Kropotkin, in Russia's Krasnodar region, already has such an event every September, which has come to the enthusiastic attention of family specialists. There is a carnival procession and athletic events, the most exemplary families in the town are honoured, marriages and births are registered, and a party is held at the Palace of Culture.[59] A similar event takes place in the small town of Kraslava, but with a stronger educational content. Young married couples don their wedding outfits each year to attend a summer party, where they receive advice on family matters from various experts and from elderly couples celebrating their silver wedding anniversaries.[60]

Yet this is still not enough. It has been argued in *Sem'ya i Shkola* that a family bureau is needed in each and every block of flats if it is to have sufficient influence, and that there should also be a voluntary system of 'social tutors', especially for one-parent families. The 'tutor', a person of exceptional personal and civic merit, would visit the family twice a week and become familiar with its personal regime, financial affairs and children's educational progress in order to help solve any problems and ensure that its upbringing function is carried out successfully.[61] Dar'yalova proposes compulsory classes for all intending couples, with diplomas awarded to successful graduates. The couples should pay for this themselves, since the cost would be less than that of divorce.[62]

Bednyi makes a particularly interesting suggestion. He complains that the family consultation services are not standardized, and hence their success-rate varies enormously from region to region. Sometimes their very existence depends on local enthusiasm. This problem would be solved if local authorities were held responsible for the demographic development of their town or area, in the same way as they are expected to ensure the fulfilment of production targets.[63] In other words, pressure would be put on local citizens to meet the requirements of the Party Plan in reproduction as well as production.

'GET-ACQUAINTED' SERVICES

'Get acquainted services' are also part of the network of agencies concerned with strengthening the family. The possibility of providing some such service to Soviet citizens was first raised in the press in 1970, when A. Rubinov reported the experience of one such organization in the GDR in *Literaturnaya Gazeta*.[64] However, it took Soviet officialdom some six years to warm to the idea.[65] It seems probable that concern about the demographic crisis prompted the change of heart. As Yu. Ryurikov puts it, the failure of millions of people to find partners is 'more than a personal tragedy: it is a social and demographic tragedy, in that there are millions of children and future workers that will never be born'.[66] This is echoed by Rubinov, who points out that the establishment of get-acquainted services will lead not just to 'the personal happiness of many millions of people', but also to 'the resolution of the difficult demographic situation, which is becoming more serious every year'.[67] Egides also argues that such services should be focused not on those who have failed to find partners, but on young people just beginning to look, since 'we need to help people create families while they are at a good child-bearing age'.[68]

Again, there are different policies for the European republics and the Caucasus and Central Asia. Family specialist A. Spirkin points out that get-acquainted services are only necessary in Russia, the Ukraine, Byelorussia and the Baltic republics (i.e. the republics suffering from the demographic crisis) since: 'In the Central Asian republics, and in Georgia, Armenia, and Azerbaijan, family problems are not acute, so they do not need such a special service yet.'[69]

The establishment of get-acquainted services has received the avid attention of the press. *Literaturnaya Gazeta* and *Rabotnitsa* have shown particular interest, discussing the organization of the various services now on offer, their pitfalls and successes, and the reasons for their need in the first place.[70] Advertisements for partners have generally been confined to the local press, but in January 1988 a column appeared for the first time in the journal *Zdorov'e*, again linking health with marital status.

Since they lack an educational dimension, get-acquainted services are not obvious forms of sex role socialization. However, the discussions in the press frequently suggest that women's excessive career ambitions and weak domestic orientation is behind their failure to find husbands. Letters like the following, which appeared in *Literaturnaya Gazeta*, are commonly quoted. The female author was an exemplary scholar at school and university, and had gone on to do post-graduate work. She was very successful, and received high praise from her supervisor. However, 'at the same time life was passing by. I didn't even notice how people my age were getting married, settling down and having children. Now I don't visit them – we have nothing to talk about. I don't want to bore them'.[71] Marriage and motherhood are presented, once more, as the sole path to real fulfilment for women, and professional ambitions an aberration that can destroy their personal lives. However successful they are in their careers, they cannot be happy without a husband and children. The editors of *Literaturnaya Gazeta* note that: 'The saddest letters were sent by women over 40. Some feel that life is already over, that there is nothing left to hope for, even though they are well-off – they live in good apartments and receive high salaries.'[72]

The get-acquainted services could thus be said to have more than one function. On the one hand, they help to ease the demographic crisis by providing partners to men and women who have failed to find them through the usual channels. There is also talk about how to remove the stigma attached to them which defines them as a last resort, so that people will see them as a perfectly acceptable way of finding a partner at any age. On the other hand, they provide another means of propagandizing the family, and of warning women of the tragic consequences of prioritizing their careers instead of family life.

DISCOURAGING DIVORCE THROUGH THE LEGAL SYSTEM

An excess of female emancipation is blamed not only for the problems some women have in finding husbands, but also for the lack of interest others show in keeping them. The high number of divorces in the Soviet Union (the figure usually quoted is one for every three marriages)[73] is a source of demographic as well as social concern. According to A. B. Sinelnikov, only one in three men and one in five women marry a second time.[74] This means that divorce results in an 'irrevocable loss' in terms of the number of children born.[75]

Around 70 per cent of divorces are initiated by women.[76] This is often due to the alcohol abuse of their partners. In a study conducted in Kiev by L. Chuiko, 47 per cent of women filing for divorce gave this as the reason.[77] Gorbachev, in his speech to the 27th Party Congress, made it clear that his anti-alcohol campaign was partly prompted by the effect of alcoholism on families.[78]

However, some Soviet commentators argue that women are abusing their right to easy divorce. L. S. Lomize, for example, explains that this right was established to ensure their protection from despotic men seeking to re-establish the old, pre-revolutionary domestic order. Yet many women now use it to free themselves from conjugal life, family duties, and their obligations to their partners and society.[79] Women have gone beyond the achievement of equality and have created a new system of matriarchy, under which men are the oppressed sex. As G. Naan puts it, 'the battle against patriarchy has been transformed into a battle against the husband, against everything that he does or likes'.[80]

The suggestion has been made repeatedly in the press that the law should begin to protect men and society from these 'over-emancipated' women. At present women are said to have nothing to lose if they divorce their husbands, since they keep the children, the apartment, and receive the child-benefit payments. If the law denied women this monopoly of rights, the divorce rate would decrease dramatically. As Egides sees it,

> If young mamas were not 100 per cent certain that, on leaving their husbands, they would take the child with them, the thought of the possibility of divorce would come into their heads more rarely. Not only legislation but also court practice must be so altered that the woman knows the child might not remain with her, that her chances are the same as her husband's – 50 : 50. Then divorce will represent for both of them a boundary which it is dangerous to approach.[81]

Such suggestions have triggered off a passionate debate in the pages of the press. When Leonid Zhukovitskii put the same case in *Literaturnaya Gazeta*, the editorial office was inundated with letters. Male readers generally denounced women's 'domestic despotism' and applauded Zhukovitskii's attempt to crush this new matriarchy,[82] while women claimed that most men are unfit for custody of their children. ('Give the child to its father? You might as well turn it out into the snow!')[83] An article by Irma Marmaladze was subsequently published, in which she argues that in previous epochs, separating women from their children was considered a sign of barbarism; now it is proposed in the name of 'strengthening the family'. This has nothing to do with concern for the welfare of children, she insists, but is a form of blackmail against women, an attempt to make them give up their emancipation and turn their sole attention to husband and family.[84]

Larisa Kuznetsova has made a surprising contribution to the debate, arguing that fathers should, indeed, be granted custody of their children more often. The reluctance of courts to do this is part of a wider problem about men's role in their children's lives. The shortage of men in the post-war years, and the consequent high number of fatherless families, resulted in a habit of seeing the mother not just as the main parent but as the only parent. The father's role has been negated. This perception has to change, and one way of achieving this is to begin considering fathers for custody.[85] Since Kuznetsova is generally an advocate of women's rights, it is surprising to find her supporting men in this case. Evidently she feels that if women are not to be tied to the confines of the family, they must also relinquish sole rights over it.

The courts already make an attempt to prevent divorce through the 'fixed term of application'. This is a delaying tactic, a compulsory wait of six months between the application for divorce and the court hearing. According to Nina Sergeeva, deputy chair of the Supreme Court of the RSFSR, in the Kirov district of Moscow an astonishing 60 per cent of applicants in one six-month period were reconciled before their cases came to court.[86] Lomize suggests that still more divorces would be prevented if special People's Courts were set up to deal only with matters concerning marriage and divorce, and had the right to refuse a divorce if the reasons behind it were not clear. He claims that this idea is supported by lawyers, educational theorists and psychologists.[87]

Although such discussions continue to appear in the press, it seems unlikely that they will prompt any major changes in the divorce laws or child custody practices. As a *Literaturnaya Gazeta* reader has noticed, the suggestion that men and women should have equal custody rights contradicts the notion, which is expressed with such alacrity elsewhere in the Soviet literature, that the woman has a peculiar fitness for child-care and an 'indissoluble link with the child'.[88] It is probable that its exponents are not even serious about its implementation. The idea is held aloft as a warning to women to keep within the parameters of their supposed personality traits – those sweet, gentle, compliant qualities of femininity, which should be intent on stoking the home fires rather than extinguishing them.

10 Sex Role Socialization in the USSR: Summary of the Past, and Prospects for the Future

This book has primarily been a study of Soviet views on sex differences in personality, and the social roles which supposedly reflect them. It has charted the discussion from its emergence in the 1960s up until the present day. The Soviet Union is now in a state of flux, and the opening up of public debate has entered this field as well as others. However, before we turn to the future and ask what might become of relations between the sexes in the Soviet Union, we should turn back the pages and summarize the story so far.

We have seen how from the time of the Revolution, Soviet psychologists, committed to the task of providing the theoretical basis for the creation of a 'new Soviet person', devoted considerable attention to understanding how personality develops. They came to the conclusion that this is a dialectical process involving four interacting factors – biology, the social environment, training, and self-training. People may be born with certain potentialities, but not with definite abilities. The potentialities find expression and develop into abilities during the course of social activity, i.e. through interaction with the social environment, combined with training and self-training. 'Social' and 'activity' are the key concepts. People are considered to be social beings from the moment of birth, in a constant state of interaction with the environment and creating myriad connections, or conditioned responses, to the environment. Personality is seen as extremely flexible. Biological input does not have a determining influence but can be adapted, developed or even transformed in the course of this social activity and in accordance with the conditions and demands of the environment.

The majority of Soviet psychologists whose work we have looked at are evidently aware of the Western theories of personality development. Psychoanalysis has generally had a fairly negative appraisal, accused of being overly biologistic and ignoring the role of the social environment in shaping personality. The Soviet emphasis on the social environment and on the flexibility of personality has made it much more compatible with social learning theory, while the importance accorded to self-training also links it with cognitive-developmental theory.

Unlike their Western counterparts, Soviet psychologists have generally shown little interest in applying their findings to an understanding of sex differences in personality. We attempted to do this for them. We then compared the resulting model of gender development to the writings which have actually appeared on the subject of sex differences in personality, penned by specialists from other disciplines.

We found a stark contrast between them. This is particularly the case with the pedagogical literature, despite the close link which has existed between pedagogy and psychology throughout the country's history. Some of the pedagogical writers could be said to adhere to Soviet psychology's four-factor framework of biology, the environment, training and self-training. However, the relative emphasis they place on these factors is completely different. Biology is elevated to the position of a determining influence. Innate abilities and psychological endowments are said to exist, and to create inevitable personality differences between men and women. These are generally, but not exclusively, connected with the different male and female reproductive functions. The influence of the social environment on male and female personality has been virtually ignored, seemingly on the grounds that in the Soviet Union it has treated men and women as equals and has offered them the same life chances.

On the other hand, the role of training and self-training have been maximized. It turns out that the biological endowments and abilities which mark men and women apart are essential for the smooth-running of society (despite psychology's promotion of the all-round personality), and their absence results in a series of social ills, not least of which is the population's failure to adequately reproduce itself. Although pedagogical writers claim these male and female traits are natural and inevitable, in the next breath they argue that they can be strangled at birth through incorrect upbringing. Teachers and parents are therefore urged to work on developing them, and to convince children of their essentialness so that they will actively seek to acquire them. It seems that no one has noticed the contradiction inherent in urging the active inculcation of what is supposed to be an inevitable gift of nature.

It is not surprising to find some disjunction between the Soviet psychological approach to personality and the pedagogical writings. Although the Soviet Union has claimed in the past that Marxism-Leninism offers a total *Weltanschauung*, some inconsistencies are to be expected. The appearance of popular assumptions in supposedly scientific theories is also not confined to the Soviet Union. However, what is surprising is the size of the chasm between the two. Despite the historically close link between psychology and pedagogy in the Soviet Union, the pedagogical writings on sex differences in personality contain virtually no reference to the serious psychological discussions on personality development. Instead they limit themselves to little more than a reproduction of popular assumptions about male and female differences, wrapped up in a pseudo-scientific guise.

The insistence on the natural, inevitable and vital basis of these stereotyped differences not only stands in stark contrast to the Marxist approach to personality which is inherent in Soviet psychology, but also to the reality of male and female personalities and behaviour in the Soviet Union. Women do not lead pampered, indolent lives while their menfolk battle on their behalf with the harsh conditions of economic life. Sociological studies have long drawn attention to the 'double burden' of women, whose dual responsibilities in the work-place and the family give them a work-load which is far greater than that of men. It is evident that to a large extent the pedagogical writings, while arguing that the traditional stereotypes are natural and inevitable, are actually a response to their erosion. This is evident in their insistence that teachers and parents should concentrate efforts on instilling these supposedly inevitable personality traits and behaviour patterns in children. The definition of sexual equality has accordingly been reworked so that it is not incompatible with the promotion of these stereotypes of male and female personality and behaviour. While feminists and social learning theorists in the West have used an understanding of personality development to challenge these stereotypes, Soviet pedagogical writers call for a better understanding of the process in order to more successfully develop them.

So what lies behind the promotion of a sex-role socialization which contradicts the basic tenets of Soviet psychology, the commitment to equality between the sexes, and the current reality of people's lives? We have posited a connection between Soviet writings on gender and sex roles, and the ideological climate in which they emerged. In other words, we linked them to certain political and demographic concerns such as the 'feminization' of men and the 'masculinization' of women, the instability of marriage, and the decrease in the birth-rate in the European republics. More recently, an economic factor has been added – it would appear that the hoped-for rationalization of the economy under *perestroika* is not compatible with women's full employment.

As we have seen, demographic problems were openly proclaimed to be a major concern in the Soviet Union in the middle of the 1970s. Demographers called for a multifaceted approach to the problem, using both ideological and material means to persuade women to have more children. Yet they also noted that material improvements do not automatically lead to an increase in the birth-rate; people have to be persuaded that they want more children. Accordingly, the most intensive battle against the birth-rate was introduced on the ideological front. Stressing the woman's natural urge for motherhood, showing how it forms the basis of her entire personality and affects all areas of her life, was one method of attempting to strengthen her desire to have children. Without them, she was told, she could not think of herself as a real woman. The introduction and content of the school course on 'the Ethics and Psychology of Family Life' reinforces this contention. So too does the fact that in Soviet Central Asia, where the birth-rate remains high, the importance of women's economic and political roles are still emphasized instead of the maternal.

The absence of clearly defined sex roles in the family has also been linked to such problems as alcoholism and hooliganism. We have seen how male alcoholism has been blamed by some writers on the man's loss of his former role as head of the family and the demise of his wife's femininity, and teenage delinquency on the placement of children in child-care institutions at too young an age. Possibly the demise of masculinity and femininity, and the inadequate fulfilment of family responsibilities, is seen as a handy explanation for these problems; or else the problems provide a useful reinforcement for the argument that sex differentiated roles are necessary. In any case, the extension of post-maternity leave is presented as a way of solving the problem of delinquency in the next generation of teenagers, as well as making it easier for women to have more children.

It would seem from the above that we are claiming a conspiratorial basis for the pedagogical writings on sex differences in personality – i.e., that they form part of a coherent government policy to prop up the family and boost the birth-rate. To some extent this may be the case.

However, we have also noted that pedagogical interest in sex differences predated the demographic crisis, or at least open discussion of it. Hence it is unlikely that pedagogical writers were briefed to provide theoretical support for the resurrection of traditional family values. What is more likely is that the climate of demographic concern provided a receptive and influential audience, which enabled the proliferation of these views.

ZAKHAROVA, POSADSKAYA AND RIMASHEVSKAYA: FOUR APPROACHES TO SEX ROLES

N. Zakharova, A. Posadskaya, and N. Rimashevskaya, of the Soviet Union's Institute of Socio-economic Problems, suggest that the Soviet literature on sex roles can be divided into four separate categories.[1] These are distinguished not by different ideal models of sex role differentiation (as we shall see, in three cases these are virtually identical), but by the problems they are aimed at solving.

They call the first approach 'patriarchal'. This is generally found in articles expressing concern about the moral state of the country. It rests on the conviction that society is based on certain natural laws, and that moral collapse ensues if these are disregarded. One of the primary natural laws is the difference in male and female roles. Nature intended women to be primarily mothers and upholders of the family, and men to be its providers and protectors. The micro world of the family and the macro world of society are distinct spheres, with men providing the link between them. Neglect of this natural law – i.e., women prioritizing work instead of the family – has led to a sharp decline in morals and the dissolution of family bonds, with children, old people and husbands being deprived of female concern and tenderness. The solution is to raise the status of motherhood and reduce women's participation in the work-force by granting them longer post-natal leave and the chance of working part-time. Mothers with three or more children should be freed from having to work at all. The image of the emancipated woman, which the media has mistakenly propagated, should be replaced by that of the happy family based on different but complementary male and female roles. Rules about child custody should also be changed to deter women from filing for divorce.

The second approach, the 'economic', is held mainly by specialists concerned with the rationalization of the economy. Women are seen as relatively ineffective elements of the economy, because their family demands lead to frequent interruptions in work and limit the development of their professional qualifications. Again, the solution is to reduce the level of their involvement in social production. Their removal from the work-force should begin by granting them a series of 'privileges' – shortening the working day, extending the period of paid leave, and so on.

The third approach, the 'demographic', looks at the woman question in the light of the need to ensure the reproduction of the population. Demographers have drawn attention to the fact that the reduction of the birth-rate has taken place in the most economically developed parts of the country, and fear that this will ultimately lead to depopulation unless strong measures are taken now. Since statistics show that the level of births are generally in reverse proportion to the level of activity of women in social production, the answer is, again, to reduce women's participation by extending post-natal leave, shortening the working day, and so on.

Hence these three different approaches to sex roles – the patriarchal, economic and demographic – produce the same practical proposals for solving the woman question. Measures should be introduced (and, indeed, have been) to reduce women's involvement in the economy so that they can devote themselves more to the family. The dominant theme in the current literature is that women should 'choose' between work or family. However, genuine choice is hindered by stereotypical ideas about women's natural role, and by considerable psychological pressure to choose the family.

The 'egalitarian' approach rejects this solution. It sees the division of labour between men and women as an outmoded patriarchal tradition based on inequality, which has to end. This can be done only by destroying the social conditions which created it. This does not involve the destruction of society itself, nor its moral bases. The current negative phenomena such as drug addiction, alcoholism, prostitution, the 'feminization' of men and the 'masculinization' of women, are not due to women's involvement in the work-force, but are the temporary result of the dislocation involved in the transition from one type of society to another. The old rules have already ceased to function, and the new ones are not yet firmly established. Instead of attempting to destroy more egalitarian relations between men and women before they have fully developed, they should be given more space and support. When the transition is complete, the authors argue, society will settle down once more.

THE DEVELOPMENT OF SOVIET VIEWS ON SEX ROLES, AND PROSPECTS FOR THE FUTURE

We would suggest that these categories can be reshuffled into a chronological order; that they constitute a sequence of responses to the emergence of specific social problems in Soviet society. We would also suggest that the first three categories are far from mutually exclusive. If viewed in this way, they offer a strong framework for the discussions we have developed throughout this book, as well as providing some ideas as to what may come to pass in the future.

The 'patriarchal' approach remains in first place. Indeed, patriarchal ideas have evidently survived since pre-revolutionary times, but proclamations about sexual equality in the early years of the Revolution pushed them beneath the surface of public discussion. This began to change in the 1960s. Discussions about the possibility of introducing some form of sex education in Soviet schools provided the pedagogical writers with a context within which to express such views. In addition, the post-Stalin thaw permitted open acknowledgement that the Soviet Union had not yet created an ideal socialist society, free of all social flaws. Hence attention was turned, in the words of Zakharova *et al.*, to 'the moral state of the country'. Since women's full employment was one of the most significant developments in the Soviet Union, this was bound to come under scrutiny as one of the possible causes of lingering social problems. This was particularly so for educationalists, confronted with an emerging youth culture which failed to espouse the country's official values.[2]

Patriarchal ideas were given new impetus when the demographic crisis became a subject of concern in the late 1970s. Since the pedagogical writings had indicated some of the causes and solutions of the crisis, they provided the basis for the 'demographic' approach. This, then, stands in second place. It can be seen not so much as a successor to the patriarchal approach, but as a combination of patriarchal ideology and demographic expedience. What followed was, as Strelyanyi puts it, a 'revolution' in propaganda and upbringing. At the centre was placed a romanticized image of the 'kitchen and family hearth' as the central feature of women's lives.[3]

In the beginning, this cosy image was complicated by the continued need for a strong female work-force. With *perestroika*, it is thought that this will no longer be the case. Indeed, attempts to rationalize the economy, and the looming spectre of unemployment, make full employment for women a highly unattractive prospect for economists. This has led to the 'economic' approach. As Zakharova et al. point out, *khozraschet*, or the need to be cost effective, demands a work-force which is both stable and adaptable to rapidly changing production needs. Women, with their family obligations, are seen as neither; 'the stereotype of women as unreliable is rapidly spreading throughout all areas [of the economy]'.[4] They will, then, be the first victims of *khozraschet*, followed by the young, disabled, and elderly.[5] Since they will no longer require qualifications for work, Zakharova et al. predict that their educational opportunities will also be severely contracted. The narrowing of women's horizons is, again, justified by reference to their natural family orientation, and the difficulty they have experienced in trying to combine this with full-time work. Patriarchal ideas, which had already been widely disseminated by the demographic approach, thus became equally intertwined with the economic.

The 'egalitarian approach' is far from new. We have seen how Andreeva insisted on the need for egalitarian relations between the sexes in her article in *Sem'ya i Shkola* in 1967, reminding readers that this was the model established by writers in the revolutionary period. The egalitarian model continued to appear in the 'biarchal' theory of sex roles, expressed by sociologists such as Matskovskii. Now, however, with the growing threat to women's role in the Soviet economy, combined with the current possibility of debate on the subject, it has found a more prominent voice in the Soviet literature. It is no longer confined to an occasional article dissenting from the mainstream position, but has even begun to appear in the editorial columns of journals. A clear example can be found in some of the articles which now appear in the women's press on International Women's Day. In the past, this day was an excuse for self-congratulatory proclamations about the Soviet Union's dedication to women's equality. In 1988, however, *Rabotnitsa* chose to look at the 9th rather than the 8th March. The husbands had finished their annual day of housework, the flowers were beginning to wilt, and life was back to back-breaking normality for the Soviet woman. The tenor of the article was rather different from those of previous years.[6]

The demographic and economic approaches continue to find vociferous support. Few writers have challenged the idea that the birth-rate needs boosting in the European republics. When Kuznetsova recently did so in *Novoe Vremya*, arguing that 'the planet is already groaning', the response of demographer Anatolii Vishnevskii was predictable; that even if there were enough children in the planet as a whole, a high birth-rate in certain regions could not compensate for its collapse in others.[7] Valentin Pokrovskii, an expert on AIDS, indicates the extent to which the demographic crisis is still thought to matter; asked by a British journalist why there is no attempt in the Soviet Union to combat AIDS by promoting use of the condom, he explains that 'we have been running a major campaign for some time to encourage a higher birth-rate in the European part of the Soviet Union'. Urging the use of a contraceptive would run counter to this aim.[8]

While the family remains primarily women's responsibility, the economic approach will also continue to find favour amongst enterprise managers concerned with balancing the books. Zakharova *et al.* suggest a number of ways of protecting women's employment. One would be the establishment of quotas of women workers, though they admit that such administrative measures rarely last long; the 1979 provision to enable women to improve qualifications and training while bringing up small children soon fell by the wayside. More effective would be such economic levers as allowing individual enterprises differential levels of profit according to their 'child burden', i.e. the ration of dependent children to members of the work-force. The extra profit kept by work collectives with a high percentage of children could form a 'child fund', used to compensate mothers who have to work part-time, and to set up more crèches and kindergartens. Enterprises could be granted still more money if they accepted into their crèches and kindergartens the children of people working elsewhere, whose own work-places lacked such facilities. At present, because of the demands of *khozraschet*, there are attempts to get rid of these so-called 'alien' children.[9]

However, the introduction of such measures presupposes a commitment on the part of the state to protect women's right to employment. At present, this does not seem to exist. No doubt it will only begin to when more women are genuinely part of the decision-making process. This is the aim of those supporting the 'egalitarian' approach. They complain that in the past, women have just passively voted for male proposals at political gatherings; now, in the words of Kuznetsova, they need to 'raise their voices and not just their hands'.[10] Some say this is already happening. Marina Lebedeva, reporting in *Izvestiya* on the 1988 plenum of the Committee of Soviet Women, said that the conduct of women delegates was like nothing she had seen before. It 'reminded me of something powerful, strong, and male . . .'.[11] There is evidence of increasing interest in the feminist movement in the West,[12] and there has recently been talk of the need and even the immanent emergence of such a movement in the Soviet Union.[13]

This, then, appears to be the shape of things to come. The presentation of a single, idealized model of sex roles, as was almost the case from the late 1970s until the dawning of *glasnost'* and *perestroika*, is no longer feasible. It is now more likely, as women's careers come under increasing threat, that there will be a greater struggle between the advocates of the patriarchal/demographic and patriarchal/economic trends on the one hand, and the egalitarian (or perhaps even feminist) on the other.

All the same, it has to be acknowledged that the egalitarian approach seems likely to remain the minority position, at least in the short term. As we have seen from the literature reviewed in this book, and as Zakharova *et al.* have acknowledged, it is not only men who support patriarchal ideas.[14] Many women agree that their full participation in the work-force has had negative consequences for the family, children and themselves, and seem happy to accept the notion that they are the repositories of a set of innate, traditionally feminine personality traits, however much at odds this is with their lived experience.[15] This can partly be attributed to the Soviet Union's intensive decade of sex-role socialization. However, it should also be noted that these ideas have intrinsic appeal for Soviet women. The emancipation they have supposedly enjoyed for the past 70 years has saddled them with a hefty double burden of work inside and outside the home, unassisted by husbands or by many of the labour-saving devices of the West; for many women, a return to more traditional female roles represents the most likely way of reducing this work-load. Although writers of the 'egalitarian' mould insist that few Soviet women would choose not to work at all,[16] it seems likely that many will be willing to comply with their removal from the labour force for lengthy periods. If this is the case, can we expect a Soviet version of *The Women's Room* or *The Captive Wife* to make its eventual appearance on the book shelves?

Notes and References

Introduction

1. V. I. Lenin, *On the Emancipation of Women* (Moscow: Progress, 1972). Appendix by C. Zetkin, 'My recollections of Lenin', p. 101.
2. Ibid.
3. A. Kollontai, *Selected Writings* (London: Allison & Busby, 1977) p. 58.
4. Ibid.
5. A. G. Khripkova and D. V. Kolesov, *Devochka-podrostok-devushka* (Moscow, 1981) p. 74.
6. Ibid.
7. Noted by I. V. Pershaeva, 'Podgotovka devochek-starsheklassnitz k lichnoi zhizni v sisteme raboty klassnogo rukovoditelya', in *O ratsionalizatsii uchebno-vospitatel'noi raboty v shkole* (Sverdlovsk, 1977) p. 143
8. V. N. Kolbanovskii, 'The Sex-upbringing of the Rising Generation', in *Soviet Education*, Vol. 1, 1964, p. 4.
9. A. G. Khripkova, 'Neobkhodima mudrost' (polovoe vospitanie – grani problemy)', in *Sovetskaya Rossiya*, 16 December 1979, p. 3.
10. Khripkova and Kolesov, *Devochka-podrostok-devushka*, p. 72.
11. V. I. Perevedentsev, 'Ne soshlis' kharakterami?', in *Literaturnaya Gazeta*, 15 February 1978, p. 13.
12. V. I. Perevedentsev, 'Population reproduction and the family', abstract in *Current Digest of the Soviet Press (CDSP)*, Vol. XXXIV, No. 19, 1982, pp. 5–6. (Originally in *Sotsiologischeskie Issledovaniya*, No. 2, 1982, pp. 80–8.)
13. Ibid., p. 6
14. Alec Nove, *The Soviet Economic System* (London: Allen & Unwin, 1977) p. 68.
15. R. Ubaidullayeva, 'One Million Unemployed', condensed text in *CDSP*, Vol. XXXIX, No. 14, 1987, p. 4. (Originally in *Sel'skaya Zhizn'*, 24 March 1987, p. 2)
16. M. Vagabor, *Islam i Sem'ya* (Moscow, 1980) p. 123.
17. A. K. Minavarov, 'Semeinoe vospitanie v respublikakh Srednei Azii', in *Sovetskaya Pedagogika*, No. 1, 1984, p. 25.
18. See, for example, Yu. Kuz'mina, 'Skvoz' plamya', in *Nauka i Religiya*, No. 11, 1988, pp. 20–25. Also L. Attwood, 'Disaster in Soviet Asia', in *Everywoman*, July 1989, pp. 12–13.
19. G. I. Litvinova and B. Ts. Urlanis, 'The Soviet Union's Demographic Policy', abstract in *CDSP*, Vol. XXXIV, No. 19, 1982, pp. 1–4. Originally in *Sovetskoe gosudarstvo i pravo*, No. 3, 1982, pp. 38–46.
20. Cited by M. Rywkin, 'Central Asia and Soviet Manpower', in *Problems of Communism*, January–February 1979, p. 8.

21. Litvinova and Urlanis, 'The Soviet Union's Demographic Policy'.
22. For example, see V. N. Kozhevnikov and A. F. Vinogradov, 'Ne men'she chem troe!' in *Zdorov'e*, No. 12, 1981, pp. 12–13.
23. Ibid.
24. G. Dimov, 'Bol'shaya sem'ya glazami medikov', in *Izvestiya*, 28 February 1987, p. 2.
25. Vagabor, *Islam i Sem'ya*, p. 123.
26. Litvinova and Urlanis, 'The Soviet Union's Demographic Policy'.
27. Ibid.; also Minavarov, 'Semeinoe vospitanie . . .'.
28. A. G. Volkov, 'Sem'ya kak faktor izmeneniya demograficheskoi situatsii', in *Sotsiologicheskie Issledovaniya*, No. 1, 1981, p. 34.
29. 'Govoryat uchastnitsy i gosti vsesoyuznoi konferentsii zhenshchin', in *Izvestiya*, 2 February 1987, pp. 2–4.
30. Litvinova and Urlanis, 'The Soviet Union's Demographic Policy', p. 1; and V. N. Shubkin, 'Chto ty dumaesh' o molodezhi?', in *Literaturnaya Gazeta*, 22 January 1986, p. 10.
31. M. S. Gorbachev, Communique on the plenary session of the Central Committee of the CPSU, *Pravda* and *Izvestiya*, 28 January 1988, p. 1; and 'Vitaly Tretyakov Defends Himself', in *Soviet Weekly*, 6 February 1988, p. 8.
32. 'V TsK KPSS i Sovete Ministrov SSSR', *Pravda* and *Izvestiya*, 31 March 1981, p. 1. Also Litvinova and Urlanis, 'The Soviet Union's Demographic Policy', pp. 1–4.
33. 'Politicheskii doklad tsentral'nogo komiteta KPSS XXVII s"ezdy kommunisticheskoi partii Sovetskogo Soyuza – doklad General'nogo Sekretarya Tsk KPSS tovarishcha Gorbacheva M. S. – 25 fevralya 1986 goda', in *Izvestiya*, 26 February 1986, pp. 2–10.
34. Mentioned in speech by V. Yu. Uzelene, head doctor of No. 1 Children's Polyclinic in Vilnius, and member of the city Women's Council, in 'Govoryat uchastnitsy i gosti vsesoyuznoi konferentsii zhenshchin', in *Izvestiya*, 2 February 1987, pp. 2–4. Also by M. Tol'ts, 'Sem'ya', in *Pravda*, 20 March 1987, p. 2.
35. See 'Politicheskii doklad tsentral'nogo komiteta . . .'.
36. G. Naan, 'Emansipatsiya, patriarkhat i "voina polov"', in *Literaturnoe Obozrenie, No.9*, 1977, pp. 57–62.
37. V. Sysenko, in 'Mnogodetnaya sem'ya: vzglyad v budushchee', round-table discussion on the multi-child family reported by O. Dmitrieva in *Komsomol'skaya Pravda*, 30 October 1981, p. 2.
38. Ada Baskina, 'Ot chego zavisit rost sem'i?' in *Sem'ya i Shkola*, No. 12, 1981, p. 28.
39. A. Antonov, 'Dvukh detei mala', in *Meditsinskaya Gazeta*, 27 September 1985, p. 4.
40. Referred to by E. Porokhnyuk and M. S. Shepeleva, 'O sovmeshchenii proizvodstvennykh i semeinykh funktsii zhenshchin-rabotnits', in *Sotsiologicheskie Issledovaniya*, No. 4, 1975, pp. 102–8.
41. T. I. Kuseleva, 'V sem'e rodilos' pyatero detei. Kak bylo?', in *Literaturnaya Gazeta*, 2 October 1986, p. 13.
42. 'Ispoved'', in K. Marks and F. Engel's, *Ob Iskusstve*, Vol. 2 (Moscow, 1957) p. 577.

43. See Chapters 6 and 7 for a number of examples.
44. V. I. Perevedentsev, 'Malysh tretii, zhelannyi', in *Nedelya*, 15–21 January 1987, p. 14.
45. A. G. Vishnevskii, S. Ya. Shcherbov, A. B. Anichkin, V. A. Grechukha, and N. V. Donets, 'Noveishie tendentsii rozhdaemosti v SSSR', in *Sotsiologicheskie Issledovaniya*, No. 3, 1988, p. 54.
46. For example, see Ann Sheehy, 'Opposition to Family Planning in Uzbekistan and Tadjikistan', *Radio Liberty Research Bulletin*, No. 159, 1988.
47. I. Bestuzhev-Lada, 'Net detei – net i budushchego u naroda', in *Nedelya*, 15–21 April 1988, pp. 20–21; and M. Malysheva, 'Postylye plody emansipatsii', in *Nedelya*, 8–14 January 1988, p. 4.
48. D. Akivis, I. Zhuravskaya, I. Skylar and A. Stepanov, 'Daite miry shans!' – Vsemirnyi Kongress Zhenshchin', in *Rabotnitsa*, No. 8, 1987, pp. 2–5.
49. See, for example, 'Vitaly Tretyakov defends himself', *Soviet Weekly*, 6 February 1988, p. 8, and I. Bestuzhev-Lada, 'O zhenshchine i dlya zhenshchiny', in *Rabotnitsa*, No. 5, 1986, p. 26.
50. See N. Zhakharova, A. Posadskaya and N. Rimashevskaya, 'Kak my reshaem zhenskii vopros', in *Kommunist*, No. 4, 1989, pp. 56–65; M. Lebedeva, 'Poka muzhchiny govoryat . . .', in *Izvestiya*, 23 October 1988, p. 6; and L. Attwood and M. McAndrew, 'Women at Work in the USSR', in M. J. Davidson and C. L. Cooper, *Working Women: An International Survey* (Chichester: John Wiley, 1984) pp. 269–304.
51. Lebedeva, ibid.
52. Zhakarova *et al.*, 'Kak my reshaem zhenskii vopros', p. 58.
53. Ibid.
54. M. S. Gorbachev, *Perestroika* (London: Collins, 1987) p. 117.

1 Western Theories of Male and Female Personality Differences

1. J. B. Rohrbaugh, *Women: Psychology's Puzzle* (London: Abacus, 1981) p. 81.
2. Ibid., p. 85.
3. Sigmund Freud, 'Some Psychical Consequences of the Anatomical Distinction Between the Sexes', in *Freud on Sexuality* (Harmondsworth: Penguin, 1977) p. 335.
4. Ibid., p. 340; and Freud, 'On the Sexual Theories of Children', in *Freud on Sexuality*, p. 195.
5. Freud, 'Some Psychical Consequences . . .', p. 340.
6. Freud, 'Female Sexuality', in *Freud on Sexuality*, p. 376.
7. Rohrbaugh, *Women: Psychology's Puzzle*, p. 89.
8. Freud, 'Female Sexuality', p. 376.
9. Ibid., p. 337.
10. Freud, 'Some Psychical Consequences . . .', p. 342.
11. Ibid., p. 337.
12. Ibid., p. 338.
13. Freud, quoted by Rohrbaugh, *Women: Psychology's Puzzle*, pp. 90–91.

14. Ibid., p. 92.
15. Freud, 'Some Psychical Consequences . . .', p. 342.
16. J. Mitchell, *Psychoanalysis and Feminism* (Harmondsworth: Penguin, 1974).
17. B. Vul'fson, 'Freudianism and Bourgeois Pedagogy', in *Soviet Education*, No. 1, 1966, p. 8.
18. J. McLeish, *Soviet Psychology: History, Theory, Content* (London: Methuen, 1975) p. 136.
19. Ibid., p. 136.
20. Ibid., p. 143.
21. V. N. Kolbanovskii, 'The Sex Upbringing of the Rising Generation', in *Soviet Education*, September 1974, p. 9.
22. Ibid.
23. See A. S. Prangishvili, A. E. Sheroziya and F. V. Bassin, *Bessozhatel'noe* (Tblisi 1978).
24. L. A. Radzhikovskii, 'Teoriya Freida: smena ustanovki', in *Voprosy Psikhologii*, No. 6, 1988, p. 101.
25. Ibid., p. 105.
26. A. Bandura, *Social Learning Theory* (Englewood Cliffs NJ: Prentice-Hall, 1977) p. 13.
27. A. Bandura and R. H. Walters, *Social Learning and Personality Development* (New York and London: Holt, Rinehart & Winston, 1964) pp. 57–8.
28. Rohrbaugh, *Women: Psychology's Puzzle*, p. 145.
29. L. A. Serbin and K. D. O'Leary, 'How Nursery Schools Teach Girls to Shut Up', in *Psychology Today*, December 1975, p. 57.
30. Bandura, *Social Learning Theory*, p. 24.
31. Rohrbaugh, *Women: Psychology's Puzzle*, p. 147. See also Rohrbaugh, p. 146; and Bandura and Walters, *Social Learning*, p. 10.
32. Ibid., p. 98.
33. E. E. Maccoby and C. N. Jacklin, *The Psychology of Sex Differences* (London: OUP, 1975) p. 147, and S. Sharpe, *Just Like a Girl* (Harmondsworth: Penguin, 1976) p. 82.
34. Bandura and Walters, *Social Learning*, p. 97; also Rohrbaugh, *Women: Psychology's Puzzle*, p. 141.
35. Bandura and Walters, *Social Learning*, p. 99.
36. Quoted by Rohrbaugh, *Women: Psychology's Puzzle*, p. 151.
37. Ibid., pp. 151–2.
38. Bandura, *Social Learning Theory*, pp. 9–10.
39. L. Kohlberg, 'A Cognitive-developmental Analysis of Children's Sex-role Concepts and Attitudes', in E. E. Maccoby (ed.) *The Development of Sex Differences* (London: Tavistock, 1967) p. 85.
40. Rohrbaugh, *Women: Psychology's Puzzle*, p. 118.
41. J. Brophy, *Child Development and Socialization* (Chicago etc.: Science Research Associates, 1977)
42. See Serbin and O'Leary, 'How Nursery Schools Teach Girls to Shut Up'.
43. Kohlberg, 'A Cognitive-developmental Analysis', p. 102.
44. Ibid., p. 111. See also Rohrbaugh, *Women: Psychology's Puzzle*, p. 127.
45. Kohlberg, 'A Cognitive-developmental Analysis', p. 163.

46. Rohrbaugh, *Women: Psychology's Puzzle*, p. 127–8.
47. Quoted by D. Spender, *For the Record* (London: The Women's Press, 1985) p. 37.
48. Ibid.
49. Cynthia Cockburn, quoted by L. Segal, *Is the Future Female?* (London: Virago, 1987) pp. xiv–xv.
50. Spender, *For the Record*; see, for example, pp. 29–30.
51. M. Barrett and M. McIntosh, *The Anti-Social Family* (London: Verso, 1982) p. 106.
52. Bandura, *Social Learning Theory*, pp. 9–10.
53. Quoted by Ann Oakley, *Subject Woman*, p. 61.
54. Segal, *Is the Future Female?*, p. 10.
55. Shulamith Firestone, *The Dialectic of Sex* (London: The Women's Press, 1979) p. 18.
56. Oakley, *Subject Woman*, p. 62.
57. Segal, *Is the Future Female?*, p. ix.
58. Ibid., p. x.
59. N. S. Yulina, 'Problemy zhenshchin: filosofskie aspekty', in *Voprosy Filosofii*, No. 5, 1988, p. 147.

2 Soviet Psychology and Personality Development

1. V. N. Kolbanovskii, 'The Sex Upbringing of the Rising Generation', in *Soviet Education*, September 1964, p. 4.
2. A. G. Khripkova and D. V. Kolesov, *Devochka-podrostok-devushka* (Moscow, 1981) p. 74.
3. B. F. Lomov, 'Sixty Years of Soviet Psychology', in *Soviet Psychology*, Vol. 17, No. 2, (Winter 1978–9) pp. 69–70.
4. G. L. Smirnov, *Soviet Man: the Making of a Socialist Type of Personality* (Moscow: Progress, 1973) p. 176.
5. A. A. Smirnov, 'Child Psychology', in Brian Simon (ed.), *Psychology in the Soviet Union* (London: RKP, 1957) p. 198.
6. J. McLeish, *Soviet Psychology: History, Theory, Content* (London: Methuen, 1975) pp. 105–6.
7. R. A. Bauer, *The New Man in Soviet Psychology* (Cambridge: Harvard Univ. Press, 1952) p. 61.
8. Quoted by Bauer, ibid., p. 73
9. See, for example, B. L. Vul'fson, 'Freudianism and bourgeois pedagogy', in *Soviet Education*, Vol. VIII, No. 3 (1966) pp. 3–14; and McLeish, *Soviet Psychology*, pp. 136–43.
10. Quoted by Bauer, *The New Man in Soviet Psychology*, p. 99.
11. Ibid., p. 99.
12. See, for example, W. H. Chamberlin, *Soviet Russia – A Living Record and a History* (London: Duckworth, 1930) p. 227, for personal observation of new Soviet schools.
13. Quoted by Bauer, *The New Man in Soviet Psychology*, p. 87.
14. Ibid.

15. Ibid., p. 87; and G. W. Lapidus, 'Educational Strategies and Cultural Revolution', in S. Fitzpatrick (ed.), *Cultural Revolution in Russia* (Bloomington, Indiana Univ. Press, 1978) pp. 95–6.
16. *Pedagogicheskie vzglyady i deyatel'nost' N. K. Krupskoi* (Moscow, 1969) pp. 135–9.
17. Ibid., pp. 135–9.
18. See A. S. Makarenko, *Road to Life: An Epic of Education* (Moscow: Progress, 1951).
19. M. Efimov, 'F. P. Petrov, Opyt issledovaniya intellektual'nogo razvitiya Chuvashskikh detei po metodu Bine-Simon, 1928', in *Pedologiya*, Nos 7–8, 1939, p. 128.
20. D. B. Elkonin, 'Some Results of the Study of the Psychological Development of Preschool-age Children', in M. Cole and I. Maltzman (eds), *A Handbook of Contemporary Soviet Psychology* (New York: Basic Books, 1969) p. 164.
21. Quoted by Bauer, *The New Man in Soviet Psychology*, p. 98.
22. Ibid., p. 146.
23. B. Simon (ed.), *Psychology in the Soviet Union* (London: RKP, 1957) p. 2 (from the Introduction).
24. Ibid., p. 14.
25. For example, see H. Cuny, *Ivan Pavlov, the Man and his Theories* (London: Souvenir Press, 1962) p. 76.
26. Ibid.
27. Ibid., p. 74.
28. Simon, *Psychology in the Soviet Union* pp. 16–17.
29. Quoted by Cuny, *Ivan Pavlov, the Man and his Theories*, p. 103.
30. Ibid., p. 106.
31. Quoted by Simon, *Psychology in the Soviet Union* p. 20.
32. Quoted by N. I. Krasnogorsky, 'The Physiology of the Development of Speech in Children', in *Soviet Psychology Bulletin*, April 1955, published by the Society for Cultural Relations with the USSR.
33. H. K. Wells, *Ivan P. Pavlov: Toward a Scientific Psychology and Psychiatry* (London: Lawrence & Wishart, 1956) p. 86.
34. Quoted by F. V. Bassin, 'Consciousness and the Unconscious', in Cole and Maltzman, *A Handbook of Contemporary Soviet Psychology*, p. 403.
35. Wells, *Ivan P. Pavlov*, p. 82.
36. Ibid., p. 93
37. Ibid., pp. 95–7.
38. Cuny, *Ivan Pavlov, the Man and his Theories*, p. 94; Wells, *Ivan P. Pavlov*, pp. 150–51; and N. P. Dubinin, I. I. Karpets and V. N. Kudryavtsev, *Genetika, Povedenie, Otvetstvennost'* (Moscow, 1982) p. 20.
39. Wells, *Ivan P. Pavlov*, p. 151.
40. Dubinin *et al.*, *Genetika, Povedenie, Otvetstvennost'*, p. 21.
41. Quoted by A. A. Smirnov, 'Child Psychology', p.*184*.
42. L. A. Radzikhovskii and E. D. Khomskaya, 'A. R. Luria and L. S. Vygotskii: Early Years of their Collaboration', in *Soviet Psychology*, Vol. XX, No. 1 (Autumn, 1981) p. 7.

43. A. Sutton, 'Cultural Disadvantage and Vygotskii's Stages of Development', in *Educational Studies*, October 1980, p. 200.
44. L. I. Bozhovich and L. S. Slavina, 'Fifty Years of Soviet Psychology of Upbringing', in J. Brozek and D. I. Slobin (eds), *Psychology in the USSR: an Historical Perspective* (New York: International Arts and Sciences Press, 1972) p. 166.
45. Sutton, 'Cultural Disadvantage . . .', p. 201
46. L. S. Vygotskii, *Mind in Society* (London and Cambridge, Mass.: Harvard Univ. Press, 1978), p. 124 (in the Afterword by V. John-Steiner and E. Souberman).
47. L. I. Bozhovich, 'Stages in the Formation of the Personality in Ontogeny (Part II)', in *Soviet Psychology*, Vol. XVIII, No. 3 (Spring, 1980) pp. 36–7.
48. Vygotskii, *Mind in Society*, p. 128 (from the Afterword).
49. Ibid., p.56.
50. Ibid.
51. V. V. Davydov and V. P. Zinchenko, 'The Principle of Development in Psychology', in *Soviet Psychology*, Vol. XX, No. 1 (Autumn, 1981) p. 43.
52. L. I. Bozhovich, 'Stages in Personality Formation', in *Soviet Psychology*, Vol. XVII, No. 3 (Spring, 1979) p. 13.
53. Bozhovich, 'Stages in the Formation of the Personality in Ontogeny (Part II)', p. 42.
54. A. N. Leont'ev, 'Intellectual Development of the Child', in R. B. Winn (ed.), *Soviet Psychology* (New York: Philosophical Library, 1961) p. 63.
55. Ibid.
56. Bozhovich, 'Stages in the Formation of the Personality in Ontogeny (Part II)', p. 43.
57. Ibid., p. 43.
58. Bozhovich and Slavina, 'Fifty Years of Soviet Psychology', p. 172.
59. Vygotskii, *Mind in Society*, p. 57.
60. Ibid., p. 27.
61. A. Z. Zaporozhets and U. D. Lukov, 'The Development of Reasoning in Young Children', in *Soviet Psychology*, Vol. XVIII, (Winter, 1979–80), No. 2, pp. 49–50.
62. Sutton, 'Cultural Disadvantage . . .', p. 205.
63. L. I. Bozhovich, 'The Personality of Schoolchildren and Problems of Education', in Cole and Maltzman, p. 216.
64. Bozhovich and Slavina, 'Fifty Years of Soviet Psychology . . .', p. 169.
65. Bozhovich, 'The Personality of Schoolchildren . . .', p. 219.
66. Ibid.
67. A. R. Luria, 'Speech Development and the Formation of Mental Processes', in Cole and Maltzman, *A Handbook of Contemporary Soviet Psychology*, pp. 125–6.
68. A. R. Luria, 'Speech and Intellect among Rural, Urban and Homeless Children', in *Soviet Psychology*, Vol. 13, No. 1 (Autumn, 1974), pp. 5–39.

69. A. R. Luria, *Cognitive Development: Its Cultural and Social Foundations* (London and Cambrige, Mass.: Harvard Univ. Press, 1976) p. 164.
70. V. V. Davydov, 'Itogi i perspektivy nauchnoi deyatelnosti instituta obshchei i pedagogicheskoi psikhologii', in *Voprosy Psikhologii*, No. 1, 1983, p. 5.
71. A. N. Leont'ev, 'The Problem of Activity in Psychology', in *Soviet Psychology*, vol. 13, No. 2, (Winter 1974–5) p. 9.
72. Ibid., p. 11.
73. See Bozhovich and Slavina, 'Fifty Years of Soviet Psychology...', pp. 167–8; and Bozhovich, 'The Personality of Schoolchildren...', p. 211.
74. Bozhovich, 'The Personality of Schoolchildren...', p. 240.
75. Ibid., p. 239.
76. Quoted by Leont'ev, 'The Intellectual Development of the Child', in Winn, *Soviet Psychology*, p. 65.
77. D. B. Elkonin, 'Some Results of the Study of the Psychological Development of Preschool-age Children', in Cole and Maltzman, *A Handbook of Contemporary Soviet Psychology*, pp. 166–7.
78. See E. V. Subbotskii, 'O genezise moral'nogo povedeniya doshkol'nikov', in *Novye issledovaniya v psikhologii*, No. 1, 1977, pp. 48–52; 'Vliyanie sverstnikov i vzroslykh na moral'noe povdenie rebenka v usloviyakh eksperimenta', in *Novye issledovaniya...*, No. 2, 1977; and 'Formironvanie moral'nogo postupka', in *Novye issledovaniya...*, No. 2, 1977.
79. Subbotskii, 'Formirovanie moral'nogo postupka', p. 50.
80. Ibid.
81. Ibid., p. 52.
82. Ibid.
83. Ibid.
84. Bozhovich, 'The Personality of Schoolchildren...', p. 240.
85. V. S. Mukhina, 'The Social Development of the Child', in *Soviet Psychology*, Vol. XX, No. 3 (Spring, 1982) p. 77.
86. Bozhovich, 'The Personality of Schoolchildren...', p. 240.
87. Mukhina cites the work of T. Shibutani and Ya. Korchak in 'The Social Devlopment of the Child', p. 67.
88. Ibid., p. 67.
89. Ibid., p. 77.
90. See Bozhovich and Slavina, 'Fifty years...', p. 167–8, and Bozhovich, 'The Personality of Schoolchildren...', p. 211.
91. D. I. Fel'dshtein, 'Psikhologo-pedagogicheskie problemy sootsosheniya biologicheskogo i sotsial'nogo', in *Sovetskaya Pedagogika*, No. 5, 1984, pp. 52–6.
92. P. N. Fedoseev, 'Problema sotsial'nogo i biologicheskogo v filosofii i sotsiologii', in *Biologischeskoe i soltsial'noe v razvitii cheloveka* (Moscow, 1977) p. 20. (It should be noted that Fedoseev is primarily a philosopher, but his views are supported by psychologists and sometimes published alongside their own, as is the case with the chapter above.)
93. Ibid., p. 8.
94. Ibid., p. 21.
95. N. F. Posnanski, 'Heredity and the Materialist Theory', in Winn, *Soviet Psychology*, p. 50.

96. N. P. Dubinin, 'Nasledovanie biologischeskoe i sotsial'noe', in *Kommunist*, No. 7, 1980, p. 71.
97. Ibid., p. 70.
98. Ibid., p. 71.
99. Ibid., p. 63.
100. Outlined by Julian Cooper, 'What is man? A new controversy in Soviet biology', unpublished paper presented at the 1983 annual conference of Birmingham's Centre for Russian and East European Studies.
101. Ibid.
102. Fel'dshtein, 'Psikhologo-pedagogicheskie problemy . . .', p. 50.
103. Ibid., p. 51.
104. Ibid.
105. For example, see Janet Sayers, 'On the Description of Psychological Sex Differences', in O. Hartnett, G. Boden and M. Fuller (eds), *Sex Role Stereotyping* (London: Tavistock, 1979) p. 48.
106. Posnanski, 'Heredity and the Materialist Theory', p. 52.

3 Soviet Psychologists on Sex Differences

1. B. G. Anan'ev, *Chelovek kak predmet soznaniya* (Leningrad, 1968) pp. 168–75.
2. Ibid., p. 185.
3. Ibid., p. 175.
4. A. A. Bodalev, 'Individual and Developmental Differences in Interpersonal Understanding', in *Soviet Psychology*, Vol. IX, No. 2 (Winter 1970–1), pp. 157–69.
5. Ibid., p. 162.
6. A. A. Bodalev, 'Subjective Significance of Another Person and its Determining Factors', in *Soviet Psychology*, Vol. XXV, No. 1 (1986) pp. 21–27.
7. Ibid., p. 27.
8. V. S. Mukhina, 'Igrushka kak sredstvo psikhicheskogo razvitiya rebenka', in *Voprosy Psikhologii*, No. 2, 1988, pp. 123–8.
9. T. G. Khashchenko, 'Rol' frustrirovannosti i pola partnerov v sovmestnom reshenii myslitel'nykh zadach', in *Voprosy Psikhologii*, No. 5, 1982, pp. 118–22.
10. A. I. Zakharov, 'Psikhologicheskie osobennosti vospriyatiya det'mi roli roditelei', in *Voprosy Psikhologii*, No. 1, 1982, pp. 59–68.
11. In a personal interview with Varga I was told that her supervisor had advised her against pursuing this subject.
12. A. Ya. Varga, 'Identifikatsiya s roditelyami i formirovanie psikhologischeskogo pola (kriticheskii podkhod k resheniyu problemy)' in A. A. Bodalev (ed.), *Sem'ya i formirovanie lichnosti – sbornik nauchnykh trudov* (Moscow, 1981) pp. 21–6.
13. Quoted by R. G. D'Anrade, 'Sex differences and cultural institutions', in E. E. Maccoby (ed.), *The Development of Sex Differences* (London: Tavistock, 1967) p. 185.
14. See, for example, J. Money and A. A. Erhardt, *Man and Woman, Boy and Girl* (Baltimore and London: Johns Hopkins University Press, 1972); and R. J. Stoller, *Sex and Gender* (London: Hogarth Press, 1968).

15. E. E. Maccoby and C. N. Jacklin, *The Psychology of Sex Differences* (London: OUP, 1977).
16. V. A. Kuts, 'Sotsial'no-psikhologicheskie razlichiya mezhdu muzhchinami i zhenshchinami v tsennostno-motivatsionnykh aspektakh stanovleniya brachnykh otnoshenii' – Candidate Dissertation at the Department of Social Psychology, Leningrad State University (LGU) (Leningrad, 1978).
17. V. P. Bagrunov and V. A. Kuts, 'K voprosu o neobkhodimosti ucheta psykhologicheskikh osobennostei pola v semeinoi vospitanii', in *Pedagogicheskie aspekty sotsial'noi psikhologii* (Minsk, 1978) pp. 214–15.
18. L. S. Sapozhnikova, 'Inculcating Moral Behaviour in Adolescents', in *Soviet Psychology*, Vol. XXIV, No. 2 (Winter 1985–6) pp. 83–95.
19. Ibid., p. 93.
20. Ibid.
21. Alison Kelly and Tat'yana Snegireva, 'Ne predopredelenie, a vybor', in *Literaturnaya Gazeta*, 23 May 1984, p. 12.
22. Ibid.
23. Ibid.
24. This claim is made by a number of feminist theorists. Dale Spender, for example, in *For the Record* (London: The Women's Press, 1985) p. 37, notes that 'the concept of socialization became popular after the publication of (Kate Millett's) *Sexual Politics*'.
25. Ann Oakley, *Subject Woman* (London: Fontana, 1982) p. 62.
26. Elizabeth Roberts, 'Soviet Psychology Today', in *Britain–USSR* (journal of the GB–USSR association) No. 74, September 1986, p. 10.

4 The Work of I. S. Kon

1. I. S. Kon, 'Pravo na tvorchestvo', in *Pravda*, 16 January 1984, p. 3.
2. For example, see Kon, 'Polovye razlichiya i differentsiatsiya sotsialnykh rolei', in *Sootnoshenie biologicheskogo i sotsial'nogo v cheloveke* (Moscow, 1975) p. 775.
3. Kon, *Lichnost' 'kak sub"ekt obshchestvennykh otnoshenii* (Moscow, 1966) pp. 4–6.
4. Ibid., p. 7.
5. Kon, 'Polovye razlichiya i differentsiatsiya sotsial'nykh rolei', p. 776. See also Kon, 'Psikhologiya polovykh razlichii', in *Voprosy Psikhologii*, No. 2, 1981, p. 48.
6. 'Psikhologiya polovykh razlichii', p. 48.
7. Ibid., p. 49.
8. 'Polovye razlichiya i differentsiatsiya . . .', p. 764.
9. Ibid., p. 49.
10. 'Psikhologiya polovykh razlichii', p. 49–50.
11. Ibid., p. 50.
12. Kon, 'Psikhologiya starsheklassnika' (Moscow, 1980) p. 113.
13. 'Psikhologiya polovykh razlichii', p. 50.
14. 'Polovye razlichiya i differentsiatsiya . . .', p. 770.
15. Ibid., p. 771.

16. 'Polovye razlichiya i differentsiatsiya . . .', p. 772.
17. Ibid., p. 774. (The text actually says 'neravenstva', i.e. *in*equality, but this must be a typographical error.)
18. From an interview with Kon in Larisa Kuznetsova, *Zhenshchina na rabote i doma* (Moscow, 1980) p. 179.
19. 'Polovye razlichiya i differentsiatsiya . . .', p. 775.
20. Kon, 'Muzhestvennye zhenshchiny? Zhenstvennye muzhchiny?', in *Literaturnaya Gazeta*, 1 January 1970, p. 12.
21. Kon, 'Ot chetyrnadtsati do vosemnadtsati', in *Vospitanie Shkol'nikov*, No. 4, 1978, p. 57.
22. 'Muzhestvennye zhenshchiny? . . .'
23. Ibid.
24. D. V. Kolesov, *Besedy o polovom vospitanii* (Moscow, 1980), p. 42.
25. From a personal visit to a school in Leningrad in 1981, discussions with teachers and pupils. However, these remarks are less applicable to rural schools, where 60 per cent of the 'trud' classes are mixed.
26. 'Muzhestvennye zhenshchiny? . . .'
27. 'Polovye razlichiya i differentsiatsiya . . .', p. 775.
28. Ibid., p. 774.
29. 'Psikhologiya polovykh razlichii', p. 54.
30. Interview with Kuznetsova, p. 188.
31. Ibid.
32. Kon, 'Zhenshchiny i muzhchiny', in *Nedelya*, 5 February 1985, pp. 14–15.
33. 'Polovye razlichiya i differentsiatsiya . . .', p. 775.
34. 'Ot chetyrnadtsati do vosemnadtsati', p. 61.
35. Interview with Kuznetsova, p. 189.
36. 'Zhenshchiny i muzhchiny', p. 14
37. Interview with Kuznetsova, p. 191.
38. Ibid.
39. 'Polovye razlichiya i differentsiatsiya . . .', p. 773.
40. Ibid., p. 772. See also Kon, 'Adam, Eva i vek-iskusitel'', in *Literaturnaya Gazeta*, 1 January 1979, p. 11.
41. Ibid., p. 773.
42. Ibid.
43. Interview with Kuznetsova, pp. 190–91.
44. Ibid., p. 191.
45. 'Polovye razlichiya i differentsiatsiya . . .', p. 774.
46. This is taken from the introduction to Kon's original manuscript, *Vvedenie v mezhditsiplinarnuyu seksologiyu*, on which his book *Vvedenie v seksologiyu* (Moscow, 1988) was based.
47. See V. N. Shubkin, 'Chto ty dumaesh' o molodezhi?', in *Literaturnaya Gazeta*, 22 January 1986, p. 10.
48. Kon, 'Where Scholarly Disciplines Meet', Abstract in *CDSP*, Vol. XXXIII, No. 50, 1982, p. 9. (Originally in *Voprosy Filosofii*, No. 10, 1981, pp. 47–55.)
49. An interview with Kon conducted by O. Moroz, 'Spravedliva li kara?', in *Literaturnaya Gazeta*, 29 March 1989, p. 11.
50. Kon, 'Nastoyashchii muzhchina', in *Nedelya*, 3–9 April 1989, pp. 14–15.

51. Ibid., p. 14
52. Ibid.
53. Ibid., p. 15.
54. Ibid.
55. Kon, 'Nastoyashchaya zhenshchina', in *Nedelya*, 17–23 April 1989, p. 15.

5 Sex Change in the Soviet Union: A. I. Belkin and the Treatment of Hermaphrodites

1. From a personal interview with Belkin in Moscow on 9 December 1984. (Much of the material in this chapter comes from, or is supported by, information provided by Belkin during this interview and a second on 13 December 1984.)
2. J. Money and A. A. Ehrhardt, *Man and Woman, Boy and Girl* (Baltimore: Johns Hopkins University Press, 1972) p. 61.
3. Cited by J. G. Raymond, *The Transsexual Empire* (London: The Women's Press, 1980) p. 6.
4. J. G. Raymond, 'Transsexualism: an Issue of Sex-role Stereotyping', in E. Tobach and B. Rosoff (eds), *Genes and Gender II* (New York: Gordon Press, 1979) p. 131.
5. See J. Money and P. Tucker, cited by Raymond, 'Transsexualism . . .', p. 133; and Money and Ehrhardt, *Man and Woman, Boy and Girl*, especially pp. 9 and 158; and R. J. Stoller, *Sex and Gender*, (London: Hogarth Press, 1968) p. 37.
6. Personal interview with Belkin.
7. Belkin, 'Biologicheskie i sotsial'nye faktory, formiruyushchie polovuyu identifikatsiyu', in *Sootnoshenie biologicheskogo i sotsial'nogo v cheloveke* (Moscow, 1975) pp. 780–81.
8. Belkin, 'Masculine, Feminine or Neutral?', in *The UNESCO Courier*, August– September 1975 (English language edition) p. 60. This article originally appeared in *Literaturnaya Gazeta*, No. 31, 1973, p. 13, as 'Muzhchina i zhenshchina: stiranie psikhologicheskikh granei?'
9. Ibid., p. 60.
10. Money and Ehrhardt, *Man and Woman, Boy and Girl*, p. 2.
11. A. I. Belkin and V. N. Lakusta, *Biologicheskaya terapiya psikhicheskikh zabolevanii* (Kishinev, 1983) pp. 123–7. See also the foreword of Belkin (ed.), *Gormony i mozg* (Moscow, 1979) pp. 8–9.
12. Belkin and Lakusta, *Biologicheskaya terapiya* . . ., p. 137.
13. Raymond, *The Transsexual Empire*, p. 54.
14. Ibid.
15. Belkin and Lakusta, *Biologicheskaya terapiya* . . ., p. 137.
16. Belkin, 'Biologicheskie i sotsial'nye faktory . . .', p. 780.
17. Ibid., p. 778–9.
18. I. V. Golubeva and A. I. Belkin, 'Sotsial'no-pravovye aspekty germafroditizma', in Belkin (ed.) *Gormony i mozg* p. 84.
19. Belkin and Lakusta, *Biologicheskaya terapiya* . . ., pp. 135–6.
20. Belkin, 'Biologicheskie i sotsial'nye faktory . . .', p. 782.
21. Ibid., p. 782.
22. From personal interviews with Belkin.

23. Unless otherwise stated, the description of these stages is taken from Belkin, 'Biologicheskie i sotsial'nye faktory . . .', pp. 782–8.
24. Personal interviews with Belkin.
25. Belkin, 'Biologicheskie i sotsial'nye faktory . . .', p. 784.
26. Belkin, 'Individual'nost i sotsializatsiya', pp. 15–16.
27. Belkin, 'Biologicheskie i sotsial'nye faktory . . .', p. 784.
28. Belkin, 'Individualnost' i sotsializatsiya', p. 22.
29. Golubeva and Belkin, 'Sotsial'no-pravovye aspekty . . .', p. 87.
30. Belkin, 'Biologicheskie i sotsial'nye faktory . . .', p. 787.
31. Ibid., p. 787.
32. For example, see Money and Ehrhardt, *Man and Woman, Boy and Girl*, p. 158.
33. Personal interviews with Belkin.
34. Unless otherwise stated, the description of 'identification' and 'distinction' is taken from Belkin, 'Individual'nost' i sotsializatisiya', pp. 19–24.
35. Personal interviews with Belkin.
36. Belkin, 'Individual'nost' i sotsializatisiya', p. 20.
37. Ibid.
38. Personal interviews with Belkin.
39. Belkin, 'Individual'nost' i sotsializatisiya', p. 21.
40. Ibid.
41. Belkin, 'Masculine, Feminine or Neutral?', p. 61.
42. M. S. Rosenhan, 'Images of Male and Female in Children's Readers', in D. Atkinson, A. Dallin and G. W. Lapidus (eds), *Women in Russia* (London: Harvester Press, 1978)
43. Belkin, 'Masculine, Feminine or Neutral?', p. 60
44. Ibid., p. 61.
45. Raymond, *The Transsexual Empire*, p. 92.
46. Belkin, 'Masculine, Feminine or Neutral?', pp. 58–61.
47. Ibid., p. 60.
48. Ibid.
49. Personal interview with Belkin.
50. Personal interview with Belkin.
51. Belkin, 'Masculine, Feminine or Neutral?', p. 61.

6 Sociological and Demographic Approaches to Sex Differences

1. D. Akivis and E. Mushkina, 'Kakaya sem'ya nam nuzhna?', report on round-table discussion on the family, in *Nedelya*, No. 47, 1987, p. 17.
2. Interview by L. Kuznetsova with A. Vishnevskii, 'Glazami zhenshchiny', in *Novoe Vremya*, No. 10, 1989, p. 33.
3. V. Shlapentokh, *Love, Marriage and Friendship in the Soviet Union* (New York: Praeger, 1984) p. 48.
4. O. A. Voronina, 'Zhenshchina v "muzhskom obshchestve"', in *Sotsiologicheskie Issledovaniya*, No. 2, 1988, p. 109.
5. See M. Buckley, 'Soviet Interpretations of the Woman Question', in B. Holland (ed.) *Soviet Sisterhood* (London: Fourth Estate, 1985) p. 40; and L. Attwood and M. McAndrew, 'Women at Work in the USSR', in

M. J. Davidson and C. L. Cooper (eds), *Working Women* (Chichester and New York: John Wiley, 1984) pp. 286–7.
6. A. G. Kharchev, *Nravstvennost' i sem'ya* (Moscow, 1981) p. 3.
7. Kharchev, *Sem'ya i brak v SSSR* (Moscow, 1979), p. 314.
8. Z. A. Yankova, 'Razvitie lichnosti zhenshchiny v Sovetskom obshchestve', in *Sotsiologischeskie Issledovaniya*, No. 4, 1975, p. 42. See also Yankova, *Izmenenie struktury sotsial'nykh rolei zhenshchin v razvitom sotsialisticheskom obshchestve i model' sem'i* (Moscow, 1972), paper given at the Soviet Sociological Association 12th International Seminar on the Study of the Family.
9. 'Razvitie lichnosti zhenshchiny . . ., p. 43.
10. R. Gurova, 'Dinamika tsennostnykh orientatsii devushek 1913–1919', in *Dinamika izmeneniya polozheniya zhenshchiny i sem'ya* (Moscow, 1972) pp. 29–39.
11. Yankova, *Sovetskaya zhenshchina* (Moscow, 1978) p. 123.
12. Ibid., pp. 121–2.
13. N. Shimin, 'Rol' zhenshchiny-materi v emotsional'no-nravstvennom razvitii detei v sem'e', in *Dinamika izmeneniya polozheniya zhenshchiny i sem'ya*, (Moscow, 1972) p. 174.
14. Ibid., p. 169.
15. E. Danilova, 'Sotsial'naya rol' zhenshchiny-materi', in *Dinamika izmeneniya polozheniya zhenshchiny i sem'ya*, (Moscow, 1972) p. 42.
16. Ibid., p. 45.
17. Yankova, *Sovetskaya zhenshchina*, pp. 123–4.
18. Ibid., p. 125.
19. Ibid., p. 123.
20. Ibid., p. 124–5.
21. Ibid., p. 128.
22. Kharchev, *Sem'ya i Brak*, p. 210.
23. Ibid., p. 209.
24. Kharchev, *Nravstvennost' i Sem'ya*, p. 22.
25. Kharchev, *Sem'ya i brak*, p. 222.
26. Ibid., p. 222.
27. Shimin, 'Rol' zhenshchiny-materi . . .', pp. 175–6.
28. For example, Yankova, in 'Razvitie lichnosti zhenshchiny . . .', pp. 44, and 48–9.
29. M. Matskovskii and T. Gurko, 'The Young Family: Problems of Formation', Abstract in *CDSP*, Vol. XXXVII, No, 5 (1984) pp. 5–6. (Originally in *Molodoi Kommunist*, June 1984, pp. 51–7.)
30. V. Perevedentsev, 'Ne soshlis' kharakterami?', in *Literaturnaya Gazeta*, 15 February 1978, p. 13.
31. L. Kuznetsova, 'Kto seichas glava sem'i?', in *My i Nasha Sem'ya* (Moscow, 1983), pp. 116–17.
32. M. S. Matskovskii, 'Podgotovka podrostkov i molodezhi k budushchei zhizhni', in *Sem'ya i sisteme nravstvennogo vospitaniya: Aktual'nye problemy vospitaniya podrostkov* (Moscow, 1979) pp. 204–13.
33. Yu. B. Ryurikov, 'Deti i obshchestvo (o nekotorykh aspektakh demografischeskoi politiki)', in *Voprosy Filosofii*, No. 4, 1977, pp. 111–21.

34. Ibid.
35. See L. Proshina, 'Muzhchiny, beregite sebya!', in *Nedelya*, 8 January 1987, p. 16. Also Yu. B. Ryurikov, 'Pochemu detei stanovitsya men'she?', in *Literaturnaya Gazeta*, 17 November 1976, and 'Pora zolotaya', in *Pravda*, 15 May 1983, p. 3.
36. Ryurikov, 'Deti i obschestvo . . .'
37. Ibid.
38. I. V. Bestuzhev-Lada, 'O zhenshchine i dlya zhenshchiny', in *Rabotnitsa*, No. 5, 1985, p. 26.
39. I. V. Bestuzhev-Lada, 'Net detei – net i budushchego u naroda', in *Nedelya*, 15–21 August 1988, p. 21.
40. Ibid.
41. N. Zakharova, A. Posadskaya and N. Rimashevskaya, 'Kak my reshaem zhenskii vopros', in *Kommunist*, No. 4, 1989, pp. 62–3.
42. Voronina, 'Zhenshchina v "muzhskom obshchestve"', p. 105.
43. M. Malysheva, 'Postylye plody "emansipatsii"', in *Nedelya*, 11–17 January 1988, p. 4.

7 The Pedagogical Approach to Sex Differences

1. A. G. Khripkova and D. V. Kolesov, *Devochka-podrostok-devushka* (Moscow, 1981) p. 72. (This book is also partly serialized in the journal *Sem'ya i Shkola*, August–December 1979. This quote is taken from the August edition, p. 28).
2. I. Dik, *Rastet v dome muzhchina* (Moscow, 1966) p. 45.
3. Ibid., p. 43.
4. Ibid.
5. Ibid., p. 45–6.
6. L. A. Levshin, *Mal'chik, muzhchina, otets* (Moscow, 1968) p. 13.
7. Ibid., p. 13–14.
8. Ibid., p. 104.
9. Ibid., p. 108.
10. Ibid., p. 109.
11. Ibid., p. 104.
12. Ibid.
13. Ibid.
14. Ibid., p. 9.
15. Ibid., pp. 69 and 72.
16. Ibid., pp. 70–82.
17. Ibid., p. 107.
18. Ibid.
19. E. G. Kostyashkin, 'Pedagogicheskie aspekty polovogo vospitaniya', in *Sovetskaya Pedagogika*, No. 7, 1964, p. 48.
20. Ibid., p. 47.
21. Ibid., p. 49.
22. Ibid.
23. Ibid., p. 51.
24. Ibid.

25. V. A. Grigoreva, 'Pedagogicheskie aspekty polovogo vospitaniya', in *Sbornik studenticheskikh nauchnykh rabot* (Blagoveshchenskogo gos.ped.in-ta, issue 11, 1974) p. 91.
26. V. Aleshina, 'Chtoby vyros nastoyashchii muzhchina', in *Sem'ya i Shkola*, No. 4, 1964, pp. 4–5; and A. G. Khripkova, *Voprosy polovogo vospitaniya* (Rostov na Dony, 1969) p. 53.
27. V. N. Kolbanovskii, 'The Sex-upbringing of the Rising Generation', in *Soviet Education*, No. 9, 1964, p. 4.
28. Ibid. p. 4.
29. Dik, *Rastet v dome muzhchina*, pp. 45–6.
30. Aleshina, 'Chtoby vyros nastoyashchii muzhchina', p. 5.
31. B. Ryabinin, 'Esli u zhenshchiny detei . . .', in *Sem'ya i Shkola*, No. 1, 1967, pp. 6–9.
32. E. Andreeva, 'Protiv patriarkhal'nykh nravov', in *Sem'ya i Shkola*, No. 1, 1967, pp. 6–9.
33. V. Mikhailova, 'Snova na kukhnyu?', in *Sem'ya i Shkola*, No. 3, 1967, pp. 4–6.
34. A. Burenkova, 'Ne ssylaites' na proshloe', in *Sem'ya i Shkola*, No. 4, 1967, p. 19.
35. S. Gazaryan, 'Ne ukhodit' ot glavnogo', in *Sem'ya i Shkola*, No. 3, 1967, pp. 4–6.
36. Yu. Shilov, 'Kazhdomy svoe', in *Sem'ya i Shkola*, No. 4, 1967, pp. 18–19.
37. Levshin, *Mal'chik, muzhchina, otets*, pp. 10–13.
38. Khripkova and Kolesov, *Devochka-podrostok-devushka* (Moscow, 1981) p. 83.
39. Ibid., p. 86.
40. Ibid., p. 73.
41. Ibid., pp. 73–80.
42. Ibid., p. 75.
43. Ibid., p. 79.
44. Ibid., p. 76.
45. Ibid., p. 87.
46. Ibid., p. 89.
47. Ibid., p. 120.
48. Ibid.
49. Ibid., p. 121.
50. Ibid., p. 120.
51. Khripkova, 'A kakov vklad pedagogiki?', in *Rabotnitsa*, No. 19, 1979, p. 14.
52. Kolesov, *Besedy o polovom vospitanii* (Moscow, 1980) p. 24.
53. Ibid., p. 24.
54. Ibid., p. 93.
55. Ibid., p. 181.
56. Ibid.
57. Ibid., p. 178.
58. Ibid., p. 221.
59. Ibid., p. 222.
60. L. Timoshchenko, 'O vospitanii devochki', in *Vospitanie Shkol'nikov*, No. 6, 1980, p. 37.
61. Ibid., p. 38.

Notes and References to pp. 152–65

62. Ibid.
63. Ibid.
64. Ibid.
65. Timoshchenko, *V sem'e rastet doch'* (Moscow, 1978) p. 6.
66. Timoshchenko, 'O vospitanii devochki', p. 38.
67. Ibid., p. 40; and *V sem'e rastet doch'*, p. 71.
68. *V sem'e rastet doch'*, pp. 58–9.
69. Ibid., p. 49.
70. Ibid., p. 77.
71. Ibid., p. 80.
72. Ibid., p. 89.
73. A. Mikaberidze, 'Osobennosti vospitaniya devochek', in *Kalendar dlya roditelei 1980* (Moscow, 1979) p. 97.
74. Kolbanovskii, 'The Sex-upbringing of the Rising Generation', p. 7.
75. Vladimir Vasil'ev, *Muzhskoi razgovor* (Moscow, 1982) pp. 26 and 90.
76. Ibid., p. 14.
77. Ibid., p. 26.
78. L. N. Gudkovich and A. M. Kondratov, *O tebe i obo mne* (Stavropol, 1977) p. 20.
79. Ibid., p. 18.
80. Ibid., p. 17.
81. V. Karakovskii, 'Uroki dlya mal'chishek', in *Sem'ya i Shkola* No. 9 1979, p. 20.
82. Gudkovich and Kondratov, *O tebe i obo mne*, p. 18.
83. Khripkova and Kolesov, *Devochka-podrostok-devushka*, p. 81.
84. Ibid., p. 75.
85. Khripkova, 'Neobkhodima mudrost' – polovoe vospitanie – grani problemy', in *Sovetskaya Rossiya*, 16 December 1979, p. 3.
86. N. N. Kuindzhi, 'Polovoe vospitanie', in *Zdorov'e*, No. 5, 1981, p. 18.
87. V. A. Sysenko, 'Zhenshchina i muzhchina', in *Zdorov'e*, No. 1, 1980, pp. 14–15.
88. A. N. Obosova and V. I. Shtil'bans, 'Budushchie muzh'ya, budushchie zheny', in *Zdorov'e*, No. 3, 1984, pp. 18–19.
89. I. V. Dorno, 'Muzhchina za 30', in *Zdorov'e*, No. 11, 1985, pp. 22–3.
90. 'Tied to Mama's Apron Strings', condensed text in *CDSP*, Vol. XXXVII, No. 15, 1985, p. 10. (Originally in *Moskovskaya Pravda*, 9 April 1985, p. 2.)
91. A. Koryakina, *Ottsy i deti* (Chelyabinsk, 1978) pp. 5–12 and 26.
92. Mikaberidze, 'Osobennosti vospitaniya devochek', p. 97.
93. For example, see I. Gyne, *Devushka prevrashchaetsya v zhenshchinu* (Moscow, 1981) p. 83, and Kolesov, *Besedy o polovom vospitanii*, p. 221.

8 The Popular Press

1. A. Strelyanyi, '"Perestavilsya" li svet?', in *Literaturnoe Obozrenie*, No. 5, 1977, p. 55.
2. N. G. Bogdanov and B. A. Vyazemski, quoted by M. McAndrew, 'Women's Magazines in the Soviet Union', in B. Holland (ed.), *Soviet Sisterhood* (London: Fourth Estate, 1985) p. 80.

3. E. P. Prokhorov, quoted by M. McAndrew, 'Women's Magazines in the Soviet Union', p. 78.
4. A. Roxburgh, *Pravda* (London: Victor Gollancz, 1987) p. 106.
5. M. W. Hopkins, *Mass Media in the Soviet Union* (New York: Pegasus, 1970) pp. 307, 300.
6. G. Belskaya, 'Otkuda berutsya plokhie zheny', in *Literaturnaya Gazeta*, 7 September 1977, p. 12.
7. 'Sila obayaniya, ili obayanie sily?', letter from V. Zolotovskii, in *Komsomol'skaya Pravda*, 30 April 1978, p. 4.
8. T. Afanas'eva, 'Muzhchina doma', in *Nedelya*, 30 May 1977, p. 6.
9. Ibid., pp. 6–7.
10. Afanas'eva, 'A byli mal'chik i devochka?', in *Zhurnalist*, No. 8, 1980, p. 43.
11. Yu. B. Ryurikov, quoted by L. Proshina, 'Muzhchiny, beregite sebya!', in *Nedelya*, 8 January 1987, p. 16.
12. Afanas'eva, 'A byli mal'chik i devochka?', p. 43.
13. Ibid., p. 41.
14. Ibid., p. 42.
15. G. Bagrazyan, 'Byt' uvazhaemym', in *Pravda*, 2 September 1984, p. 6.
16. L. Zhukovitskii, 'Kuda ischezayut nastoyashchie muzhchiny?', in *Literaturnaya Gazeta*, 10 October 1984, p. 12.
17. Bagrazyan, 'Byt' uvazhaemym', p. 6.
18. 'Sovremmenaya zhenshchina', in *Komsomol'skaya Pravda*, 13 October 1978, p. 4.
19. L. Tarkhova, 'Chto sluchilos' s muzhchinoi?', in *Komsomol'skaya Pravda*, 17 August 1986, p. 4.
20. Larisa Proshina, 'Muzhchiny, beregite sebya!', in *Nedelya*, 8 January 1987, pp. 16–17.
21. Ibid.
22. Afanas'eva, 'Muzhchina doma', pp. 6–7.
23. Ibid.
24. M. Tol'ts, 'Sem'ya', in *Pravda*, 20 March 1987, p. 2; and A. Zakharov, 'Mama na rabote', in *Sem'ya i Shkola*, No. 8, 1987, pp. 23–5.
25. Letter from Elena T., 'Svobodna. Ot chego?', in *Rabotnitsa*, No. 4, 1985, p. 29.
26. Letter from Lyubov' Gr-va, *Rabotnitsa*, No. 9, 1985, p. 25.
27. Letter from A. Katicheva, *Rabotnitsa*, No. 1, 1986, p. 29.
28. Letter from A. Lagunova, ibid., p. 29.
29. Letter from Popova, ibid., p. 28.
30. Letter from L. Goncharova, *Rabotnitsa*, No. 9, 1985, p. 25.
31. Ibid.
32. V. Alekseeva, 'Liki emansipatsii', ibid., p. 24.
33. I. Golubeva, 'Stepen' vnimania', ibid., p. 25.
34. I. Bestuzhev-Lada, 'O zhenshchine i dlya zhenshchiny', ibid., p. 26.
35. V. Stolin, 'Vybiraya – vybirai', ibid., p. 27.
36. V. N. Kozhevnikov and A. F. Vinogradov, 'Ne men'she chem troe!', in *Zdorov'e*, No. 12, 1981, pp. 12–13.
37. Ibid.; also 'Ne men'she chem troe!' (readers letters), in *Zdorov'e*, No. 12, 1982, pp. 18–19.

38. 'Mnogodetnaya sem'ya', in *Komsomol'skaya Pravda*, 30 October 1981.
39. Kozhevnikov and Vinogradov, 'Ne men'she chem troe!'.
40. Ibid.
41. See, for example, Polina Solovei, 'Pero zhar-ptitsy', in *Pravda*, 5 December 1983, p. 7.
42. T. Afanas'eva, 'Zhenshchina doma', in *Nedelya*, 9–15 December 1976, pp. 18–19.
43. See, for example, Michael Binyon, *Life in Russia* (London: Panther, 1983) pp. 56–7.
44. Alla Moiseikova, 'Schastlivaya zhenshchina – eta ... ya', in *Rabotnitsa*, No. 9, 1986, p. 20.
45. V. Lavrentsova, 'Mamoi nado stat'', in *Pravda*, 4 June 1984, p. 7.
46. I. Langueva, 'A vse-taki – lyubov'', interview with actress Natal'ya Gundareva in *Komsomol'skaya Pravda*, 8 February 1981, p. 4.
47. O. Dmitrieva, 'Domovodstvo', *Komsomol'skaya Pravda*, 24 September 1981, p. 2.
48. G. W. Lapidus, *Women in Soviet Society* (Berkeley and London: University of California Press, 1978) p. 330.
49. L. Kuznetsova, *Zhenshchina na rabote i doma* (Moscow, 1980), pp. 174 and 176.
50. Ibid., pp. 127 and 151.
51. Ibid., pp. 174–5.
52. Ibid., p. 177
53. Ibid., p. 163.
54. Ibid., p. 167.
55. A. Oakley, *Subject Woman* (London: Fontana, 1982) pp. 215–6.
56. Kuznetsova, *Zhenshchina na rabote i doma*, p. 162.
57. Ibid., p. 170.
58. Deputy chair of the Supreme Court of the RSFSR Nina Yu. Sergeeva answers questions put by L. Kuznetsova, 'Otets est' – otsa net', in *Literaturnaya Gazeta*, 3 April 1985, p. 12.
59. Kuznetsova, 'V zashchitu zhenskoi kar'ery', in *Novoe Vremya*, 19 June 1987, pp. 22–4.
60. Kuznetsova, 'Tretii pol?', in *Novoe Vremya*, 9 September 1988, p. 46.
61. Ibid.
62. Ibid., p. 47.
63. M. Lebedeva, 'Poka muzhchiny govoryat ...', in *Izvestiya*, 23 October 1988, p. 6.
64. Kuznetsova, 'Igra v korolevu?' in *Nedelya*, 2 January 1989, pp. 18–19.
65. Kuznetsova, 'Tretii pol?', p. 47.
66. I. Marmaladze, 'Poslednyaya privilegiya', in *Literaturnaya Gazeta*, 23 January 1985, p. 11.
67. Ibid.
68. Ninel' Maslova and El'vira Novikova, 'Parametry "zhenskogo voprosa"', in *Novoe Vremya*, 11 December 1987, p. 28.
69. Ibid.
70. Interview with T. E. Abova, conducted by L. Derun, 'Vernetsya li ona na kukhnyu?', in *Sovetskaya Zhenshchina*, No. 7, 1988, p. 9.
71. I. Zhuravskaya, 'Razgovor 9 Marta', in *Rabotnitsa*, No. 3, 1988, p. 7.

72. O. Voronina, 'Muzhchiny sozdali mir dlya sebya . . .', in *Sovetskaya Zhenshchina*, No. 11, 1988, p. 14.
73. Zhuravskaya, 'Razgovor 9 Marta'.
74. D. Akivis, 'Materinstvo i "otchestvo"', in *Rabotnitsa*, No. 6, 1988, pp. 21–3.
75. E. Cherenakhova, 'Opyat' subbota bez mamy', in *Rabotnitsa*, No. 11, 1987, p. 16.
76. Introduction to article by N. Azhgikhina, 'Volshebnaya vetka, mimozy', in *Komsomol'skaya Pravda*, 30 May 1982, p. 2.
77. L. S. Lomize, 'Molodezhi o semeinoi zhizhni', in *Sovetskaya Pedagogika*, No. 1, 1984, p. 23.

9 The Practical Application of Soviet Ideas on Sex Differences

1. For example, G. Naan, 'Emansipatsiya, patriarkhat i "voina polov"', in *Literaturnoe Obozrenie*, No. 9, 1977, pp. 57–62; and V. Sysenko, in 'Mnogodetnaya sem'ya: vzglyad v budushchee', round-table discussion on the multi-child family reported by O. Dmitrieva in *Komsomol'skaya Pravda*, 30 October 1981, p. 2.
2. A. Inin (script-writer of film 'One day 20 years later'), participant in *Komsomol'skaya Pravda*'s round-table discussion on the multi-child family, reported in 'Mnogodetnaya sem'ya', 30 October 1981.
3. Interview with A. Egides, conducted by T. Ostrovskaya, 'Sovet i podderzhka', in *Sem'ya i Shkola*, No. 12, 1988, pp. 28–31.
4. G. Belskaya, 'Otkuda berutsya plokhie zheny', in *Literaturnaya Gazeta*, 7 September 1977, p. 12.
5. T. I. Yufereva, 'Obrazy muzhchin i zhenshchin v soznanii podrostkov', in *Voprosy Psikhologii*, No. 3, 1985, p. 84.
6. A. S. Krasovskii, *Eticheskie besedy so starsheklassnikami o brake i sem'e* (Minsk, 1983) p. 6.
7. This suggestion came up during a discussion following a paper I gave on 'Gender and Soviet Pedagogy' at a conference held by the Soviet Education Study Group at CSEES in London on 15 November 1986. It is borne out by figures offered by R. Ubaidulleva, 'Sotsial'nye aspekty ispol'zovaniya zhenskogo truda', in *Kommunist Uzbekistana*, No. 7, 1979, p. 34.
8. Yufereva, 'Obrazy muzhchin i zhenshchin . . .', p. 90.
9. Ibid., p. 90.
10. T. Snegireva, 'Ne predopredlenie, a vybor', *Literaturnaya Gazeta*, 23 May 1984, p. 12.
11. This was reproduced in a series 'Etika i psikhologiya semeinoi zhizni' in *Vospitanie Shkol'nikov*, Nos 1 and 2, 1982 ('experimental version'), and Nos 1–6, 1983 (Course Outline for Teachers).
12. *Vospitanie Shkol'nikov*, No. 1, 1982, pp. 29–30.
13. Ibid., 1983, p. 36.
14. Ibid., p. 37.
15. Ibid., p. 38.
16. *Vospitanie Shkol'nikov*, No. 3, 1983, pp. 28–9.
17. Ibid., No. 4, 1983, p. 36.

18. Ibid., No. 1, 1982, p. 32.
19. I. V. Bestuzhev-Lada, 'Itak, nachinaem', in *Izvesitya*, 31 August 1985, p. 6.
20. L. Kovalenko, 'Vysokoe i prekrasnoe prednaznachenie zhenshchiny', in *Vospitanie Shkol'nikov*, No. 1, 1986, pp. 66–8.
21. I. Orchinnikova, 'Milye branyatsya', in *Vospitanie Shkol'nikov*, No. 5, 1986, pp. 68–9.
22. A. Kotlyar, 'Muzhskaya otvetstvennost'', in *Vospitanie Shkol'nikov*, No. 4, 1986, pp. 69–71.
23. L. Kuznetsova, 'O domashnikh zabotakh', in *Vospitanie Shkol'nikov*, No. 5, 1988, pp. 64–6.
24. For example, V. Cherednichenko, 'Iz opyta prepodovaniya etika i psikhologiya semeinoi zhizni', in *Vospitanie Shkol'nikov*, No. 3, 1986, pp. 75–7. Also, personal conversation with teacher in Moscow.
25. L. Kovaleva, 'Otmetki vystavit zhizn'', in *Vospitanie Shkol'nikov*, No. 5, 1986, pp. 69–70.
26. Ibid.
27. Personal conversations with teachers in Moscow and Kalinin.
28. Egides, 'Sovet i podderzhka', p. 30.
29. L. S. Lomize, 'Vsemerno ukreplyat' sovetskuyu sem'yu', in *Sovetskaya Pedagogika*, No. 6, 1986, p. 57.
30. L. Velikanova, 'Sem'ya – sem' "ya"!', interview with A. Spirkin, in *Literaturnaya Gazeta*, 1 May 1978, p. 12. Also A. G. Kharchev, *Sem'ya i brak v SSSR* (Moscow, 1979), p. 203.
31. Cheslovas Grizitskas, in an interview with N. Tyurina, 'Grozdiki po sredam', in *Komsomol'skaya Pravda*, 6 February 1976, p. 2.
32. M. Bednyi, 'Sem'ya i demografiya', in *Pravda*, 6 December 1984, p. 3.
33. L. S. Lomize, 'Molodezhi o semeinoi zhizhni', in *Sovetskaya Pedagogika*, No. 1, 1984, p. 20; and Elena Mushkina, 'Sluzhba sem'i i demografiya', in *Nedelya*, 12–18 January 1981, pp. 2–3, 10–11.
34. Lomize, 'Vsemerno ukreplyat' . . .', p. 22; and Grizitskas, 'Grozdiki po sredam', p. 2.
35. Grizitskas, 'Grodzdiki po sredam', p. 2.
36. Bednyi, 'Sem'ya i demografiya', p. 3.
37. Lomize, 'Vsemerno ukreplyat' sovetskuyu sem'yu', in *Sovetskaya Pedagogika*, No. 6, 1986, p. 54.
38. Velikanova's interview with Spirkin, 'Sem'ya – sem' "ya"!', and Kharchev, *Sem'ya i brak v SSSR*, p. 203.
39. Grizitskas, 'Grozdiki po sredam', p.2.
40. Egides, 'Sovet i podderzhka', p. 28.
41. Grizitskas, 'Grozdiki po sredam', p.2.
42. Ibid.
43. Ibid.
44. Ibid.
45. A. Poleev, 'V poiskakh sovmestimosti', in *Rabotnitsa* No. 3, 1987, p. 31.
46. Ibid.
47. Ibid.
48. N. Efremenko, 'Klub molodoi sem'i', in *My i nasha sem'ya* (Moscow, 1983), pp. 84–6, and E. S. Kalmykova, 'Psikhologisheskie problemy

pervykh let supruzheskoi zhizni', in *Voprosy Psikhologii*, No. 3, 1983, pp. 83–8.
49. N. Dar'yalova, 'Svad'bu pishem, razvod – v ume', in *Literaturnaya Gazeta*, 28 August 1985, p. 13.
50. Ibid.
51. I. V. Dorno, 'Pochti zhenat ili pochti kholost?', in *Zdorov'e*, No. 9, 1986, pp. 22–3.
52. V. Stolin, 'Vybiraya – vybirai' in *Rabotnitsa*, No. 5, 1986, p. 27.
53. Ibid.
54. Ibid.
55. Lomize, 'Molodezhi o semeinoi zhizhni', p. 21.
56. Ibid.
57. O. Dmitrieva, 'Domovodstvo', in *Komsolol'skaya Pravda*, 24 September 1981, p. 2.
58. S. Antonova, 'Studentka vyshla zamuzh', in *Pravda*, 10 December 1984, p. 7.
59. Mushkina, 'Sluzhba sem'i i demografiya', p. 10.
60. Lomize, 'Molodezhi o semeinoi zhizhni', p. 21.
61. 'Sluzhba sem'i – kakoi ei byt'?' (editorial article), in *Sem'ya i Shkola*, No. 8, 1987, pp. 1–2.
62. Dar'yalova, 'Svad'bu pishem, razvod – v ume'.
63. Bednyi, 'Sem'ya i demografiya, p. 3.
64. A. Rubinov, 'Lyubov' po ob"yavleniyu?', in *Literaturnaya Gazeta*, 20 May 1970, p. 13.
65. Velikanova's interview with Spirkin, 'Sem'ya – sem' "ya"!'.
66. Yu. Ryurikov, 'Love and Family Today – Sharp and Controversial Questions', Abstract in *CDSP*, Vol. XXVIII, No. 15, 1976, p. 3. (Originally in *Molodoi Kommunist*, No. 10, 1975.)
67. A. Rubinov, 'Schast'e tak vozmozhno', in *Literaturnaya Gazeta*, 8 March 1978, p. 12.
68. Egides, 'Sovet i podderzhka', p. 28–9.
69. Velikanova's interview with Spirkin, 'Sem'ya – sem' "ya"!'.
70. In addition to articles mentioned elsewhere, see also 'Pozvol'te poznakomit'sya', in *Literaturnaya Gazeta*, 30 November 1977, p. 12; E. Fedoseeva, '"SM-120 khotel by naznachit' svidanie SZH-40 . . ." - iz opyta raboty sektsii supruzheskikh znakomstv', in *Literaturnaya Gazeta*, 25 October 1978, p. 13.; L. Malinovskii, 'Zaochnyi klub "druzhba"', in *Literaturnaya Gazeta*, 22 December 1976, p. 13; Nina Rusakova, 'Retsept ot odinochestva', in *Rabotnitsa*, No. 7, 1985, pp. 26–8; Nina Rusakova, 'Troe i odna', in *Rabotnitsa*, No. 3, 1986, pp. 26–8; S. Golikova, 'Abonent No. 0000308 – ochen' schastliv!', in *Rabotnitsa*, No. 12, 1986, p. 26; E. Mushkina, 'Sluzhba sem'i i demografiya', in *Nedelya*, 12–18 January 1981, pp. 2–3, 10–11; O. Fin'ko, 'Kak naiti lyubimogo', in *Komsomol'skaya Pravda*, 14 October 1980, p. 2; and O. Fin'ko, 'Prikhodite svatat'sya', in *Komsomol'skaya Pravda*, 14 October 1980, p. 4.
71. 'Bud'te znakomy! – o chem povedali pervye 500 pisem', in *Literaturnaya Gazeta*, 22 December 1976, p. 13.
72. Ibid.

Notes and References to pp. 199–210

73. For example, 'Love and Marriage' – a series of articles on the subject in *Soviet Weekly*, 9 April 1988, pp. 5–11.
74. Quoted by A. G. Volkov, 'Sem'ya kak faktor izmeneniya demograficheskoi situatsii', in *Sotsiologicheskie Issledovaniya*, No. 1, 1981, p. 39.
75. Ibid.
76. Leonid Zhukhovitskii, 'Kuda ischezayut nastoyashchie muzhchiny?', in *Literaturnaya Gazeta*, 10 October 1984, p. 12.
77. Cited by V. Perevedentsev, 'Ne soshlis' kharakterami?', in *Literaturnaya Gazeta*, 15 February 1978, p. 13.
78. Christopher Walker, 'Gorbachev Sets the Seal on New Era of Reform', in *The Times*, 27 February 1986, p. 7.
79. L. S. Lomize, 'Vsemerno ukreplyat' sovetskuyu sem'yu', in *Sovetskaya Pedagogika*, No. 6, 1986, p. 56.
80. G. Naan, 'Emansipatsiya, patriarkhat i "voina polov"', in *Literaturnoe Obozrenie*, No. 9, 1977, p. 58.
81. A. Egides, 'Lider nachinaet i . . . proigryvaet', in *Literaturnaya Gazeta*, 2 October 1986, p. 13.
82. 'O pape, mame i semeinoi drame', in *Literaturnaya Gazeta*, 26 December 1984, p. 13.
83. Ibid.
84. I. Marmaladze, 'Poslednyaya privilegiya', in *Literaturnaya Gazeta*, 23 January 1985, p. 11.
85. L. Kuznetsova, 'Otets est' – ottsa net', interview with deputy chair of the Supreme Court of the RSFSR, Nina Yu. Sergeeva, in *Literaturnaya Gazeta*, 3 April 1985, p. 12.
86. Ibid.
87. L. S. Lomize, 'Vsemerno ukreplyat' sovetskuyu sem'yu', in *Sovetskaya Pedagogika*, No. 6, 1986, p. 56.
88. 'O pape, mame i semeinoi drame', p. 13.

10 Sex Role Socialization in the USSR: Summary of the Past, and Prospects for the Future

1. N. Zakharova, A. Posadskaya, and N. Rimashevskaya, 'Kak my reshaem zhenskii vopros', in *Kommunist*, No. 4, 1989, pp. 56–9.
2. See T. Frisby, 'Soviet Youth Culture', in J. Riordan (ed.), *Soviet Youth Culture* (London: Macmillan, 1989) pp. 1–15.
3. A. Strelyanyi, '"Perestavilsya" li svet?', in *Literaturnoe Obozrenie*, No. 5, 1983, p. 3.
4. Zakharova *et al.*, 'Kak my reshaem zhenskii vopros', p. 60.
5. Ibid., p. 59–60.
6. I. Zhuravskaya, 'Razgovor 9 Marta', in *Rabotnitsa*, No. 3, 1988, p. 7.
7. L. Kuznetsova, 'Glazami zhenshchiny', interview with A. Vishnevskii, in *Novoe Vremya*, 10 March 1989, p. 33.
8. S. Kauffmann, 'USSR still Touchy about its Gays', in *The Guardian Weekly*, 3 April 1988, p. 14.
9. Zakharova *et al.*, 'Kak my reshaem zhenskii vopros', p. 60.

10. L. Kuznetsova, 'Tretii pol?', in *Novoe Vremya*, 9 September 1988, p. 47.
11. M. Lebedeva, 'Poka muzhchiny govoryat . . .', in *Izvestiya*, 23 October 1988, p. 6.
12. See, for example, N. S. Yulina, 'Problemy zhenshchin: filosofskie aspekty (feministskaya mysl' v S.SH.A)', in *Voprosy Filosofii*, No. 5, 1988, pp. 137–47; and T. A. Klimenkova, 'Filosofskie problemy neofeminizma 70-kh godov', in *Voprosy Filosofii*, No. 5, 1988, pp. 148–57.
13. Kuznetsova, 'Glazami zhenshchiny', p. 34.
14. Zakharova *et al.*, 'Kak my reshaem zhenskii vopros', p. 57.
15. Personal conversations with Russian women. Also, see the speeches given at the All Union Conference of Women held in Moscow in 1987, reported in 'Vsesoyuznaya konferentsiya zhenshchin – Doklad V. V. Tereshkovoi', in *Izvesitya*, 1 February 1987, pp. 3–4; 'Govoryat uchastnitsy i gosti vsesoyuznoi konferentsii zhenshchin', in *Izvestiya*, 2 February 1987, pp. 2–4; and 'Khozyaiki zemli rodnoi', in *Rabotnitsa*, No. 3, 1987.
16. For example, Zakharova *et al.*, 'Kak my reshaem zhenskii vopros', p. 57; and N. Maslova and E. Novikova, 'Parametry "zhenskogo voprosa"', in *Novoe Vremya*, 11 December 1987, pp. 28–9.

Bibliography

List of Soviet Journals and Newspapers Used

Fizkul'tura i Zdorov'e
Izvestiya
Kommunist
Komsomol'skaya Pravda
Krestyanka
Literaturnaya Gazeta
Literaturnoe Obozrenie
Meditsinskaya Gazeta
Nedelya
Novoe Vremya
Novye Issledovaniya v Psikhologii
Novyi Mir
Pravda
Rabotnitsa
Sem'ya i Shkola
Sotsiologicheskie Issledovaniya
Sovetskaya Pedagogika
Sovetskaya Rossiya
Sovetskoe Zdravookhranenie
Uchitel'skaya Gazeta
Voprosy Filosofii
Voprosy Psikhologii
Vospitanie Shkol'nikov
Yunost'
Zhurnalist
Zdorov'e

Material in Russian

ABOVA, T. E., interviewed by L. Derun, 'Vernetsya li ona na kukhnyu...?', in *Sovetskaya Zhenshchina*, No. 7, 1988, p. 9.

AIDAROVA, K., 'Eshche raz o ravnopravii', in *Pravda*, 31 July 1977, p. 3.

AFANAS'EV, A., 'Maminy chasy', in *Komsomol'skaya Pravda*, 7 October 1981, p. 2.

AFANAS'EVA, T., 'Zhenshchina doma', in *Nedelya*, 9–15 December 1976, pp. 18–19.

AFANAS'EVA, T., 'Muzhchina doma', in *Nedelya*, 30 May 1977, pp. 6–7.

AFANAS'EVA, T., 'A byli mal'chik i devochka?', in *Zhurnalist* No. 8, 1980, pp. 41–4

AFANAS'EVA, T., 'Sem'ya v zerkale sotsiologii', in *Vospitanie Shkol'nikov*, No. 1, 1986, pp. 65–66.
AFANAS'EVA, T., 'Dvoe', in *Vospitanie Shkol'nikov*, No. 3, 1986, pp. 73–5.
AKIVIS, D., ZHURAVSKAYA, I., SKYLAR, I. and STEPANOV, A., 'Daite miru shans! – Vsemirnyi kongress zhenshchin', in *Rabotnitsa*, No. 8, 1987, pp. 2–5.
AKIVIS, D. and MUSHKINA, E., 'Kakaya sem'ya nam nuzhna?', in *Nedelya*, No. 47, 1987, p. 17.
AKIVIS, D., 'Materinstvo i "otchestvo"', in *Rabotnitsa*, No. 6, 1988, pp. 21–3.
ALEKSANDROV, G., 'Lechit' sem'yu, kogda ona zabolela', in *Literaturnaya Gazeta*, 11 October 1978, p. 12.
ALEKSEEVA, V., 'Liki emansipatsii', *Rabotnitsa*, No. 5, 1986, p. 24.
ALESHINA, V., 'Chtoby vyros nastoyashchii muzhchina', in *Sem'ya i Shkola*, No. 4, 1964, pp. 4–5.
ANAN'EV, B. G., *Chelovek kak predmet soznaniya* (Leningrad, 1968).
ANDREEVA, E., 'Protiv patriarkhal'nykh nravov', in *Sem'ya i Shkola*, No. 1, 1967, pp. 6–9.
ANTONOV, A., 'Dvukh detei mala', in *Meditsinskaya Gazeta*, 27 September 1985, p. 4.
ANTONOVA, S., 'Studentka vyshla zamuzh', in *Pravda*, 10 December 1984, p. 7.
ANUFRIEVA, A., 'Razgovor na trudnuyu temy', in *Uchitel'skaya Gazeta*, 19 January 1982, p. 3.
ASMOLOV, A. G., 'O predmete psikhologii lichnosti', in *Voprosy Psikhologii*, No. 3, 1983, pp. 118–30.
AZHGIKHINA, N., 'Volshebnaya vetka, mimozy', in *Komsomol'skaya Pravda*, 30 May 1982, p. 2.
BAGRAZYAN, G., 'Byt' uvazhaemym', in *Pravda*, 2 September 1984, p. 6.
BAGRUNOV, V. P. and KUTS, V. A., 'K voprosu o neobkhodimosti ucheta psikhologicheskikh osobennostei pola v semeinoi vospitanii', in *Pedagogicheskie aspekty sotsial'noi psikhologii* (Minsk, 1978) pp. 214–15.
BASKINA. A., 'Ot chego zavisit rost sem'i?', in *Sem'ya i Shkola*, No. 12, 1981, p. 28.
BEDNYI, M., 'Sem'ya i demografiya', in *Pravda*, 6 December 1984, p. 3.
BELKIN, A. I., 'Biologicheskie i sotsial'nye faktory, formiruyushchie polovuyu identifikatsiyu', in *Sootnoshenie biologicheskogo i sotsial'nogo v cheloveke* (Moscow, 1975).
BELKIN, A. I., (ed.), *Gormony i mozg* (Moscow, 1979).
BELKIN, A. I. and LAKUSTA, V. N., *Biologicheskaya terapiya psikhicheskikh zabolevanii* (Kishinev, 1983).
BELSKAYA, G., 'Otkuda berutsya plokhie zheny', in *Literaturnaya Gazeta*, 7 September 1977, p. 12.
BESTUZHEV-LADA, I., 'Sem'ya – izvechnaya tsennost'', in *Novyi Mir*, No. 7, 1980, pp. 264–8.
BESTUZHEV-LADA, I., 'O zhenshchine i dlya zhenshchiny', *Rabotnitsa*, No. 5, 1985, p. 26.
BESTUZHEV-LADA, I. V., 'Itak, nachinaem', in *Izvestiya*, 31 August 1985, p. 6.

BESTUZHEV-LADA, I. V., 'Net detei – net i budushchego u naroda', in *Nedelya*, 15–21 August 1988, pp. 20–21.
BOGUSLAVSKAYA, Z., 'Kakie my, zhenshchiny?', in *Literaturnaya Gazeta*, 5 August 1987, p. 12.
BOITKO, I., 'V interesakh sem'i', in *Pravda*, 18 May 1984, p. 3.
'Bud'te znakomy! – o chem povedali pervye 500 pisem', in *Literaturnaya Gazeta*, 22 December 1976, p. 13.
BURENKOVA, A., 'Ne ssylaites' na proshloe', in *Sem'ya i Shkola*, No. 4, 1967, p. 19.
'Chelovek byudushchego – kakov on?' (collection of short articles), in *Literaturnaya Gazeta*, 11 October 1978, p. 12.
CHEREDNICHENKO, V., 'Iz opyta prepodavaniya etiki i psikhologiya semeinoi zhizni', in *Vospitanie Shkol'nikov*, No. 3, 1986, pp. 75–7.
CHEREPAKHOVA, E., 'Opyat' subbota bez mamy', in *Rabotnitsa*, No.11, 1987, pp. 15–17.
DANILOVA, E., 'Sotsial'naya rol' zhenshchiny-materi', in *Dinamika izmeneniya polozheniya zhenshchiny i sem'ya* (Moscow, 1972).
DAR'YALOVA, N.,'Svad'bu pishem, razvod – v ume', in *Literaturnaya Gazeta*, 28 August 1985, p. 13.
DAR'YALOVA, N., 'Pozhar', in *Literaturnaya Gazeta*, 4 February 1987, p. 13.
DAVYDOV, V. V., 'Itogi i perspektivy nauchnoi deyatelnosti instituta obshchei i pedagogicheskoi psikhologii', in *Voprosy Psikhologii*, No. 1, 1983, pp. 5–22.
'Dela domashnie' (readers' letters), in *Komsomol'skaya Pravda*, 22 October 1981, p. 2.
DIK, IOSIF, *Rastet v dome muzhchina* (Moscow, 1966).
DIMOV, G., 'Bol'shaya sem'ya glazami medikov', in *Izvestiya*, 28 February 1987, p. 2.
DMITRIEVA, O., 'Domovodstvo', in *Komsomol'skaya Pravda*, 24 September 1981, p. 2.
DMITRIEVA, O., 'Mnogodetnaya sem'ya: vzglyad v budushchee', in *Komsomol'skaya Pravda*, 30 October 1981, p. 2.
DOLINA, N., 'Ne pri vsekh', *Komsomol'skaya Pravda*, 15 December 1964, p. 2.
DORNO, I. V., 'Muzhchina za 30', in *Zdorov'e*, No. 11, 1985, pp. 22–3.
DORNO, I. V., 'Pochti zhenat ili pochti kholost?', in *Zdorov'e*, No. 9, 1986, pp. 22–3.
DRYAKHOV, N. I., LITVINOVA, I. V. and PAVLOVA, V. V., 'Otsenki muzhchinami i zhenshchinami uslovii truda: sblizhenie ili differentsiatsiya?', in *Sotsiologicheskie Issledovaniya*, No. 4, 1987, pp. 111–14.
DUBININ, N. P., 'Nasledovanie biologishceskoe i sotsial'noe', in *Kommunist*, July 1980, pp. 62–74.
DUBININ, N. P., KARPETS, I. I. and KUDRYAVTSEV, V. N., *Genetika, povedenie, otvetstvennost'* (Moscow, 1982).
EFIMOV, M., 'F. P. Petrov, Opyt issledovaniya intellektual'nogo razvitiya Chuvashskikh detei po metodu Bine-Simon, 1928', in *Pedologiya*, Nos 7–8, 1939, p. 128.
EFREMENKO, N., 'Klub molodoi sem'i', in *My i nasha sem'ya* (Moscow, 1983) pp. 84–6.

EGIDES, A., 'Lider nachinaet i . . . proigryvaet', in *Literaturnaya Gazeta*, 2 October 1986, p. 13.
EGIDES, A., interviewed by T. Ostrovskaya, 'Sovet i podderzhka', in *Sem'ya i Shkola*, No. 12, 1988, pp. 28–31.
EL'SHTEIN, N. V., 'On i ona', in *Fizkul'tura i Zdorov'e*, No. 1, 1984, pp. 60–3.
'Eta trudnaya semeinaya zhizn' . . .' (readers' letters), in *Yunost'*, No. 10, 1978, pp. 56–9.
'Etika i psikhologiya semeinoi zhizhni', in *Vospitanie Shkol'nikov* Nos 1–6, 1983.
FEDOSEEV, P. N., 'Problema sotsial'nogo i biologicheskogo v filosofii i sotsiologii', in *Biologicheskoe i sotsial'noe v razvitii cheloveka* (Moscow, Academiya Nauk SSSR, Institut Psikhologii, 1977) pp. 5–30.
FEDOSEEVA, E., '"SM-120 khotel by naznachit' svidanie SZH-40 . . ." – iz opyta raboty sektsii supruzheskikh znakomstv', in *Literaturnaya Gazeta*, 25 October 1978, p. 13.
FEL'DSHTEIN, D. I., 'Psikhologo-pedagogicheskie problemy sootnosheniya biologicheskogo i sotsial'nogo', in *Sovetskaya Pedagogika*, No. 5, 1984, pp. 52–6.
FIN'KO, O., 'Kak naiti lyubimogo', in *Komsomol'skaya Pravda*, 8 August 1980, p. 2.
FIN'KO, O., 'Prikhodite svatat'sya', in *Komsomol'skaya Pravda*, 14 October 1980, p. 4.
FLORES, M., interviewed by V. Sobolev, 'Mat' i "macho"', in *Novoe Vremya*, 22 July 1988, pp. 38–9.
GARBUZOV, V., 'Trudnye voprosy', in *Sem'ya i Shkola*, No. 5, 1986, pp. 32–3.
GAZARYAN, S., 'Ne ukhodit' ot glavnogo', in *Sem'ya i Shkola*, No. 3, 1967, pp. 4–6.
GOLIKOVA, S., 'Abonent No. 0000308 – ochen' schastliv!', in *Rabotnitsa*, No. 12, 1986, p. 26.
GOLUBEVA, I. V. and BELKIN, A. I., 'Sotsial'no-pravovye aspekty germafroditisma', in A. I. Belkin (ed.) *Gormony i mozg* (Moscow, 1979) pp. 82–90.
GOLUBEVA, I. V., 'Stepen' vnimaniya', in *Rabotnitsa*, No. 5, 1985, p. 25.
GORBACHEV, M. S., Communiqué on the plenary session of the Central Committee of the CPSU, *Pravda & Izvestiya*, 28 January 1987, p. 1.
'Govoryat uchastnitsy i gosti vsesoyuznoi konferentsii zhenshchin', in *Izvestiya*, 2 February 1987, pp. 2–4.
GRAFOVA, L., 'Vernut' muzha?', in *Literaturnaya Gazeta*, No. 42, 1981, p. 12.
GRIZITSKAS, Ch., 'Iskusstvo zhit' vdvoem', in *Vospitanie Skhol'nikov*, No. 5, 1986, p. 68.
GUDKOVICH, L. N. and KONDRATOV, A. M., *O tebe i obo mne* (Stavropol', 1977).
GUROVA, R., 'Dinamika tsennostnykh orientatsii devushek 1913–1919' in *Dinamika izmeneniya polozheniya zhenshchiny i sem'ya* (Moscow, 1972) pp. 29–39.
GYNE, I., 'Zhenstvennost'', in P. Peter, V. Shebek and I. Gyne, *Devushka prevrashchaetsya v zhenshchinu* (Moscow, 1960).
GYNE, I., *Yunosha prevrashchaetsya v muzhchinu* (Moscow, 1960).

ILLARIONOVA, I., 'Troe detei – sem'ya mnogodetnaya', *Zdorov'e*, No. 11, 1983, p. 4.
IMELINSKII, K., *Psikhogigiena polovoi zhizhni* (Moscow, 1972).
ISCHENKO, A., 'Ne zrya zhivy na zemle', in *Pravda*, 4 June 1984, p. 7.
IVANOVA, V., 'Edinstvennyi rebenok', in *Sovetskaya Rossiya*, 20 November 1983, p. 3.
KACHUK, G., 'Zhena vinovata', *Nedelya*, 22–28 July 1985, p. 12.
'Kak pomoch' Ol'ge?' (readers' letters), in *Komsomol'skaya Pravda*, 20 September 1981, p. 2.
'Kakaya sem'ya nam nuzhna' (readers' letters) in *Nedelya*, 20–26 November 1987, pp. 17–18.
KALMYKOVA, E. S., 'Psikhologisheskie problemy pervykh let supruzheskoi zhizni', in *Voprosy Psikhologii*, No. 3, 1983, pp. 83–9.
KARAKOVSKII, V., 'Uroki dlya mal'chishek', in *Sem'ya i Shkola*, No. 9, 1979, pp. 18–21.
KARSAEVSKAYA, T. V., 'O sotsial'nykh i biologicheskikh aspektakh razvitiya rebenka', in *Sootnoshenie biologicheskogo i sotsial'nogo v razvitii cheloveke* (Moscow, 1974) pp. 50–52.
'Kazhdoi sem'e – otdel'nuyu kvartiru' (readers' letters), in *Literaturnaya Gazeta*, 14 January 1987, p. 11.
KELLY, A. and SNEGIREVA, T., 'Ne predopredelenie, a vybor', *Literaturnaya Gazeta*, 28 May 1984, p. 12.
KHARCHEV, A. G., *Sem'ya i brak v SSSR* (Moscow, 1979).
KHARCHEV, A. G., *Nravstvennost' i sem'ya* (Moscow, 1981).
KHASHCHENKO, T. G., 'Rol' frustrirovannosti i pola partnerov v sovmestnom reshenii myslitel'nykh zadach', in *Voprosy Psikhologii*, No. 5, 1982, pp. 118–22.
'Khozyaiki zemli rodnoi' (report from the All-Union Women's Conference), in *Rabotnitsa*, No. 3, 1987, pp. 2–6.
KHRIPKOVA, A. G., *Voprosy polovogo vospitaniya* (a lecture given to teachers in the town of Rostov) (Rostov na Donu, 1969).
KHRIPKOVA, A. G., 'Voprosy polovogo vospitaniya', *Sovetskaya Pedagogika*, No. 3, 1970, p. 106.
KHRIPKOVA, A. G., *Razgovor na trudnuyu temu* (Moscow, 1970).
KHRIPKOVA, A. G., 'Ne toropis', devushka ...', in *Krestyanka*, No, 5, 1979, p. 26.
KHRIPKOVA, A. G., 'A kakov vklad pedagogiki?', in *Rabotnitsa*, No. 19, 1979, pp. 12–15.
KHRIPKOVA, A. G., 'Neobkhodima mudrost'' (polovoe vospitanie – grani problemy), in *Sovetskaya Rossiya*, 16 December 1979, p. 3.
KHRIPKOVA, A. G. and KOLESOV, D. V., *Devochka-podrostok-devushka* (Moscow, 1981). This book is also partly serialized in the journal *Sem'ya i Shkola*, Nos 8–12, 1979.
KHRIPKOVA, A. G. and KOLESOV, D. V., *Mal'chik-podrostok-yunosha* (Moscow, 1982).
KHUTORNAYA, T., 'Prazdnik, posvyashchennii Dnyu 8 Marta', in *Vospitanie Skhol'nikov*, No. 1, 1985, pp. 73–4.
KIRYUSHCHENKOV, A. P., 'Tol'ko ne abort', in *Zdorov"*, No. 12, 1981, pp. 26–7.

KISELEVA, T. I., 'V sem'e rodilos' pyatero detei. Kak bylo?', in *Literaturnaya Gazeta*, 2 October 1986, p. 13.
KLIMENKOVA, T. A., 'Filosofskie problemy neofeminizma 70-kh godov', in *Voprosy Filosofii*, No. 5, 1988, pp. 148–57.
KNIZHNIK, S., 'Razvod . . .s synom', in *Literaturnaya Gazeta*, 23 January 1985, p. 11.
KOLESOV, V., *Besedy o polovom vospitanii* (Moscow, 1980).
KON, I. S., *Lichnost kak sub"ekt obshchestvennykh otnoshenii* (Moscow, 1966).
KON, I. S., 'Muzhestvennye zhenshchiny? Zhenstvennye muzhchini?', in *Literaturnaya Gazeta*, 1 January 1970, p. 12.
KON, I. S., 'Polovye razlichiya i differentsiatsiya sotsial'nykh rolei', in *Sootnoshenie biologicheskogo i sotsial'nogo v cheloveke* (Moscow, 1975) pp. 763–76.
KON, I. S., 'Ot chetyrnadtsati do vosemnadtsati', in *Vospitanie Skhol'nikov*, No. 4, 1978, pp. 57–63.
KON, I. S., 'Adam, Eva i vek-iskusitel'', in *Literaturnaya Gazeta*, 1 January 1979, p. 11.
KON, I. S., 'O ser'eznom – vserez', in *Komsomol'skaya Pravda*, 21 October 1981, p. 4.
KON, I. S., *Psikhologiya starsheklassnika* (Moscow, 1980).
KON, I. S., 'Psikhologiya polovykh razlichii', in *Voprosy Psikhologii*, No. 2, 1981, pp. 47–57.
KON, I. S., 'Pravo na tvorchestvo', in *Pravda*, 16 January 1984, p. 3.
KON, I. S., 'Zhenshchiny i muzhchiny', in *Nedelya*, 5 February 1985, pp. 14–15.
'I. S. Kon: Vvedenie v seksologiyu', review of Kon's book by I. S. Andreeva, in *Voprosy Filosofii*, No. 1, 1989, pp. 170–74.
KON, I. S., 'Spravedliva li kara?', in *Literaturnaya Gazeta*, 29 March 1989, p. 11.
KON, I. S., 'Nastoyashchii muzhchina: mifi i realii', in *Nedelya*, 3–9 April 1989, pp. 14–15.
KON, I. S., 'Nastoyashchaya zhenshchina: mifi i realii', in *Nedelya*, 17–23 April 1989, pp. 14–15.
KONOVALOV, O. E., 'Mediko-demograficheskie aspekty vnebrachnoi rozhdaemosti', in *Sovetskoe Zdravookhranenie*, No. 7, 1984, pp. 39–42.
KORYAKINA, A., *Ottsy i deti* (Chelyabinsk, 1978).
KOSHELEVA, L., 'A babushka sorok vsego . . .', in *Izvestiya*, 6 July 1984, p. 6.
KOSTYASHKIN, E. G., 'Pedagogicheskie aspekty polovogo vospitaniya', in *Sovetskaya Pedagogika*, 1964, No. 7, pp. 43–51.
KOTLYAR, A., 'Muzhskaya otvetstvennost'', in *Vospitanie Shkol'nikov*, No. 4, 1986, pp. 69–71.
KOVALENKO, L., 'Vysokoe i prekrasnoe prednaznachenie zhenshchiny', *Vospitanie Shkol'nikov*, No. 1, 1986, pp. 66–8.
KOVALEVA, L., 'Otmetki vystavit zhizn'', in *Vospitanie Shkol'nikov, No.5*, 1986, pp. 69–70.
KOVALEVSKII, V., 'Eleny XX veka', in *Komsomol'skaya Pravda*, 11 April 1985, p. 49.

KOZHEVNIKOV, V. N. and VINOGRADOV, A. F., 'Ne men'she chem troe!', in *Zdorov'e*, No. 12, 1981, pp. 12–13.
KRASKOVSKII, A. S., *Eticheskie besedy so starsheklassnikami o brake i sem'e* (Minsk, 1983) p. 6.
KUDRYAVTSEV, V. N., 'Sotsial'noe i biologicheskoe v antiobshchestvennom povedenii', in *Biologicheskoe i sotsial'noe v razvitii cheloveka* (Moscow, 1977) pp. 152–8.
KUINDZHI, N. N., 'Polovoe vospitanie', in *Zdorov'e*, No. 5, 1981, pp. 18–19.
KUNTS, O., 'Kak vospityvat' devochku', in *Vospitanie Shkol'nikov*, No. 4, 1982, p. 80.
KUTS, V. A., 'Sotsial'no-psikhologicheskie razlichiya mezhdu muzhchinami i zhenshchinami v tsennostno-motivatsionnykh aspektakh stanovleniya brachnykh otnoshenii' (Leningrad, 1978). (Candidate dissertation at the department of social psychology, Leningrad State University.)
KUTSYI, V., 'Nuzhna li stat'ya 35', in *Pravda*, 25 July 1977, p. 3.
KUZNETSOVA, L., 'Semeinaya zhizn' Konstantina Zorina', in *Literaturnoe Obozrenie*, No. 5, 1977, pp. 56–60.
KUZNETSOVA, L., 'Kto glava sem'i?', in *Nedelya*, No. 26, 1977, p. 12.
KUZNETSOVA, L., *Zhenshchina na rabote i doma* (Moscow, 1980).
KUZNETSOVA, L., 'Kto seichas glava sem'i?', in *My i nasha sem'ya* (Moscow, 1983) pp. 116–17.
KUZNETSOVA, L., 'Otets est' – ottsa net', interview with deputy chair of the Supreme Court of the RSFSR Nina Yu. Sergeeva, in *Literaturnaya Gazeta*, 3 April 1985, p. 12.
KUZNETSOVA, L., 'V zashchitu zhenskoi kar'ery', in *Novoe Vremya*, 19 June 1987, pp. 22–4.
KUZNETSOVA, L., 'Lishnee rebro Adama', in *Novoe Vremya*, 18 September 1987, pp. 16–17.
KUZNETSOVA, L., 'Tretii pol?', in *Novoe Vremya*, 9 September 1988, pp. 46–7.
KUZNETSOVA, L., 'O domashnikh zabotakh', in *Vospitanie Shkol'nikov*, No. 5, 1988, pp. 65–6.
KUZNETSOVA, L., 'Igra v korolevu?', in *Nedelya*, 2–8 January 1989, pp. 18–19.
KUZNETSOVA, L., in dialogue with A. Vishnevskii, 'Glazami zhenshchiny', in *Novoe Vremya*, 10–17 March 1989, pp. 33–5.
LANGUEVA, I., 'A vse-taki – lyubov'', interview with actress Natal'ya Gundareva in *Komsomol'skaya Pravda*, 8 February 1981, p. 4.
LAPTEVA, S., 'Spasibo za tsvety', in *Pravda*, 4 May 1984, p. 6.
LAPUTINA, O., 'Nepolnyi rabochii den': blazh' ili neobkhodimost'?', in *Rabotnitsa*, No. 11, 1988, pp. 18–20.
LAVRENTSOVA, V., 'Mamoi nado stat'', in *Pravda*, 4 June 1984, p. 7.
LEBEDEVA, M., 'Poka muzhchiny govoryat . . .', in *Izvestiya*, 23 October 1988, p. 6.
LEONT'EV, A. N., *Deyatel'nost', soznanie, lichnost'* (Moscow, 1975).
LEVSHIN, L. A., *Mal'chik, muzhchina, otets* (Moscow, 1968).
LOMIZE, L. S., 'Molodezhi o semeinoi zhizhni', in *Sovetskaya Pedagogika*, No. 1, 1984, pp. 19–23.

LOMIZE, L. S., 'Vsemerno ukreplyat' sovetskuyu sem'yu', in *Sovetskaya Pedagogika*, No. 6, 1986, pp. 53–7.
LOSOTO, Ye., 'Snovo o vtorom rebenke', in *Komsomol'skaya Pravda*, 2 February 1980, p. 2.
LYNEV, P., 'Gryaz'', in *Komsomol'skaya Pravda*, 24 September 1966, p. 4.
MALINOVSKII, A. A., 'Problema sootnosheniya sotsial'nogo i biologicheskogo', in *Biologicheskoe i sotsial'noe v razvitii cheloveka* (Moscow, 1977) pp. 220–26.
MALINOVSKII, L., 'Zaochnyi klub "druzhba"', in *Literaturnaya Gazeta*, 22 December 1976, p. 13.
MALYSHEVA, M., 'Postylye plody "emansipatsii"', in *Nedelya*, 11–17 January 1988, p. 4.
MARKS, K. and ENGEL'S, F., 'Ispoved'', in *Ob Iskusstve*, Vol 2 (Moscow, 1957) p. 577.
MARMALADZE, I., 'Poslednyaya privilegiya', in *Literaturnaya Gazeta*, 23 January 1985, p. 11.
MASLOVA, N. and NOVIKOVA, E., 'Parametry "zhenskogo voprosa"', in *Novoe Vremya*, 11 December 1987, pp. 28–9.
MATSEKHA, E., 'Dariteli i potrebiteli', in *Pravda*, 28 July 1984, p. 3.
MATSKOVSKII, M. S., 'Sem'ya – dlya svoego blaga', in *Sem'ya i Shkola*, January 1979, pp. 28–30.
MATSKOVSKII, M. S., 'Podgotovka podrostkov i molodezhi k budushchei zhizhni', in *Sem'ya i sistema nrastvennogo vospitaniya: aktual'nye problemy vospitaniya podrostkov* (Moscow, 1979) pp. 204–13.
MATSKOVSKII, M. S. and ZOLOTOVA, T., 'Lyubov' i byt', *Vospitanie Shkol'nikov*, No. 4, 1986, pp. 72–3.
MELIKSETYAN, A., 'Ot chego zavisit prochnost' braka?', in *Vospitanie Shkol'nikov*, No. 6, 1988, pp. 63–7.
MERETUKOVA, M. KH. and FLOROVSKII, Yu. V., 'Voprosy polovogo vospitaniya v rabote klassnogo rukovoditel'ya', in *Problemy obucheniya i vospitaniya v sel'skoi natsional'noi shkole* (Rostov na Dony, 1976) pp. 48–58.
MIKABERIDZE, A., 'Osobennosti vospitaniya devochek', in *Kalendar dlya roditelei 1980* (Moscow, 1979) p. 97.
MIKHAILOVA, L., 'Chuzhoi?', in *Pravda*, 4 June 1984, p. 7.
MIKHAILOVA, V., 'Snova na kukhnyu?', in *Sem'ya i Shkola*, No. 3, 1967, pp. 4–6.
MINAVAROV, A. K., 'Semeinoe vospitanie v respublikakh Srednei Azii', in *Sovetskaya Pedagogika*, No. 1, 1984, p. 25.
'Mnogodetnaya Sem'ya' (readers' letters), in *Komsomol'skaya Pravda*, 30 October 1981, p. 2.
MOISEIKOVA, ALLA, 'Schastlivaya zhenshchina – eta . . . ya', in *Rabotnitsa*, No. 9, 1986, p. 20.
MUKHINA, V. S., 'Igrushka kak sredstvo psikicheskogo razvitiya rebenka', in *Voprosy Psikhologii*, No. 2, 1988, pp. 123–8.
MUSHKINA, E., 'Sluzhba sem'i i demografiya', in *Nedelya*, 12–18 January 1981, pp. 2–3, 10–11.
MUSHKINA, E., 'Bez ottsa . . .', interview with M. Bednyi in *Nedelya*, 9–15 April 1984, pp. 16–17.

MUSHKINA, E., 'V zerkale demografii', in *Nedelya*, 9–15 April 1987, pp. 15–16.
MUSINA, I. M., 'Nekotorye voprosy polovogo vospitaniya v sem'e i shkole', in *Sanitarno-gigienicheskoe vospitanie shkol'nikov* (Minsk, 1979) pp. 114–19.
My i nasha sem'ya (Kniga dlya molodykh suprugov) (Moscow, 1983).
NAAN, G., 'Emansipatsiya, patriarkhat i "voina polov"', in *Literaturnoe Obozrenie*, No. 9, 1977, pp. 57–62.
'Ne men'she chem troe!' (readers' letters), *Zdorov'e*, No. 12, 1982, pp. 18–19.
NOVIKOVA, E., 'Dvoinaya nosha', in *Pravda*, 16 July 1984, p. 7.
'Nuzhdaetsya li v zashchite sil'noi pol?', in *Literaturnaya Gazeta*, 3 April 1985, p. 12.
'Nuzhny li Dzhul'etty?' (readers' letters) in *Komsomol'skaya Pravda*, 29 June 1978, p. 4.
'O pape, mame i semeinoi drame', in *Literaturnaya Gazeta*, 26 December 1984, p. 13.
OBOZOVA, A, N. and SHTIL'BANS, V. I., 'Budushchie muzh'ya, budushchie zheny', in *Zdorov'e*, No. 3, 1984, pp. 18–19.
'On i ona – smena rolei?', in *Literaturnaya Gazeta*, 15 October 1986, p. 12.
ORLOVA, T., 'Vozrastnoi podkhod v podgotovke shkol'nikov k semeinoi zhizhni', in *Vospitanie Skhol'nikov*, No. 5, 1983, pp. 38–9.
OVCHINNIKOVA, I., 'Milye branyatsya', in *Vospitanie Skhol'nikov*, No. 5, 1986, pp. 68–9.
OVCHINNIKOVA, I., 'Kak za kamennoi stenoi', in *Izvestiya*, 8 October 1986, p. 3.
OVCHINNIKOVA, I., 'Idti navstrechu zhelaniyam drug druga', in *Vospitanie Skhol'nikov*, No. 3, 1988, pp. 67–8.
PAVLOV, B., 'Snimy kvartiru', in *Pravda*, 14 January 1985, p. 7.
Pedagogicheskie vzglyady i deyatel'nost' N. K. Krupskoi (Moscow, 1969).
PEREVEDENTSEV, V. I., 'Ne soshlis' kharakterami?', in *Literaturnaya Gazeta*, 15 February 1978, p. 13.
PEREVEDENTSEV, V. I., 'Dvoe v semeinoi lodke', in *Yunost'*, No. 8, 1979, pp. 67–72.
PEREVEDENTSEV, V. I., 'Malysh tretii, zhelannyi', in *Nedelya*, 15 January 1987, p. 14.
PERSHAEVA, I. V., 'Podgotovka devochek-starsheklassnits k lichnoi zhizni v sisteme raboty klassnogo rukovoditelya', in *O ratsionalizatsii uchebno-vospitatel'noi raboty v shkole* (Sverdlovsk, 1977) pp. 142–7.
PETER, R., SHEBEK, V. and GYNE, I., *Devushka prevrashchaetsya v zhenshchinu* (Moscow, 1960).
PIRADOVA, M. D., *Yunosha i devushka* (Moscow, 1965).
POLEEV, A., 'V poiskakh sovmestimosti', in *Rabotnitsa*, No. 3, 1987, pp. 30–31.
'Politicheskii doklad tsentral'nogo komiteta KPSS XXVII s"ezdy kommunisticheskoi partii Sovetskogo Soyuza – doklad general'nogo sekretarya TsK KPSS tovarishcha Gorbachev M. S. 25 fevralya 1986 goda', in *Izvestiya*, 26 February 1986, pp. 2–10.
POLYAKOVA, R., 'Portret v semeinom inter'ere', in *Nedelya*, 9 April 1987, p. 20.

'Popolnenie v kruge chteniya', in *Pravda*, 1 January 1988.
POPOV, A. A., 'Kontrol' reproduktivnoi funktsii sem'i i faktory ego opredelyayushchie', in *Sovetskoe Zdravookhranenie*, No. 7, 1984, pp. 36–8.
POROKHNYUK, E. and SHEPELEVA, M. S., 'O sovmeshchenii proizvodstvennykh i semeinykh funktsii zhenshchin-rabotnits', in *Sotsiologicheskie Issledovaniya*, No. 4, 1975, pp. 102–8.
POSTNIKOVA, T., 'Babushka ili studentka?', in *Rabotnitsa*, No. ,2 1987, p. 15.
POTUPOV, E., 'On i ona', in *Literaturnaya Gazeta*, 17 December 1986, p. 5.
'Pozvol'te poznakomit'sya', in *Literaturnaya Gazeta*, 17 November 1976, p. 13.
PRELOVSKAYA, I., 'Sluzhba sem'i', in *Izvestiya*, 27 January 1982, p. 3.
PROSHINA, L., 'Muzhchiny, beregite sebya!', in *Nedelya*, 8 January 1987, p. 16.
'Pust' nash trud tozhe vov'etsya v trud pyatiletki', letter from women in Orenburg, in *Izvesitya*, 11 April 1976, p. 1.
RADZIKHOVSKII, L. A., 'Teoriya Freida: smena ustanovki', in *Voprosy Psikhologii*, No. 6, 1988, pp. 100–105.
RYABUSHKIN, T. V., 'Demograficheskaya politika i nauka', in *Sotsiologicheskie Issledovaniya*, No. 3, 1978, pp. 46–55.
RUBINOV, A., 'Lyubov' po ob"yavleniyu?', in *Literaturnaya Gazeta*, 20 May 1970, p. 13.
RUBINOV, A., 'Schast'e tak vozmozhno', in *Literaturnaya Gazeta*, 8 March 1978, p. 12.
RUDENKO, I., 'Odnazhdy, posle bala', in *Komsomol'skaya Pravda*, 14 May 1978, p. 2.
RUSAKOVA, NINA., 'Retsept ot odinochestva', in *Rabotnitsa*, No. 7, 1985, pp. 26–8.
RUSAKOVA, N., 'Troe i odna', in *Rabotnitsa*, No. 3, 1986, pp. 26–8.
RYABININ, B., 'Esli u zhenshchiny deti . . .', in *Sem'ya i Shkola*, No. 1, 1967, pp. 6–9.
RYURIKOV, YU. B., 'Deti i obshchestvo (o nekotorykh aspektakh demograficheskoi politiki)', in *Voprosy Filosofii*, No. 4, 1977, pp. 111–21.
RYURIKOV, YU. B., 'Pochemu detei stanovitsya men'she?', in *Literaturnaya Gazeta*, 17 November 1976, p. 13.
RYURIKOV, YU. B., 'Pora zolotaya', in *Pravda*, 15 May 1983, p. 3.
'Sem'ya i plany gosudarstva', in *Sem'ya i Shkola*, No. 2, 1986, pp. 1–3.
SERMYAZHKO, E. I., 'Vospitanie detei v sem'e', in *Sovetskaya Pedagogika*, No. 2, 1988, pp. 113–16.
SHCHERBAK, Y., 'Zmievyi valy', in *Pravda*, 20 January 1987, p. 3.
SHLYAPENTOKH, V., 'Problemy svoi chuzhie', in *Literaturnaya Gazeta*, 30 November 1977, p. 12.
SHOROKHOVA, E. V., 'O estestvennoi prirode i sotsial'noi sushchnosti cheloveka', in *Biologicheskoe i sotsial'noe v razvitii cheloveka* (Moscow, 1977) pp. 65–78.
SHILOV, YU.,'Kazhdomy svoe', in *Sem'ya i Shkola*, No. 4, 1967, pp. 18–19.
SHIMIN, N., 'Rol' zhenshchiny-materi v emotsional'no-nravstvennom razvitii detei v sem'e', in *Dinamika izmeneniya polozheniya zhenshchiny i sem'ya* (Moscow, 1972).

SHUBKIN, V., 'Chto ty dumaesh' o molodezhi?', in *Literaturnaya Gazeta*, 22 January 1986, p. 10.
'Sila obayaniya, ili obayanie sily?' (readers' letters) in *Komsomol'skaya Pravda*, 30 August 1978, p. 4.
'Sluzhba sem'i – kakoi ei byt'? (editorial article), in *Sem'ya i Shkola*, No. 8, 1987, pp. 1–2.
SOLOVEI, P., 'Pero zhar-ptitsy', in *Pravda*, 5 December 1983, p. 7.
'Sovremennaya zhenshchina' (readers' letters) in *Komsomol'skaya Pravda*, 13 October 1978, p. 4.
'SPID: voprosov bol'she, chem otvetov', in *Literaturnaya Gazeta*, 7 May 1986, p. 15.
SPIVAKOVSKAYA, A. S., *Igra – eto ser'ezno* (Moscow, 1981)
STEPUNINA, S., 'Babushka otkupilas'', in *Sovetskaya Rossiya*, 16 March 1984, p. 2.
STARYGINA, E., 'Babushka v dzhinsakh', in *Literaturnaya Gazeta*, 1 December 1982, p. 12.
STOLIN, V., 'Psikhologicheskie osnovy semeinoi terapii', in *Voprosy Psikhologii*, No. 4, 1982, p. 104.
STOLIN, V., 'Vybiraya-vybirai', *Rabotnitsa*, No. 5, 1985, p. 27.
STRELYANYI, A., '"Perestavilsya" li svet?', in *Literaturnoe Obozrenie*, No. 5, 1977, pp. 51–60.
SUBBOTSKII, E. V., 'O genezise moral'nogo povedeniya doshkol'nikov', in *Novye issledovaniya v psikhologii*, No. 1, 1977, pp. 48–52.
SUBBOTSKII, E. V., 'Vliyanie sverstnikov i vzroslykh na moral'noe povedenie rebenka v usloviyakh eksperimenta', in *Novye issledovaniya v psikhologii*, No. 2, 1977, pp. 47–50.
SUBBOTSKII, E. V., 'Formirovanie moral'nogo postupka', in *Novye issledovaniya v psikhologii*, No. 2, 1977, pp. 48–50.
SUKHOMLINSKII, V. A., *Serdtse otdayu detyam* (Kiev, 1974)
'Svobodna. Ot chego?', in *Rabotnitsa*, No. 4, 1985, p. 29, No. 9, 1985, p. 24, and No. 1, 1986, p. 29.
SYSENKO, V. A., 'Zhenshchina i muzhchina', in *Zdorov'e*, No. 1, 1980, pp. 14–15.
SYSENKO, V. A., 'Zhenshchina i muzhchina', in *Zdorov'e*, No. 5, 1981, p. 18.
TALALAI, M., 'Chei detskii sad', in *Pravda*, 7 May 1984, p. 7.
TARKHOVA, L.,'Chto sluchilos' s muzhchinoi?', in *Komsomol'skaya Pravda*, 17 August 1986, p. 4.
TELEN', L., 'Kakaya zhe ona, zhenskaya dolya?', in *Sotsialisticheskaya Industriya*, 22 January 1988, pp. 2–3.
TERESHKOVA, V. V., 'Vsesoyuznaya konferentsiya zhenshchin – Doklad V.V. Tereshkovoi', in *Izvestiya*, 1 February 1987, pp. 3–4.
TIMOSHCHENKO, L., *V sem'e rastet doch' (Moscow, 1978)*
TIMOSHCHENKO, L., 'O vospitanii devochki', in *Vospitanie Shkol'nikov*, No. 6, 1980, pp. 37–40.
TOL'TS, M., 'Sem'ya', in *Pravda*, 20 March 1987, p. 2.
TUTORSKAYA, S., 'Zhenskaya dolya', in *Nedelya*, 6–13 February 1989, pp. 14–15.
TYURINA, N., 'Grozdiki no sredam', interview with Ch. Grizitskas in *Komsomol'skaya Pravda*, 6 February 1976, p. 2.

URLANIS, B., 'Zhelannyi rebenok', in *Nedelya*, 1–7 December 1980, p. 16.
USHANOV, S., 'Net, i muzhchinam, i zhenshchinam luchshe idti putem, nachertannym prirodoi', in *Literaturaya Gazeta*, 15 October 1986, p. 12.
'V Prezidiume Verkhovnogo Soveta SSSR – o rabote, provodimoi v Latviiskoi SSR po soblyudeniyu trebovanii zakonodatel'stva ob ukreplenii sem'i i povyshenii ee otvetstvennosti za vospitanie detei', in *Pravda*, 29 May 1986, p. 2, and *Izvestiya*, pp. 1–2.
'V TsK KPSS i Sovete Ministrov SSSR', *Pravda* and *Izvesitya*, 31 March 1981, p. 1.
'V TsK KPSS i Sovete Ministrov SSSR i VTsSPS', in *Pravda*, 19 January 1988, pp. 1–2.
VAGABOR, M., *Islam i Sem'ya* (Moscow, 1980)
VARGA, A. Ya., 'Identifikatsiya s roditelyami i formirovanie psikhologicheskogo pola (kriticheskii podkhod k resheniyu problemy)', in A. A. Bodalev (ed.), *Sem'ya i formirovanie lichnosti – sbornik nauchnykh trudov* (Moscow, 1981) pp. 21–6.
VASEKHA, V., 'Chisto muzhskoi razgovor', in *Rabotnitsa*, No. 10, 1986, p. 21.
VASIL'EV V., *Muzhskoi razgovor* (Moscow, 1982).
VEDENEVA, I., 'Dochki-materi', *Komsomol'skaya Pravda*, 16 August 1981, p. 4.
VELIKANOVA, L., 'Sem'ya – sem' "ya"!' (interview with A. Spirkin), in *Literaturnaya Gazeta*, 1 May 1978, p. 12.
VOINA, V., 'Studentka s rebenkom', in *Literaturnaya Gazeta*, 27 March 1985, p. 11.
VOLKOV, A. G., 'Sem'ya kak faktor izmeneniya demograficheskoi situatsii', in *Sotsiologicheskie Issledovaniya*, No. 1, 1981, pp. 34–42.
VOLKOVA, A. N., 'Semeinye krizisy', in *Zdorov'e*, No. 9, 1986, pp. 24–5.
VINOGRADOVA, M. D., 'A vam deti pomogayut?', in *Zdorov'e*, No. 12, 1984, pp. 8–9.
VISHNEVSKII, A. G., 'Brak: mozhno li im upravlyat'?', in *Literaturnaya Gazeta*, No. 43, 1976, p. 13.
VISHNEVSKII, A. G., SHCHERBOV, S. YA., ANICHIN, A. B., GRECHUKHA, V. A. and DONETS, N. V., 'Noveishie tendentsii rozhdaemosti v SSSR', in *Sotsiologicheskie Issledovaniya*, No. 3, 1988, pp. 54–67.
VORONINA, O. A., 'Zhenshchina v "muzhskom obshchestve"', in *Sotsiologicheskie Issledovaniya*, No. 2, 1988, pp. 104–10.
VORONINA, O. A., 'Muzhchiny sozdali mir dlya sebya', in *Sovetskaya Zhenshchina*, No. 11, 1988, pp. 14–15.
YANKOVA, Z. A., *Izmenenie struktury sotsial'nykh rolei zhenshchin v razvitam sotsialisticheskom obshchestve i model' sem'i* (Moscow, 1972) p. 2 (paper given at the Soviet Sociological Association 12th International Seminar on the Study of the Family).
YANKOVA, Z. A., 'Razvitie lichnosti zhenshchiny v sovetskom obshchestve', in *Sotsiologicheskie Issledovaniya*, No. 4, 1975, p. 42.
YANKOVA, Z. A., *Sovetskaya Zhenshchina* (Moscow, 1978).
YAROVSHEVSKII, M. G., *Istoria Psikhologii* (Moscow, 1976).
YUFEREVA, T. I., 'Obrazy muzhchin i zhenshchin v soznanii podrostkov', in *Voprosy Psikhologii*, No. 3, 1985, p. 84.

YULINA, N. S., 'Problemy zhenshchin: filosofskie aspekty (feministskaya mysl' v S.SH.A.), in *Voprosy Filosofii*, No. 5, 1988, pp. 137–47.
YURCHENKO, A., 'Dorozhit' lyubov'yu', in *Vospitanie Shkol'nikov*, No. 2, 1988, pp. 59–61.
ZAKHAROV, A. I., 'Psikhologischeskie osobennosti vospriyatiya det'mi roli roditelei', in *Voprosy Psikhologii*, No. 1, 1982, pp. 59–68.
ZAKHAROV, A. I., 'Mama na rabote', in *Sem'ya i Shkola*, No. 8, 1987, pp. 23–5.
ZAKHAROVA, N., POSADSKAYA, A. and RIMASHEVSKAYA, N., 'Kak my reshaem zhenskii vopros', in *Kommunist*, No. 4, 1989, pp. 56–65.
'Zhenshchiny iz Orenburga pravil'no stavyat vopros: pust' nash trud tozhe vov'etsya v trud pyatiletki', readers' letters to *Izvestiya*, 17 April 1976, p. 2.
ZHUKOVITSKII, L., 'Odinochestvo obshchitel'nogo cheloveka?', in *Komsomol'skaya Pravda*, 16 December 1981, p. 4.
ZHUKOVITSKII, L., 'Kuda ischezayut nastoyashchie muzhchiny?', in *Literaturnaya Gazeta*, 10 October 1984, p. 12.
ZHURAVSKAYA, I., 'Razgovor 9 Marta', in *Rabotnitsa*, No. 3, 1988, p. 7.

Russian Texts in English Translation

ANAN'EV, B. G., 'Bilateral regulation of ontogenetic development in humans', in *Soviet Psychology*. Vol. IX, No. 2 (Winter 1970–71) pp. 108–123.
BASKINA, A., 'Suppose You Get Married . . .', in *Soviet Weekly*, 9 April 1988, p. 6.
BASSIN, F. V., 'Consciousness and the Unconscious', in M. Cole and I. Maltzman, *A Handbook of Contemporary Soviet Psychology* (New York: Basic Books, 1969) pp. 399–420.
BELKIN, A. I., 'Masculine, Feminine or Neutral?', in *The UNESCO Courier*, August–September 1975 (English language edition) pp. 58–61.
BODALEV, A. A., 'Individual and Developmental Differences in Interpersonal Understanding', in *Soviet Psychology*, Vol. IX, No. 2, (Winter 1970–71) pp. 157–69.
BODALEV, A. A., 'Subjective Significance of Another Person and Its Determining Factors', in *Soviet Psychology*, Vol. XXV, No. 1, (Autumn 1986) pp. 21–7.
BOZHOVICH, L. I., 'The Personality of Schoolchildren and Problems of Education', in M. Cole and I. Maltzman (eds) *A Handbook of Contemporary Soviet Psychology*, (New York: Basic Books, 1969) pp. 209–49.
BOZHOVICH, L. I. and SLAVINA, L. S., 'Fifty Years of Soviet Psychology of Upbringing', in Josef Brozek and Dan I. Slobin (eds) *Psychology in the USSR: an Historical Perspective* (New York: International Arts and Sciences Press, 1972) pp. 161–76.
BOZHOVICH, L. I., 'Stages in Personality Formation', in *Soviet Psychology*, Vol. XVII, No. 3 (Spring 1979) pp. 3–24.
BOZHOVICH, L. I., 'Stages in the Formation of the Personality in Ontogeny (Part II)', in *Soviet Psychology*, Vol. XVIII, No. 3 (Spring 1980) pp. 35–52.

BRONISLAVOVNA SEGLENIECE, KLARA, 'Is Induced Abortion Murder?' in *CDSP*, Vol. XXXIII, No. 5, 1981, pp. 11–13.
DAVYDOV, V.V., 'The Category of Activity and Mental Reflection in the Theory of A.N. Leont'ev', in *Soviet Psychology*, Vol. XIX, No. 4 (Summer 1981) pp. 3–29.
DAVYDOV, V.V. and ZINCHENKO, V.P., 'The Principle of Development in Psychology', in *Soviet Psychology*, Vol. XX, No. 1 (Autumn 1981) pp. 22–46.
ELKONIN, D.B., 'Some Results of the Study of the Psychological Development of Preschool-age Children', in M. Cole and I. Maltzman (eds) *A Handbook of Contemporary Soviet Psychology*, (New York: Basic Books, 1969) pp. 163–202.
FEL'DSHTEIN, D., 'Psychological Laws of the Social Development of the Personality in Ontogeny', in *Soviet Psychology*, Vol. XXV, No. 3 (Spring 1987) pp. 45–65.
GORBACHEV, M., *Perestroika* (London: Collins, 1987).
'Homework!' (about full-time housewife) in *Soviet Weekly*, 12 March 1988, p. 7.
KELLE, V.Zh., in *The Great Soviet Encyclopaedia*, Vol. 10 (New York and London: Macmillan, 1978) p. 120.
KOLBANOVSKII, V.N., 'The Sex-upbringing of the Rising Generation', in *Soviet Education*, Vol. 1, 1964, pp. 3–13.
KON, I.S.,'Where Scholarly Disciplines Meet', Abstract in *CDSP*, Vol. XXXIII, No. 5 (1981) pp. 9–10.
KOSTIUK, G.S., 'Problems of the Child's Personality Formation', in R.B. Winn (ed.) *Soviet Psychology* (New York: Philosophical Library, 1961) pp. 86–8.
KRASNOGORSKY, N.I., 'The Physiology of the Development of Speech in Children', in *Soviet Psychology Bulletin*, April 1955.
LENIN, V.I., *On the Emancipation of Women* (Moscow: Progress, 1972).
LEONT'EV, A.N., 'The Intellectual Development of the Child', in Ralph B. Winn (ed.) *Soviet Psychology* (New York: Philosophical Library, 1961) pp. 57–65.
LEONT'EV, A.N., 'The Problem of Activity in Psychology', in *Soviet Psychology*, Vol. XIII, No. 2 (Winter 1974–5) pp. 4–33.
LEVITIN, K., 'The Best Path to Man', in *Soviet Psychology*, Vol. XVIII, No. 1 (Autumn 1980), pp. 11–26.
LITVINOVA, G.I. and URLANIS, B.TS., 'The Soviet Union's Demographic Policy', Abstract in *CDSP*, Vol. XXXIV, No. 19, 1982, pp. 1–4.
LOMOV, B.F., 'Sixty Years of Soviet Psychology', in *Soviet Psychology*, Vol. XVII, No. 2 (Winter 1978–79) pp. 68–82.
LURIA, A.R., 'Speech Development and the Formation of Mental Processes', in M. Cole and I. Maltzman (eds) *A Handbook of Contemporary Soviet Psychology*, (New York: Basic Books, 1969) pp. 121–62.
LURIA, A.R., 'Speech and Intellect among Rural, Urban and Homeless Children', in *Soviet Psychology*, Vol. XIII, No. 1 (Autumn 1974) pp. 5–39.
LURIA, A.R., *Cognitive Development: Its Cultural and Social Foundations* (London and Cambridge Mass.: Harvard Univ. Press, 1976).
MAKARENKO, A.S., *Road to Life: An Epic of Education* (Moscow: Progress, 1951).

MATSKOVSKII, M. and GURKO, T., 'The Young Family: Problems of its Formation', Abstract in *CDSP*, Vol. XXXVII, No. 5, 1985, pp. 5–6.
MENCHINSKAYA, V.S., 'Some aspects of the Psychology of Teaching', in Brian Simon (ed.) *Psychology in the Soviet Union* (London: RKP, 1957) pp. 190–96.
MERLIN, V.S., 'Problems in the Integrated Study of Individual Differences', in *Soviet Psychology*, Vol. XX, No. 3 (Winter, 1981–2) pp. 49–72.
MUKHINA, V.S., 'The Social Development of the Child', in *Soviet Psychology*, Vol. XX, No. 3 (Spring, 1982) pp. 60-79.
PEREVEDENTSEV, V.I., 'Population Reproduction and the Family', abstract in *CDSP*, Vol. XXXIV, No. 19, 1982, pp. 5–6.
POLCHANOVA, S.L., 'Midwives' Counseling about Hazards of Abortions should be more Aggressive', précis in *CDSP*, Vol. XXXVI, No. 45, 1984, p. 18.
POSNANSKI, N.F., 'Heredity and the Materialist Theory', in R.B. Winn (ed.), *Soviet Psychology* (New York: Philosophical Library, 1961) pp. 49–54.
RADZIKHOVSKII, L.A. and KHOMSKAYA, E.D., 'A.R. Luria and L.S. Vygotskii: Early Years of their Collaboration', in *Soviet Psychology*, Vol. XX, No. 1 (Autumn 1981) pp. 3–21.
RYURIKOV, YU., 'Love and Family Today – Sharp and Controversial Questions', Abstract in *CDSP*, Vol. XXVIII, No. 15, 1976, pp. 1–3.
RYURIKOV, YU., 'The Source of Humanism', in *Soviet Weekly*, 9 April 1988, p. 7.
SAPOZHNIKOVA, L.S., 'Inculcating Moral Behaviour in Adolescents', in *Soviet Psychology*, Vol. XXIV, No. 2 (Winter 1985–1986), pp. 83–95.
SMIRNOV, A.A., 'Psychological Research 1953-5', in B. Simon (ed.), *Psychology in the Soviet Union* (London:RKP, 1957) pp. 29–45.
SMIRNOV, A.A., 'Child Psychology', in B. Simon (ed.), *Psychology in the Soviet Union* (London:RKP, 1957) pp. 183–9.
SMIRNOV, G.L., *Soviet Man: the Making of a Socialist Type of Personality* (Moscow: Progress, 1973).
SOKOLOVA, E., 'Keep Your Distance', in *Soviet Weekly*, 9 April, p. 10.
'Tied to Mama's Apron Strings', condensed text in *CDSP*, Vol. XXXVII, No. 15, 1985, p. 10.
TRETYAKOV, V., 'Vitaly Tretyakov Defends Himself', in *Soviet Weekly*, 6 February 1988, p. 8.
TURSUNOV, A., 'Atheism and Culture', in *CDSP*, Vol. XXXIX, No. 3, 1987, pp. 7–8.
UBAIDULLAYEVA, R., 'One Million Unemployed', in *CDSP*, Vol. XXXIX, No. 14, 1987, p. 4.
VENGER, L. and MUKHINA, V., 'Basic Patterns in the Mental Development of Children', in *Soviet Education*, May 1974, p. 48.
VOINOV, L., 'Is Sex Education Inadequate in Latvia?', in *CDSP*, Vol. XXXVI, No. 40, 1984, p. 11.
VUL'FSON, B., 'Freudianism and Bourgeois Pedagogy', in *Soviet Education*, Vol. VIII, No. 3, 1966, pp. 3–14.
VYGOTSKII, L.S., *Mind in Society* (London and Cambridge, Mass.: Harvard Univ. Press, 1978).

ZAPOROZHETS, A. Z. and LUKOV, U. D., 'The Development of Reasoning in Young Children', in *Soviet Psychology*, Vol. XVIII, (Winter 1979–1980), No. 2, pp. 47–66.
ZVEREV, I. D., 'On the Problem of the Sex Education of Schoolchildren in Connection with the Study of Human Physiology', in *Soviet Education*, Vol. XI, No. 8, 1968, pp. 50–52.

Material in English

ARCHER, J. and LLOYD, B., *Sex and Gender* (Harmondsworth: Pelican, 1982).
ATTWOOD, L. and MCANDREW, M., 'Woman at Work in the USSR', in M. J. Davidson and C. L. Cooper (eds), *Working Women* (Chichester: John Wiley, 1984) pp. 269–304.
BANDURA, A., *Social Learning Theory* (Englewood Cliffs NJ: Prentice-Hall, 1977).
BANDURA, A. and WALTERS, R. H., *Social Learning and Personality Development* (New York, London: Holt, Rinehart & Winston, 1964).
BARRETT, M. AND MCINTOSH, M., *The Anti-Social Family* (London: Verso, 1982).
BAUER, R. A., *The New Man in Soviet Psychology* (Cambridge: Harvard University Press, 1952).
BINYON, M., *Life in Russia* (London: Panther, 1983).
BLEKHER, F., *The Soviet Woman in the Family and in Society* (New York: Halsted Press, 1979).
BROOKS-GUNN, J. and SCHEMPP-MATTHEWS, W., *He and She* (Englewood Cliffs NJ: Prentice-Hall, 1979).
BROPHY, J., *Child Development and Socialization* (Chicago: Science Research Associates, 1977).
BROWNING, GENIA, 'Soviet Politics – Where are the Women?', in B. Holland (ed.), *Soviet Sisterhood* (London: Fourth Estate, 1985) pp. 202–36.
BROZEK, J., 'Spectrum of Soviet Psychology', in *American Psychologist*, Vol. 24, 1969, pp. 944–6.
BUCKLEY, MARY, 'Soviet Interpretations of the Woman Question', in B. Holland (ed.), *Soviet Sisterhood* (London: Fourth Estate, 1985) pp. 24–53.
CHAMBERLIN, W. H., *Soviet Russia – a Living Record and a History* (London: Duckworth, 1930).
COLE, M. and MALTZMAN, I., (eds), *A Handbook of Contemporary Psychology* (New York: Basic Books, 1969).
COOPER, J., 'What is Man? A New Controversy in Soviet Biology', unpublished paper for the CREES annual conference of 1983.
COOTE, A. and CAMPBELL, B., *Sweet Freedom* (London: Picador, 1982).
D'ANRADE, R., 'Sex Differences and Cultural Institutions', in E. E. Maccoby (ed.), *The Development of Sex Differences* (London: Tavistock, 1967) pp. 173–204.
FIRESTONE, S., *The Dialectic of Sex* (London: Women's Press, 1979).

FREUD, S., *Introductory Lectures on Psychoanalysis* (Harmondsworth: Penguin, 1975).
FREUD, S., *Freud on Sexuality* (Harmondsworth: Penguin, 1977).
GOLDMAN, W. Z., review of Vladimir Shlapentokh's book, *Love, Marriage and Friendship in the Soviet Union: Ideals and Practices*, in *Russian Review*, Volume 45, No. 4, 1986, pp. 452–4.
HARTNETT, O., BODEN, G. and FULLER, M., (eds), *Sex Role Stereotyping* (London: Tavistock, 1979).
HOPKINS, M. W., *Mass Media in the Soviet Union* (New York: Pegasus, 1970).
KOHLBERG, L., 'A Cognitive-developmental Analysis of Children's Sex-role Concepts and Attitudes', in E. E. Maccoby (ed.), *The Development of Sex Differences* (London: Tavistock, 1967) pp. 82–173.
LAPIDUS, G., *Women in Soviet Society* (Berkeley and London: University of California Press, 1979).
LEE, P. C. and SUSSMAN STEWART, R., (eds), *Sex Differences: Cultural and Developmental Dimensions* (New York: Urizen Books, 1976).
MACCOBY, E. E., (ed.), *The Development of Sex Differences* (London: Tavistock, 1967).
MACCOBY, E. E. and JACKLIN, C. N., *The Psychology of Sex Differences* (London: OUP, 1975).
MARCUSE, H., *Soviet Ideology* (London and Aylesbury: RKP, 1968).
MCANDREW, M., 'Soviet Women's Magazines', in B. Holland (ed.), *Soviet Sisterhood* (London: Fourth Estate, 1985) pp. 78–115.
MCLEISH, J., *Soviet Psychology: History, Theory, Content* (London: Methuen, 1975).
MEYER, A., 'The Functions of Ideology in the Soviet Political System', in *Soviet Studies*, Vol. XVII, January 1966, No. 3, pp. 273–85.
MITCHELL, J., *Psychoanalysis and Feminism* (Harmondsworth: Penguin, 1974).
MONEY, J. and EHRHARDT, ANKE A., *Man and Woman, Boy and Girl* (Baltimore and London: Johns Hopkins University Press, 1972).
NOVE, A., The Soviet Economic System *(London: Allen & Unwin, 1977)*.
OAKLEY, A., *Subject Woman* (London: Fontana, 1982).
PEERS, J., 'Demographic policy, Modernisation and Social Development in Soviet Central Asia', unpublished paper presented to the TAGS symposium on Soviet Central Asia, SOAS, 1981.
RAYMOND, J. G., 'Transsexualism: an Issue of Sex-role Stereotyping', in E. Tobach and B. Rosoff (eds), *Genes and Gender II* (New York: Gordon Press, 1979) pp. 131–41.
RAYMOND, J. G., *The Transsexual Empire* (London: The Women's Press, 1980).
ROHRBAUGH, J. B., *Women: Psychology's Puzzle* (London: Abacus, 1981).
ROSENHAN, M. S., 'Images of Male and Female Children in Children's Readers', in D. Atkinson, A. Dallin and G. W. Lapidus (eds), *Women in Russia* (London: Harvester Press, 1978) pp. 292–305.
RYWKIN, M., 'Central Asia and Soviet Manpower', in *Problems of Communism*, January–February 1979, pp. 1–13.

SAYERS, JANET, 'On the Description of Psychological Sex Differences', in O. Hartnett, G. Boden and M. Fuller (eds), *Sex Role Stereotyping* (London: Tavistock, 1979) pp. 46–56.

SEGAL, L., *Is the Future Female?* (London: Virago, 1987).

SERBIN, A. and O'LEARY, K. D., 'How Nursery Schools Teach Little Girls to Shut Up', in *Psychology Today*, December 1975, pp. 57–8, 102–3.

SEVE, L., *Man in Marxist Theory and the Psychology of Personality* (London: Harvester Press, 1978).

SHARPE, S., *Just Like a Girl* (Harmondsworth: Penguin, 1976).

SIMON, B., (ed.), *Psychology in the Soviet Union* (London: RKP, 1957).

SOUTH, J., 'To the Backstreet by the Backdoor', in *The New Statesman*, 22 November 1985, pp. 14–15.

SPENDER, D., *For the Record* (London: Women's Press, 1985).

STITES, R., *The Women's Liberation Movement in Russia* (Princeton NJ: Princeton University Press, 1978).

STOLLER, R. J., *Sex and Gender* (London: Hogarth Press, 1968).

STRICKLAND, L. H.,'Applied Social Psychology in the USSR – Excerpts from interviews at Leningrad State University', in *Soviet Psychology*, Vol. XX, No. 1 (August 1981) pp. 81–90.

SUTTON, A., 'Measures and Models in Developmental Psychology', in *Educational Studies*, Vol. 6, No. 2, June 1980.

SUTTON, A., 'Cultural Disadvantage and Vygotskii's Stages of Development', in *Educational Studies*, Vol. 6, No. 1, October 1980, pp. 199–209.

SUTTON, A., 'Soviet Developmental Psychology in English Translation', unpublished paper, August 1982.

WALKER, C., 'Gorbachev Sets the Seal on New Era of Reform', *The Times*, 27 February 1986, p. 7.

WALKER, M., 'Russians Finally Let the Gays Come Out', in *Guardian*, 25 January 1987, p. 1.

WELLS, H. K., *Ivan Pavlov: Towards a Scientific Psychology and Psychiatry* (London: Lawrence & Wishart, 1956).

ZETKIN, C., 'My Recollections of Lenin', Appendix in V. I. Lenin, *On the Emancipation of Women* (Moscow: Progress, 1972) pp. 97–123.

Index

abortion, 177
Abova, Tamara, 179
Academy of Pedagogical
 Sciences, 82, 86, 131, 137, 185, 196
Academy of Sciences, 62, 128
adolescence, 52, 91–2, 94, 98, 136, 138–40, 155, 190
adult reinforcement of behaviour deemed inappropriate in children
 in the Soviet literature, 39, 51, 52, 79, 95, 102, 113
 in the Western literature, 22, 25, 78
Afanas'eva, Tamara, 168, 169, 173
aggression as a male attribute, 22, 73, 94, 98, 103, 111, 155
AIDS, 98, 211
Akivis, Dalina, 180–1
alcohol abuse, 115, 161, 169, 173, 177, 195, 200, 206, 208
 as contributing cause of divorce, 195, 200
Alekseeva, A. G., 171
Aleshina, V., 139
Anan'ev, B. G., 40, 68–70, 93
Andreeva, E., 141–5, 155, 157, 210
Anisimov, E., 168
Anna Karenina, 187
anti-alcohol campaign, 200
Antonov, A., 7
Armenia, 199
Azerbaijan, 199

Bagrazyan, G., 168
Baltic republics
 and family consultation services, 191, 197
 and family size, 181, 191
 and 'get acquainted' services, 199
 and 'The Ethics and Psychology of Family Life', 184
Bandura, A., 21–4, 74

Barrett, Michele and Mary McIntosh, 28
Baskina, A., 7
Bauer, R. A., 39
beauty contests, 177–8
Bednyi, M., 191–2, 198
Belkin, A. I., 78, 79, 100–18, 156
 and adult reinforcement of sex differences in personality, 102, 113
 and biological factors in the development of sex differences in personality, 102, 117
 and 'identification' and 'distinction', 111–13
 and role models in the development of sex differences in personality, 102, 111, 113, 117
 and social factors in the development of sex differences in personality, 102
 and training and self-training in the development of sex differences in personality, 102, 111
Belskaya, G., 167, 184
Bestuzhev-Lada, I., 10–11, 119, 129–31, 171, 188
'biarchy', 128–30, 179, 210
birth-rate, Soviet, ix, 3, 6, 9, 96, 98, 119, 120, 129, 169, 181, 210
Blonskii, P. P., 33–4
Bodalev, A. A., 68, 69–70, 73, 93, 196
Bozhovich, L. I., 48, 49, 50, 52, 56, 57
Bowlby, John, 175
Brezhnev, Leonid, 6, 9, 116
Bulgaria's introduction of paternity leave, 180–1
Burenkova, A., 144
Byelorussia
 and family size, 181
 and 'get acquainted' services, 199

capitalism and oppression of
  women, 187
Caucasus, 199
Central Asia, Soviet
  and birth-rate, 4–6, 10, 129, 206
  and bride price (*kalym*), 5
  and female employment, ix, 6
  and 'get acquainted' services, 199
  and health problems, 5
  and 'The Ethics and Psychology of
    Family Life', 184–5
  and Soviet ideology, ix, 6
  and unemployment, 4
  see also Uzbekistan
Cherenakhova, E., 181
Chernenko, Konstantin, 62
child birth, 172, 177
child care
  and maternal role, 128, 130–2,
    151, 170, 180, 188
  and paternal role, 91, 114, 127,
    132, 140, 141, 153, 175, 180–1,
    194, 201
child custody, 183, 201–2, 207
chivalry as a male attribute, 135,
  139–40, 141, 144, 176, 177
choice for women between work and
  family, 99, 129–32, 170–2, 180,
  197, 208
cognitive-development theory, 24–6
  in relation to social learning
    theory, 25
  in relation to Soviet writings, 67,
    74, 76, 77, 89–90, 111, 113, 204
Committee of Soviet Women, 177,
  211
Communist Party Congresses
  26th (1981), 5, 6
  27th (1986), 7, 9, 10, 200
Constitution, Soviet, ix, 186
Consultation Centre of Psychological
  Help for the Family,
    Moscow, 196
contraception, 211
crèches, *see* preschool child-care
  institutions

Danilova, E., 123–4
Dar'yalova, N., 195, 198

dating services, *see* 'get acquainted'
  services
delinquency, 128, 170, 206
demographic crisis, ix, 4–6, 181,
  183, 189, 199, 200, 206, 207, 209,
  211
demography, 119–20, 127, 183, 208,
  209, 210
'developed socialism', 125
Dewey, John, 36
Dik, Iosif, 133–4, 139, 155
divorce, 3–4, 98, 120, 148, 156, 168,
  176, 177, 180, 183, 184, 190, 193,
  195, 200–2, 207
  and remarriage, 4, 200
  see also marriage, factors
    contributing to failure of
Dmitrieva, O., 174
Dorno, I. V., 161, 195
double-burden, *see* over-burdening
  of Soviet women
drug abuse, 208
Dubinin, N. P., 61–2

economic changes and their effect on
  women's employment, 11–13,
  132, 210–11
education, *see* Ethics and Psychology
  of Family Life (school course);
  sex education; 'sex upbringing';
  schools; pedagogy
educational opportunities for women,
  contraction of, 210
Efimov, M., 38, 151
egalitarianism, *see* sexual equality
Egides, A., 183, 190, 193, 199, 201
Elkon'in, D.B., 57
emotionality as a negative
  psychological attribute, 64, 81,
  92, 124, 152, 163
emotionality as a female
  psychological attribute, 27, 64,
  81, 91, 92, 120, 122, 124, 138,
  146, 148, 152, 161, 163, 194
employment, female (paid), 7, 90,
  92, 93, 94, 112, 115, 120, 121,
  122, 124, 125, 130–2, 140, 144,
  199, 208, 209, 211

Index 257

combined with family roles, 88, 91–6, 99, 115, 120, 121, 122, 124, 125, 127, 128, 129, 130, 140, 164, 167, 170–3, 180, 181, 187, 188, 196
part-time, 7, 10, 11, 140, 141, 144, 171, 179, 180, 186, 189, 208
performed at home, 171
preferences for certain types of, 82–4, 93, 131, 151, 156, 161, 164
threat to, 176–7, 179, 180
and the work collective, 37, 124, 125
endocrinology and sex differences, 100–18
equality between the sexes, *see* sexual equality; 'biarchy'
Estonia and family consultation services, 192
Ethics and Psychology of Family Life (school course), 8, 83, 184–91, 206

family
as 'basic cell' of Soviet society, 185, 190
concern about instability of, 85, 87, 94, 96, 98, 99, 114, 120, 125, 128, 148, 166, 181–2, 183–4, 191, 206
consultation centres, 183, 191–8
'head of', 75, 76, 154, 161, 166, 168, 175, 189, 195
and health, 161–2, 169, 172, 188, 192, 199
optimum size, 5–6, 119, 129, 167, 172–3, 192
and relationship between husband and wife, 70, 121, 125, 127–30, 135, 141–4, 148, 153–4, 156, 168, 175, 186–7, 191–8, 200–2, 210
role of in sex-role socialization, 153–4, 155, 156, 158, 161, 204, 205
see also marriage; multi-child family

Fedoseev, P. N., 60
Feld'shtein, D. I., 62–3
female personality traits, 18–19, 22–31, 70, 71, 73, 79, 80, 81–4, 91–4, 109, 113, 114–15, 120–7, 135, 145–8, 152–4, 160–1, 163, 166, 167, 175–6, 186–7, 189, 194, 196, 202, 212
changes in, 93–6, 121, 124–5, 167, 170, 171, 175, 176, 178
femininity, 94, 107, 108, 113, 114, 115, 122, 123, 124, 125, 126, 127, 132, 135, 136, 137, 142–4, 148, 151, 152, 155, 156, 158, 162, 163, 165, 167, 168, 170, 171, 174, 176, 178, 179, 184, 186, 187, 189, 193, 196, 202, 206, 212
feminism, Soviet, 129, 141, 144, 174, 212
feminism, Western, 27–31, 78, 84–5, 149, 205
and Soviet attitudes to, 31, 67, 83, 143, 212
feminization of males, 3, 8, 79, 97, 114, 116, 126, 149, 161, 162, 166, 169, 175, 206, 208
Firestone, Shulamith, 29
Freud, Sigmund, 16–21, 35, 44, 163
in relation to Pavlov, 44
Soviet views on, 20–1, 32, 53, 76, 89, 150, 203–4
functionalist sociology, 87, 90, 91, 119, 160

Gazaryan, S., 144
Georgia, 199
'get acquainted' services, 183, 198–200
glasnost', x, 9, 56, 97, 159, 165, 176, 212
Golubeva, I. A., 171
Gorbachev, Mikhail
on women, x, 7, 9–13
and anti-alcohol campaign, 200
Grigorova, V. A., 139
Grizitskas, Cheslovas, 191, 192, 193–4, 195
Gudkovich, L. N. and A. M. Kondratov, 156

Gurko, T., 128
Gurova, R., 122

hermaphroditism, 78, 100–19
homosexuality, 98, 114, 115, 116
hooliganism, *see* delinquency
Hopkins, Mark, 166
housewives, *see under* housework
housework
  and differential contribution of men and women, 153, 180, 186, 188
  and female contribution, 128, 132, 136, 137, 142–4, 170–2, 173–4, 179, 189
  and the full-time housewife, 131, 132, 140, 143, 144, 171, 173–4, 207
  and labour-saving devices and services, 153, 186, 212
  and male contribution, 125, 127–9, 130, 136–7, 141–4, 148, 153, 169, 180, 186, 189
housing
  and birth-rate, 7
  shortage and inadequacy of, 6

intelligence testing, 39–40
International Women's Congress (Moscow 1987), 10, 11
International Women's Day, 210
Islam, 4–6, 102
  see also Central Asia, Soviet
Izvestiya, 11, 211

journalists, 165, 167–8
Jung, Carl Gustav, 53, 68

kalym, *see under* Central Asia, Soviet
Karakovskii, V., 156
Kelly, Alison, 81–2
Kharchev, A. G., 120, 121, 125–6
Khashchenko, T. G., 71–4
khozraschet (self-financing), 11, 132, 210, 211
Khripkova, A. G., 2, 133, 139, 145–9, 150, 156, 157, 159

kindergartens, *see* preschool childcare institutions
Kohlberg, Lawrence, 24–6, 33, 67, 74, 76, 113
  see also cognitive-development theory
Kolbanovskii, V. N., 2, 139
Kolesov, D. V., 133, 145–51, 156, 157, 159, 160
Kollontai, Alexandra, 1
Kommunist, 11, 61, 62
Komsomol, 92, 136, 138, 156, 181, 190
Komsomol'skaya Pravda, 165, 168, 174, 181, 187, 193
Kon, I. S., 40, 86–99, 116, 119, 158, 176
Kondratov, A. M., 156
Koryakina, A., 162
Kornilov, K. N., 33–4
Kostyashkin, E. K., 2, 137–9
Kovalenko, L., 188
Kovalev, Yu., 168
Kozhevnikov, V. N. and A. F. Vinogradov, 173
Krupskaya, Nadezhda, 33, 37, 141
Kuindzhi, N. N., 160
Kuts, V. A. and V. P. Bagrunov, 78–9
Kuznetsova, Larisa, 174–8, 179, 189, 201–2, 210, 211

labour shortage, 4, 9, 120
Langueva, I., 174
Latvia, and family consultation services, 191, 192, 197
Lavrentsova, V., 173
leadership, female, *see* power, women in positions of
Lebedeva, Marina, 211
Lenin, V. I., 1, 140
  on sex, 1
  on sexual equality, 141, 176
  on women and productive work, 179
Leont'ev, A. N., 44–5, 50, 54–5, 57, 58, 62, 65
Levshin, L. A., 134–7, 144

Index

Literaturnaya Gazeta, 7, 8, 81, 98, 145, 165, 168, 184, 195, 198, 199, 201, 202
Lithuania
  and family consultation services, 192, 193, 197
  and pro-family propaganda, 181
Lomize, L. S., 181, 190, 200, 202
Luria, A. R., 47, 53
L'vov, Mikhail, 134
Lysenko, T. D., 39

Maccoby, E. E., and C. Jacklin, 78, 79, 91, 147, 155
Makarenko, Anton, 37, 56–7, 117, 139
male personality traits, 18–19, 22–31, 70, 71, 73, 78, 79, 80, 81–4, 91–4, 113, 125, 133–9, 141, 143, 145–8, 152, 156, 157, 160, 161, 162, 166, 167, 175, 186, 194, 196
  see also aggression as a male attribute; child care, and paternal role; chivalry as a male attitude; feminization of men; masculinity; strength as a male attribute
Malysheva, M., 132
Marmaladze, Irma, 178–9, 201
marriage
  factors contributing to failure of, 94, 121, 128, 142, 148, 156, 161, 168, 170, 193–5, 206
  factors contributing to success of, 78, 148, 187, 193–5
  Soviet psychologists on, 70, 78–9, 85
  see also divorce; family
Marx Karl
  on personality, 186
  on sex differences, 8, 95, 126, 133–5, 137, 154, 171, 175
  and Soviet psychology, 33–6, 46–7, 48, 53, 54, 55, 61, 66, 86, 95, 205
Marxism-Leninism, 205
masculinity, 92, 94, 95, 98, 99, 107, 113, 114, 115, 126, 127, 135, 136, 143, 144, 148, 151, 152, 155, 156, 158, 161, 163, 165, 167, 176, 184, 186, 187, 189, 196, 206
masculinization of females, 3, 79, 97, 114, 116, 124, 125, 148, 149, 154, 161, 166, 168, 206, 208
Maslova, Ninel', and El'vira Novikova, 179, 182
maternal deprivation, 175
maternal instinct, 136, 140, 146, 151, 156, 189
maternity, see motherhood
maternity benefits, 6, 7
maternity leave, 6, 7, 70, 180, 186, 189, 206
matriarchy in the Soviet Union, 200–1
Matskovskii, M. I., 128–210
Mead, Margaret, 77
media, see press
medical profession on sex differences in personality, 159–62
men and combination of work and family roles, 180
Mikaberidze, A., 163
Mikhailova, V., 143–4
Millett, Kate, 27
Minavarov, A.K., 5
Mitchell, Juliet, 19
modelling, see role models in child development
Moiseikova, Alla, 173
Money, John and Anke Eherhardt, 100–1, 102
moral state of the Soviet Union, 207, 209
moral upbringing, 2–3
morality, women as custodians of, 109, 162, 187
Moskovskaya Pravda, 162
motherhood, 113, 120, 122, 123, 124, 128, 129, 130–2, 135, 153, 171, 176, 179, 180, 181, 188, 194, 199, 207
Mukhina, V. S., 50, 58–9, 64, 70–1, 92
multi-child family, 172–3, 186

Naan, G., 7, 200
name-giving ceremonies, 197

Nedelya, 98, 119, 165
New Soviet Person, 29, 34–5, 56, 63, 64, 203
Nove, Alec, 4
Novoe Vremya, 119, 176, 210
nurseries, *see* preschool child-care institutions

Oakley, Ann, 29–30, 84
Obozova, A. N. and V. I. Shtil'bans, 161
Odnazhdy dvadtsat' let spustya (One Day 20 Years Later), 174
O'Leary, K. D., 22
one-child family, 4, 5, 173, 187, 190
one-parent family, 198
Ovchinnikova, I., 188
over-burdening of women, 127, 170–1, 177, 178, 205, 212
'over-emancipated' Soviet women, *see* matriarchy in the Soviet Union

Parsons, Talcott, *see* functionalist sociology
paternity leave, 180–1
patriarchy, 27, 128, 129, 141, 143, 176, 194, 200, 207, 209, 211
Pavlov, Ivan, 34, 35, 40–7, 60, 63, 65
  and conditioned reflexes, 41–4
  and Freud, 44
  and Marxism, 46–7
  and second-signalling system, 44
  and sex differences, 44
  and temperament types, 45–6, 65
pedagogy, Soviet, 2–3, 8, 96, 133–64
  and biology, 159
  and genetics, 63
  and the medical profession, 159–62
  and psychology, 2–3, 32, 34, 36, 39, 48, 50, 52, 56, 81, 82, 83, 86, 92, 95, 96, 133, 155, 156, 157–8, 159, 204
  and sex differences, 133–64, 184–91, 206–7, 209
  see also Ethics and Psychology of Family Life (school course);

sex education; 'sex upbringing'; schools
pedology, 36, 38, 40
'People's Universities' (adult education centres), 197
Petrov, F. P., 38
perestroika, x, 6, 9–13, 130, 172, 177, 206, 209, 212
Perevedentsev, Victor, 4, 9, 119, 128
Piaget, Jean, 24, 48, 150
Pokrovskii, V., 211
Poleev, A., 194
Polynin, V. M., 61
population, *see* birth-rates; demography
power, women in positions of, 73–4, 131, 139, 154, 177, 211
Pravda, 86, 165, 173, 178, 191, 197
preschool child-care institutions, 130, 131, 140, 186, 211
  changes in provision of, 7, 8, 10
  criticisms of, 170, 206
press, the Soviet, 165–82
  and the CPSU, 166
  and ideology, 165–6
  and the image presented of women, 170, 172, 207
  and the pro-family campaign, 165–82
  and readers' letters, 166, 168, 169, 170–1, 173–5, 178, 186, 187, 196, 199, 201, 202
Proshina, Larisa, 169
prostitution, 208
psychoanalysis, *see* Freud
psycho-physiology, Soviet references to, 39, 40, 120
psychology, Soviet, 32–99
  and 'activity', 49–50, 54–5, 65, 66, 203
  and the 'all-round personality', 33, 64, 117, 121, 123, 138, 186, 204
  and biological input into sex differences, 3, 68–9, 82–3, 87, 88, 90–3, 96–7
  and biology/physiology, 34, 35, 39, 40, 60–3, 203
  and the collective, 52, 56–7, 117

and competition, 58–9, 98
and Darwinism, 62
and the head of the family, 169
and family consultation services, 193, 196
and the four-factor theory of personality development, 39, 157–8, 203, 204
and Freudianism, 32, 35–6, 66, 76, 77
and Marxism, 33, 34, 48, 53
and moral attitudes and behaviour, 56–9, 80–1
and pedagogy, 2–3, 32, 34, 36, 39, 56, 81, 92, 95, 205
and self-training, 39, 155, 158, 169, 203, 204
and sex differences, 2, 3, 47, 50, 60, 63–6, 67–85, 86–99
and social influences in the development of sex differences in personality, 68, 76–8, 87–90, 92–9
and training, 39, 156, 158, 164, 169, 203, 204
and the two-factor theory of personality development, 36, 39, 61
and Western feminism, 67, 78, 95–6, 97
and Western psychology, 34, 36, 39, 40, 64, 67, 74, 77, 78, 79, 86, 89–90, 97, 156
see also adult reinforcement of behaviour deemed appropriate in children; role models in child development; status, the concept of in theories of child development
psychology, Western, 16–31
and sex differences, 16–31
and Soviet psychology, 34, 36, 39, 40
psychotherapy, 196

Rabotnitsa, 10, 11, 149, 168, 170–2, 173, 180, 194, 199, 210
rape, *see* sex crimes
Raymond, Janice, 101, 103–4, 114
reproduction, *see* motherhood

Rohrbaugh, Janice, 16, 18, 22, 23, 25, 26
role models in child development
in the Soviet literature, 51, 74–7, 78, 102, 107–8, 111, 113, 117, 152, 155, 156, 158
in the Western literature, 22–3, 26, 74, 107
Rosenhan, M. S., 113
Roxburgh, Angus, 165
Rubinov, A., 198, 199
Russia
and family size, 181
and family consultation services, 191, 197
and 'get acquainted' services, 199
and 'The Ethics and Psychology of Family Life', 184
Ryabinin, B., 140–1, 143–4
Ryurikov, Yu. B., 129, 179, 198

Sapozhnikova, L.S. 80–1
schools, 36–7, 38, 52, 56–63, 67, 83, 86, 141, 183
Tsarist, 37, 142
and the collective, 52
and training in sex roles, 8, 83, 95, 135, 184–91
see also Ethics and Psychology of Family Life (school course); sex education; 'sex-upbringing'; schools
science, women in, 81–2
Sechenov, I.M., 40
Segal, Lynne, 29–30
Sem'ya i Shkola, 140, 143, 145, 159, 198, 210
Serbin, A., 22
Sergeeva, Nina (of the Supreme Court of the RSFSR), 202
Sève, Lucien, 62
sex, 1, 88, 95, 97, 98, 159, 161–2, 189, 190, 192
double standard in, 95, 98, 109
Lenin's views on, 1
as part of marriage, 189, 192
pre-marital, 195
sex change, 101–18
sex crimes, 2, 98, 136, 176

sex differences in children's
  literature, 113, 116
sex differences in children's
  play, 50–1, 65, 71, 75, 156, 158
sex differences in personality in the
  Soviet literature
  and the influence of biology, 3,
    68–9, 82–3, 87, 88, 90–3, 96–7,
    102–4, 135, 136, 137, 138, 140,
    145, 149, 150, 152, 154, 155,
    158, 161, 167, 171, 204
  and the influence of social
    factors, 68, 76–8, 87–90,
    92–9, 109, 138, 149, 150, 152,
    154, 159, 160, 167–8, 175, 187
  see also female personality traits;
    male personality traits
sex education, 2, 133, 159, 193, 209
sex-role differentiation in family and
  society, 77, 88, 91, 93–6, 99,
  113–16, 125–32, 137, 140–4, 151,
  153–4, 157, 160–4, 167–72,
  175–82, 184–9, 193–7, 199,
  201–2, 207–8
  see also child-care; family;
    housework; sex differences in
    personality in the Soviet
    literature
sex roles, children's attitudes
  towards, 185
sex-role socialization, see 'sex
  upbringing'
'sex upbringing', 2–3, 6–8, 78, 79,
  88, 98, 102, 133–64, 183, 186,
  191, 199, 203–12
sexology, see Kon, I. S.
sexual equality, early Soviet attitudes
  towards, 141–2, 144, 148, 151
  perceived negative consequences
    of, ix, 31, 79, 83, 96, 119,
    120, 125, 126, 136, 138, 140,
    144, 148, 151, 152, 156–7,
    161–2, 167, 168
  promotion of, 94, 95, 128–9,
    141–3, 174–81, 208, 211, 212
  redefinition of, ix, 31, 79, 83, 96,
    116, 125, 126, 151, 167, 168,
    171, 187, 189, 205

supposed improvements in, 128,
  187
see also 'biarchy'; matriarchy
Shlapentokh, Vladimir, 119
social duties in Soviet
  writings, 115–16, 117, 118, 188,
  189, 200
Sotsiologicheskie Issledovaniya, 120
Sovetskaya Zhenshchina, 179
Shilov, Yu., 144
Shimin, N. D., 123, 127
Shul'gin, V. N., 36
Sinelnikov, A. B., 200
Snegireva, T., 81–4, 185
social learning theory, 21–4, 25, 205
  and feminism, 28
  in relation to Soviet writings, 29,
    74, 77, 89, 156, 204
sociologists on sex differences, 2,
  119–32
Spirkin, A., 199
Stalin, Joseph, 38, 39
  and education, 38, 142
  and psychology, 21, 38–9, 40, 60
status, the concept of in theories of
  child development
  in the Soviet literature, 52–3, 57,
    59, 70, 75, 76, 92
  in the Western literature, 22–3
Stolin, I., 172, 196, 197
Strelyanyi, Anatoli, 165, 209
strength as a male attribute, 8, 94,
  98, 133–9, 141, 143, 148, 161, 168
Subbotskii, E. V., 57–8, 117
Sutton, Andrew, 48
Sysenko, V. A., 7, 160–1

Tarkhova, L., 169
teachers, role of in sex-role
  socialization, 136, 138, 152,
  156, 158, 185–91, 204, 205
  life styles of, 190
  need for more male teachers, 156
Tereshkova, Valentina, 107
thaw, the (post Stalin), 209
Timoshchenko, L., 139, 151
transsexualism, 101, 114

'trial marriage', 195
Trud (school class), 92, 164

Ukraine
  and family size, 181
  and 'get-acquainted' services, 199
unemployment, 4, 10–11, 206, 209
UNESCO Courier, 116
Uzbekistan, 54
Uznade Psychology Institute, Tbilisi, 21

Vasil'ev, V., 155
Vagabor, M., 5
Varga, A. Ya., 77–8
Vishnevskii, A.G., 9, 119, 210
Volkov, A. G., 6, 119
Voprosy Filosofii, 31
Voprosy Psikhologii, 70
Voronina, O.A., 131
Vospitanie Shkol'nikov, 188, 190
Vul'fson, B. L., 20
Vygotskii, L. S., 47–55, 56, 60, 63, 64, 65, 66, 117, 163
  compared with Piaget, 48

war games in Soviet education, 156
weakness as a female attribute, 8, 131–9, 141, 143–4, 149, 160, 161, 163, 168, 176
Wells, H. K., 44, 46
'woman question', the, 1, 120, 208
Women's Councils (*zhensovety*), 12
women's liberation, *see* feminism

Yankova, Zoya, 115, 121, 122, 124, 125, 158, 176
youth culture, 209
Yufereva, T. I., 185
Yulina, N. S., 31
Yunost', 165

Zakharov, A. I., 74–7, 79
Zakharova, N., A. Posadskaya and N. Rimasheveskaya, 11, 131, 207–12
Zarya (Moscow state organization of domestic service), 197
Zdorov'e, 159, 160, 162, 192, 195, 199
Zetkin, Clara, 1
Zhukovitskii, Leonid, 168, 201
Zhuravskaya, I., 180